# Channel Waypoint Guide

*A comprehensive waypoint pilot for both sides of the English Channel, from the Isles of Scilly to Ramsgate, and Calais to the Chenal du Four*

Includes the Channel Islands and over 50 cross-Channel routes

Peter Cumberlidge

Charts devised by Jane Cumberlidge

Imray Laurie Norie & Wilson

Published by
Imray Laurie Norie & Wilson Ltd
Wych House St Ives
Cambridgeshire PE27 5BT England
℡ +44 (0)1480 462114
Fax +44 (0)1480 496109
Email ilnw@imray.com
www.imray.com
2011

1st edition 2011

© Peter Cumberlidge

Peter Cumberlidge has asserted his right to be identified as the author of this work in accordance with the Copyright, Designs and Patents Act 1988.

© Plans Imray Laurie Norie & Wilson Ltd 2011

© Aerial photographs Patrick Roach and Imray Laurie Norie & Wilson Ltd except where credited otherwise. All other photographs Peter Cumberlidge except where credited otherwise

ISBN 978 184623 383 8

British Library Cataloguing in Publication Data.
A catalogue record for this book is available from the British Library.

PLANS
The plans in this guide are not to be used for navigation. They are designed to support the text and should at all times be used with navigational charts.

The plans and tidal information have been reproduced with the permission of the Hydrographic Office of the United Kingdom (Licence No. HO151/951101/01) and the Controller of Her Britannic Majesty's Stationery Office.

CAUTION
Whilst every care has been taken to ensure accuracy, neither the Publishers nor the Author will hold themselves responsible for errors, omissions or alterations in this publication. They will at all times be grateful to receive information which tends to the improvement of the work.

CORRECTIONAL SUPPLEMENTS
This pilot book will be amended at intervals by the issue of correctional supplements which will be published on our website www.imray.com and may be downloaded free of charge.

Printed in Singapore by Star Standard Industries Ltd

# Contents

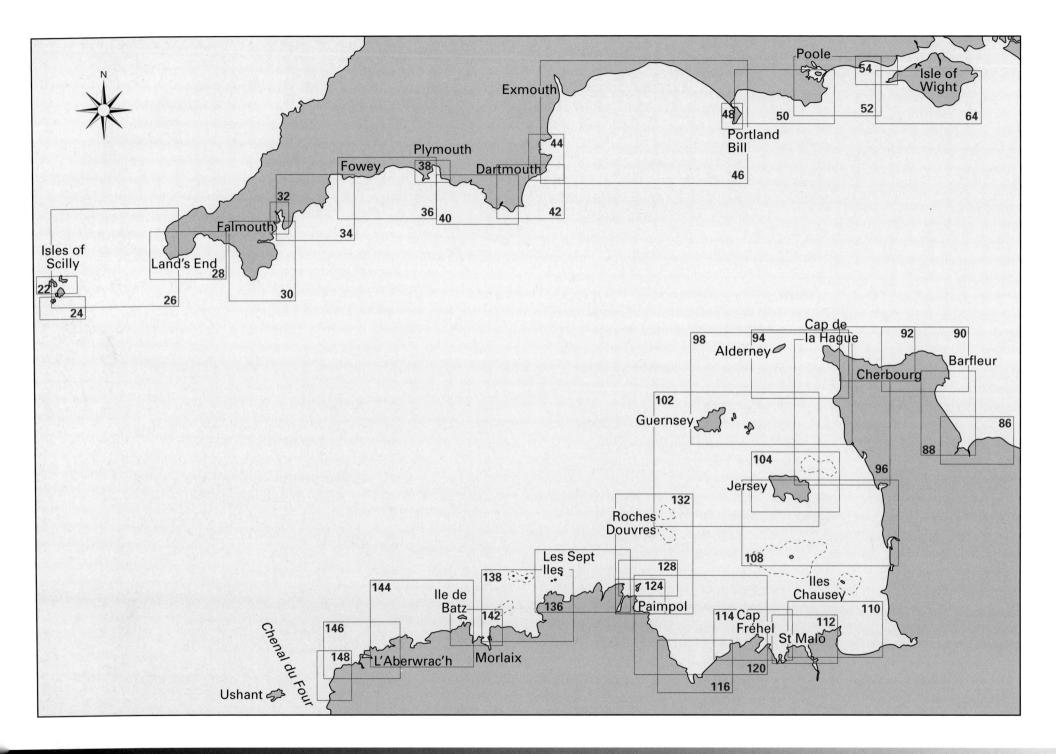

N

Poole

Isle of Wight

54

52

Exmouth

48

50

64

Portland Bill

44

Plymouth

46

Fowey

38

Dartmouth

32

36      40      42

Falmouth

34

Isles of Scilly

Land's End      28

22

26

30

24

Cap de la Hague

98      94

Alderney

92      90

Barfleur

Cherbourg

102

Guernsey

86

104

88

Jersey

96

132

Roches Douvres

108

Iles Chausey

128

Les Sept Iles

144      138

124

110

Ile de Batz

142      136      Paimpol

114 Cap Fréhel

112

146

St Malo

120

148      L'Aberwrac'h

Morlaix      116

Chenal du Four

Ushant

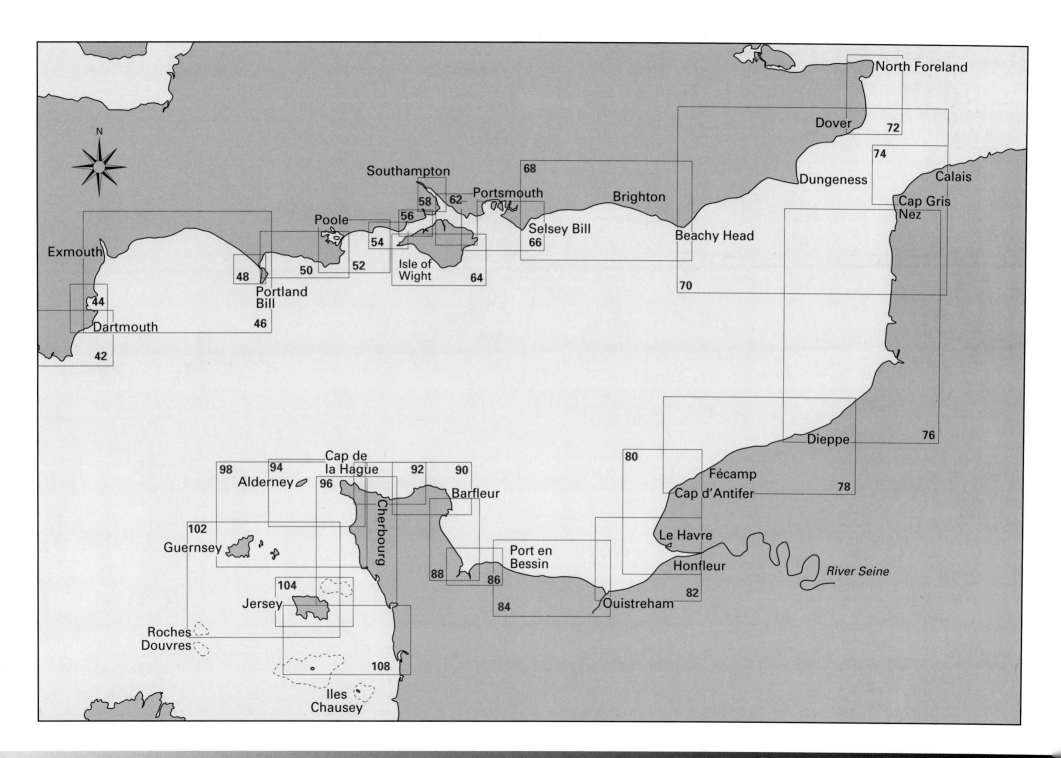

N

North Foreland

Dover 72

74

Dungeness

Calais

Cap Gris
Nez

Southampton

68

Portsmouth

Brighton

58
62

Poole

56

Selsey Bill

Beachy Head

54

66

70

52

Isle of
Wight

64

76

Exmouth

48

50

Portland
Bill

44

46

Dartmouth

42

Dieppe

Cap de
la Hague

98
94

92
90

80

Fécamp

Alderney

96

Cap d'Antifer

78

Barfleur

102

Cherbourg

Le Havre

Guernsey

River Seine

Honfleur

88

104

86

82

Jersey

84

Ouistreham

Roches
Douvres

Port en
Bessin

108

Iles
Chausey

# Introduction

## ELECTRONIC NAVIGATION

All navigation, whether 'pencil and dividers' or high-tech digital, has the common purpose of conducting a vessel safely from place to place and keeping track of where you are on the way. The aims of modern electronic navigation are identical to those of traditional navigation. Technology simply enables us to do this more easily, more accurately and, on the whole, more safely. Remember the basic objectives of any navigation:

1. Planning a safe and efficient route to avoid charted dangers

2. Position fixing and monitoring your route while on passage

3. Safe landfall pilotage until you are moored at your destination.

Traditional principles of seamanship don't change for electronic navigation. Linked to the basic skills and an informed awareness of error must be a sense of passage-making strategy and an understanding of the potential risks posed by a particular sea area at a given time in the conditions likely to be prevailing.

Whether you are using simple GPS, chart plotters or highly integrated systems, the first navigational priority will be to give a wide berth to dangerous reefs and banks, passing down-tide or to leeward if possible. You should be wary of certain headlands in wind-over-tide conditions, and cautious about approaching rocky coasts at night, in murky visibility or in strong onshore winds.

You have to allow for possible weather shifts, make the best use of tidal streams, plan landfalls carefully and work out possible bolt holes for different stages of your passage. Keeping a flexible strategy is becoming increasingly easy with each new generation of nav system, but despite this assistance navigators must always remain a bit pessimistic, ready for unforeseen complications and prepared for diversions in the event of mechanical problems or a threatening forecast.

It certainly makes sense for navigators to use technology to best advantage and there is now every reason to make GPS or plotter systems central to your navigation, so long as you maintain some basic seamanlike precautions:

a Always carry a set of paper charts for all stages of your passage, plus the relevant tidal atlases, pilot books and a current almanac.

b Make sure your GPS or plotter systems are carefully installed and located to reduce the risk of power failure, aerial problems or damage by seawater or corrosion.

c Ideally your GPS systems should be duplicated for safety, but at least always keep a hand-held GPS on board in a safe dry place, with plenty of spare batteries wrapped up carefully against damp.

d As part of normal navigation routine, keep a regular manual log of displayed latitude and longitude, at least every hour for displacement boats and more frequently aboard high-speed boats, so that if all systems should fail you can carry on navigating manually.

## WAYPOINT THINKING

Although navigators have always used buoys and other seamarks as signposts on passage, the waypoint concept has taken on a wider meaning since its incorporation into GPS route planning software. Waypoints are used to represent both tangible navigation marks along a route and more arbitrary positions that serve as convenient, safe and also efficient turning points between stages of a passage.

Figure 1 shows examples of three different types of waypoint, using a coastal passage eastward round Tangle Point and Bull Head

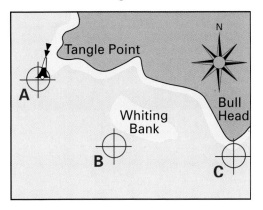

Waypoint A is the south-cardinal buoy off Tangle Point, either its actual latitude and longitude or a position slightly to seaward of the buoy. Waypoint B is a clearing waypoint set a safe distance seaward of Whiting Bank so that the passage legs approaching and leaving 'B' both take you through safe water. Waypoint C is a headland clearing waypoint whose distance offshore will depend on local factors and conditions, such as how steep the coast is, the wind direction at the time and whether there are any tidal overfalls or crab-pots to avoid.

When you use waypoints routinely, it soon becomes apparent that the safe placing of different types of waypoint depends not only on the extent and severity of the charted dangers involved, but also on the 'shape' of your passage and the angles each passage leg makes when approaching, passing and leaving an area of danger.

### Seamark waypoints

Seamark waypoints may be buoys, beacons, light-floats, lightships, and so on. Some navigators set actual positions for seamark waypoints, to maximise the chance of actually finding the mark. Others prefer offset waypoints, to be sure of staying in safe water and, in poor visibility, to reduce the risk of collision with the waypoint!

### Clearing waypoints

Danger clearing waypoints are set a safe but arbitrarily judged distance clear of navigational dangers such as sandbanks, reefs, headlands or races off headlands. Because clearing waypoints are often positions at which you change course, they must be set so that your tracks approaching and leaving the waypoint both lie in safe water, with no dangerous cutting of corners.

The distance off for clearing waypoints may depend on weather and sea-state, wind direction, visibility, whether the headland is a popular area for crab-pots, the type of boat (deep or shallow draught) and her general manoeuvrability and cruising speed.

Setting the right distance off involves judgment and experience. You obviously don't want to shave a danger area too close, and yet taking too wide a sweep adds extra distance and time that may be crucial later in the passage. Even an extra half an hour at sea may have a significant bearing on future events in the lottery of changing weather and sea conditions.

### Turning waypoints

Some waypoints are arbitrarily chosen positions at which it is simply convenient to alter course: for example, off a bulge in the coast where the shoreline changes direction, or perhaps on the edge of a traffic separation scheme within which your heading is constrained at right-angles to the direction of the scheme.

### Departure waypoints

When starting an open sea passage, navigators have traditionally taken a final departure from some convenient known point, such as an outer channel buoy or a fix position off a headland. You should also set a clear departure waypoint when using GPS, rather than just allowing the system to take its own departure from wherever you switch on. The cross-track error display will then make logical sense throughout the passage, showing current displacement from the direct track between your departure and landfall waypoints.

### Landfall waypoints

These are carefully chosen positions out in safe water, perhaps within a few miles of the coast you are heading for. Landfall waypoints may be seamarks, such as fairway buoys or outer channel buoys, but they may also just be convenient positions on the chart that are far enough offshore to be safe destinations in any weather, but close enough inshore that you can identify landmarks and get your bearings before closing the coast.

When specifying landfall waypoints, much depends on the type of coastline you are approaching: whether steep-to or gradually shoaling; whether it is free of offshore dangers or littered with rocks or sandbanks; whether it is high and fairly easy to identify or low, featureless and enigmatic. Also consider what the tide will be doing as you approach the coast. Where streams are powerful, as in the Dover Strait, around the Channel Islands or along the North Brittany coast, it's usually best to arrive a little up-tide of your destination (easier by far to drop down half-a-mile with a three-knot stream than push back against it).

### Approach waypoints

You need to have done your homework for the final approach and carefully worked out any inshore waypoints that may be useful, for example, in leading along a harbour entrance channel or into a river mouth in poor visibility. Don't worry about over-preparing an approach. To my mind, it doesn't make sense to use GPS to arrive precisely at an outer fairway buoy and then risk getting lost or confused in the more intricate coastal buoyage simply through lack of preparation. Used with care, GPS waypoints can be extremely helpful in close-quarters pilotage, keeping you oriented while you try to identify important marks visually.

I prefer to enter a complete set of waypoints for a passage – a door-to-door route that can, if necessary, take you right up to the marina entrance. You will appreciate such detailed waypoint planning if the weather turns foul during a landfall, perhaps when the coast you have successfully found and identified vanishes in driving rain, along with the next critical buoy you thought you'd just spotted a mile away.

Of course you must be careful using waypoints close inshore and along narrow channels, since the normal limits of system accuracy can sometimes take you the wrong side of a buoy as easily as the right side. However, close-quarters waypoints can at least set you off in the right direction towards the next mark, until you identify it for certain by eye.

### Marking waypoints on the chart

Having decided on a set of waypoints for a passage, I like to pencil them on the charts in black-and-white, using the now conventional waypoint symbol and with the GPS identifier written against each waypoint for example P001, P002, P003, P004 etc, or the relevant reference numbers from this Waypoint Guide.

## Entering and checking waypoints

Using electronic systems as primary means of position fixing, it's vital to double-check, slowly and carefully, that you have entered your selected waypoints accurately. One wrong digit can lead you into trouble, and a slight error in a waypoint position can be more dangerous than a large error that may often reveal itself as such in good time.

Make sure you key in the decimal point correctly, and check that you are entering latitude when your system is expecting latitude, and longitude when it is expecting longitude. Most longitudes in this book are west of Greenwich, so you need to know whether your program assumes west or east longitude as a default entry – remember to change this if necessary with the ± or E/W key.

Once all waypoints for a passage have been entered, scroll them across the display to double-check the latitudes and longitudes against your list. Check and double-check are the watchwords with electronic navigation, a way of thinking that should continue throughout a passage. At sea, you should be frequently scanning your GPS displays, or different 'pages', to verify that what they are showing is consistent with your route plan and the tidal effects that you are expecting to experience.

## Monitoring tidal effects

A gradually increasing discrepancy between a charted course to steer and the displayed 'course to next waypoint' is usually the result of a cross-tide. So if you know from the tidal atlas what the stream should be doing and if the difference between the displayed and charted courses to steer develops as expected, you have an explainable consistency between different sources of information which strengthens the reliability of the navigational conclusions you can draw. The habit of looking for consistency, or inconsistency, between different sources of navigational information is just as important as it always was in traditional navigation, indeed even more important now that we are using electronic systems as the primary means of finding our way about.

## Conclusions on choosing and using waypoints

Waypoint thinking has now become a normal part of modern navigation, but it's important to remember that routing information given by GPS displays depends crucially on the care and accuracy with which waypoints are specified, stored and handled.

While some traditional navigational methods and skills are falling naturally into disuse, many new kinds of expertise are emerging. Perhaps the most important relate to the whole business of passage planning and setting up a navigation system so that it can easily handle possible changes of route without significant data entry at sea. A vital consideration here lies in specifying safe, carefully considered individual waypoints that when linked together create safe and efficient routes.

Although the process of setting a waypoint may seem routine and straightforward, there can be many strategic implications in the selection of even a single waypoint, especially off a tricky coast. How a number of waypoints then fit together to form a route can be critical to the value and flexibility of a passage plan.

## ELECTRONIC NAVIGATION IN PRACTICE

The power of GPS comes not just from the still amazing facility of having your position displayed continuously to within a few metres, but also from the slick passage planning software which has introduced the concepts of 'waypoint' and 'cross-track error', and which brings into sharp focus the idea of 'course and speed made good'.

GPS displays of 'distance to next waypoint' and 'bearing to next waypoint' are important route monitoring features, and electronic navigators now visualise, and hence plan, their passages in a different kind of way. Destinations seem more precise, with waypoints normally specified to two or three decimal places of a minute.

One side effect of such theoretically accurate navigation comes from greatly increased expectations of a precisely ordered passage. Even fairly minor incidents or problems causing deviations from plan can now cause feelings of 'distress' in relatively inexperienced navigators, where they would once have been accepted as a normal part of passage-making and being at sea. Always remember that you are not necessarily in danger just because a GPS system has failed and you suddenly don't know exactly where you are. Anyone who goes to sea should have traditional navigation skills that can take over effortlessly and without any great stress if any electronic navigation system should fail.

## Allowing for tide

Tide doesn't vanish off the scene just because you are using a precise position-fixing system. When planning longish passages in tidal waters, you still have to assess the net tidal effect in advance, as you would if navigating the traditional way. Indeed a full appreciation of tidal streams throughout all stages of a passage is important for interpreting changing GPS displays, especially 'cross-track error' displays.

Novice navigators sometimes interpret 'cross-track error' as kind of a *navigational* error or an off-course warning needing immediate correction, but this is usually not the case on a longish passage. Cross-track error is not an error if, for example, the tide is setting west for the first half of a Channel crossing, then slack for an hour, then setting east for the second half. Designing navigational software from scratch, it would be best not to use the term 'cross-track error' at all, but perhaps 'cross-track shift' which doesn't imply that anything is wrong, but simply that for one reason or another you have drifted off the direct line between two waypoints.

On a longish passage, working out the most efficient course to start steering involves the same tide calculations as if you were navigating by traditional methods. The tidal vectors are compounded for the estimated duration of your passage, and the course to steer laid off on the chart in the usual way. For fast motor boats, however, this process isn't usually worth the bother and it's simplest, although strictly speaking not optimal, to simply stay on the direct track between waypoints and steer by the 'rolling road' GPS display.

## Monitoring tide

Accurate position-fixing systems allow you to monitor the effect of tidal streams quite precisely. With GPS interfaced to an electronic compass and log, some systems can display the tidal direction and rate you are experiencing at any given time, by calculating the vector difference between the course steered and speed through the water and your actual course and speed made good.

Even without this facility, an experienced navigator can soon tell from the 'cross-track error' and 'bearing to next waypoint' displays whether he is experiencing more or less tide than predicted and can then adjust his course in good time.

## GPS landfalls

The satisfaction of a good landfall never palls, although a landfall on instruments has a different quality to the traditional style of arrival when you were often not too sure which section of coast would lift above the horizon.

Using GPS, and especially watching a chart plotter, you make a landfall more gradually, well in advance of actually seeing land. The flashing icon edges closer to your approach waypoint, converging with the video outline of the coast. The first radar echoes of the coast may turn up long before you glimpse land over the bow. Compared to a plotter display of charted land, a radar scan somehow has a genuine solid feel about it, a real but invisible sighting. Yet even knowing your position every step of the way, and despite the advance warning of various displays, it's exhilarating when the first smudge of land appears ahead.

As you draw closer inshore, it's prudent to plot your GPS latitude and longitude in pencil on a fairly large-scale landfall chart from time to time and project your track forwards, so that you can check your approach line against the big picture that only a paper chart can provide. Remember that an approach waypoint may have been set slightly in error and you want to discover this sooner rather later, before getting close in amongst hazards.

A traditional and long recognised danger about landfalls, especially with inexperienced navigators, is that once you see solid land up ahead, the passage may suddenly feel almost over and you can start to relax, imagining yourself practically to have arrived just as the boat is entering the most risky part of the trip. This tendency to lose focus is equally relevant to instrument landfalls, sometimes more so because a navigator using GPS usually feels certain about his position and highly confident about picking up whatever marks he has set

as waypoints. But guard against over-confidence and keep double-checking the navigation until you really do arrive. It's easy to see what you expect to see, but don't jump to premature conclusions about which lighthouse is which, or which headland has just lifted above the horizon.

## Landfalls and the visual picture

When your attention has been focused on relatively small GPS displays during the main part of a passage, it's important to try and build up a clear mental picture of where your landfall and final approach waypoints will lead you. This aspect of pilotage develops gradually with experience, the facility to draw upon all available sources of data to enhance the developing image in your mind of how all the coastal features, landmarks, seamarks and navigational dangers fit together, and what everything should look like as you arrive.

Fig. 2 shows an imaginary landfall fairly typical of many arrivals around the Channel Islands or the rocky coasts of North Brittany. You have a distant background of land with various rocks and islets dotted about the approaches, buoys and beacons leading the way in and a strong tide across the entrance. In clear visibility you'd see the land, islets and larger beacon towers from well offshore, but the buoys and slimmer spar beacons would only gradually pop up as you drew closer in.

As with any complex puzzle, it's useful to identify with certainty at least one pretty unambiguous feature and work outwards from there, as with a surveyor triangulating from a known point. For this kind of landfall decoding, a full-sized paper chart is immeasurably better, clearer and more easily apprehended than a tiny plotter screen, which gives little sense of context. At the same time, setting waypoints all the way inshore gives you confidence to press on safely while you are trying to work things out.

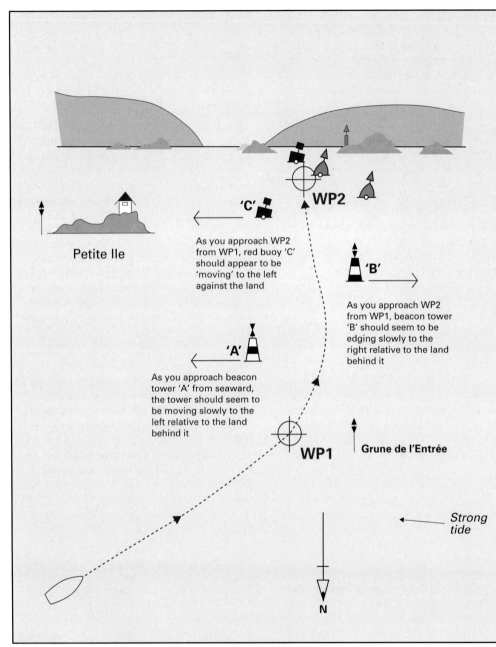

**FIGURE 2 - INTERPRETING LANDFALL FEATURES**

Labels in figure:
Petite Ile

'C' — As you approach WP2 from WP1, red buoy 'C' should appear to be 'moving' to the left against the land

WP2

'B' — As you approach WP2 from WP1, beacon tower 'B' should seem to be edging slowly to the right relative to the land behind it

'A' — As you approach beacon tower 'A' from seaward, the tower should seem to be moving slowly to the left relative to the land behind it

WP1

Grune de l'Entrée

Strong tide

N

In Figure 2, given the angle of approach, Petite Ile will probably be the first feature to identify clearly, a fair way offshore with its small but recognisable house on its highest end. As you approach the outer entrance waypoint ⊕1 from the direction shown, the colours or topmarks of beacon towers 'A' and 'B' may not be obvious from a couple of miles off, but by watching how these marks 'move' against the land and relative to each other, you'll soon be able to work out which is which.

Because tower 'A' has to be left well to port going in and there's a strong tidal stream on your starboard bow, you should hold, by your plotter displays, just a little up-tide of ⊕1 on the approach and then keep just up-tide of the new track once you start heading towards ⊕2 from ⊕1. On both these legs you also need to keep in mind that, with any close-quarters waypoint opposite a fairly narrow entrance gap, there's always scope for slight error in how the waypoint was originally placed. Coming in towards ⊕1 from seaward, while monitoring your 'distance to waypoint' and 'cross-track error' displays, also watch ahead by eye how tower 'A' seems to be 'moving' relative to the vista of islets and land behind it. For your track to leave 'A' safely to port, this tower should seem to be moving *to the left* against the land as you draw closer to ⊕1.

It's good to cultivate this habit of watching relative visual shifts throughout a landfall approach, to check you are 'on the glide path'. As you round tower 'A', with the tide trying to set you east, it's best to hold up to starboard for a while towards beacon tower 'B'. But even as you steer by GPS towards the inner waypoint ⊕2 and keep an eye on the new cross-track-error, your attention should also be visually focused on the red lateral buoy 'C' up ahead and how it seems to be moving relative to the land behind it. Buoy 'C' should seem to be edging slightly left against the land if your track is to leave 'C' to port.

When you think about these shifting visual patterns of various marks and what they mean for your pilotage, how much more critical (yet at the same time more simple!) everything would be in murky visibility. Approaching gingerly on instruments, suppose you saw nothing of this landfall scene until spotting beacon tower 'A' on the port bow, with maybe a ghostly hint of tower 'B' behind it. Then it would take real care and judgment to gauge the effect of strong cross-tide from your GPS displays and give tower 'A' safe clearance.

## Heavy weather

Good navigation systems really come into their own in heavy weather, especially when your GPS receiver is duplicated for peace of mind. The main requirement for navigation in heavy weather is that your passage planning should be even more conscientious than usual. The classic landfall risk, of trying to reach a nearby harbour that is inherently unsafe in the prevailing conditions, can actually be increased when you have accurate position-fixing systems when anything seems possible. This is a question of seamanship rather than navigation, but there are cases every season where skippers using GPS have diverted, in deteriorating weather, for potentially dangerous entrances they would never have considered if navigating by traditional methods.

Even with high technology, prudent seamanship should rule the day. Beware of closing a tide-swept rocky coast in rising onshore winds, or making for a shallow river mouth where the seas are liable to break over a bar. Don't risk being guided with unerring digital accuracy into a traditional seaman's death-trap.

## The danger of 'auto-steering'

Perhaps one of the greatest hazards from increasingly integrated systems is the risk from boats being steered on autopilot directly from GPS, when you select a particular waypoint and tell the boat to go there automatically. This auto-track facility must be used with great caution, not only in terms of always keeping a good lookout at sea, but also in the care given to data input so that you are not sent off inadvertently in a dangerous direction.

## Regular manual back-up

Even if you have fully duplicated position-fixing systems, it's vital to keep a regular note of the minimum data that would enable you to carry on navigating manually should all your equipment fail. The minimum safe record is to write down every hour (every half-hour for fast motor boats) the time, your course, log reading and latitude and longitude by GPS, having first checked that, if you have duplicate systems, the two displays are giving practically the same readings. By keeping up this minimum log as a routine, you'll never be far away from an accurate position, and you can quickly use your course steered and present log reading to work out an estimated position if your electronics go down.

## USING THE WAYPOINT GUIDE

This Waypoint Guide has been compiled for the convenience of anyone who uses electronic systems for navigating the popular cruising areas of the English Channel, under sail or power. As I have indicated, choosing and specifying waypoints, especially landfall waypoints, needs care and judgment. The waypoints presented in this guide have certainly been set with safety in mind, but they have also been chosen to be practical in all kinds of passage-making circumstances, whether yachts are pottering fairly close inshore within a local area, cruising between neighbouring coastal areas, or arriving on a particular stretch of coast after a longish offshore passage. Near the front of the guide is a set of charts, waypoints and routes for crossing different sections of the English Channel.

It is not enough to present published waypoints in a long numbered list with rather vague labels. A navigator has to understand exactly where a waypoint lies in relation to a harbour entrance, in relation to coastal dangers and in relation to other waypoints. Each double-page spread in this

book therefore covers a particular section of coast in detail. A scale chart on each right-hand page shows the location of my chosen waypoints in that area, while the precise positions and descriptions of these waypoints are given in a table on the corresponding left-hand page.

The latitude and longitude of waypoints is given to three decimal places of a minute, ready for immediate entry into a GPS database. Also, because it's important for navigators to know exactly where each waypoint can be located and plotted on a paper chart, a description of each waypoint's charted position is included in the tables, usually related by bearing and distance to some readily identifiable landmark or seamark. You therefore know exactly which waypoint you are dealing with and can readily judge whether it is safe and suitable for your purpose.

Together with the detailed waypoint table on each left-hand page, I have given a brief summary of the most significant coastal dangers in that area, together with a list of the relevant paper charts, so that navigators have this information conveniently to hand.

## WAYPOINTS FOR CHART PLOTTERS

Compact chart plotters and computer-based navigation systems are widely used as the principal means of navigating boats of all sizes. Their accuracy and clarity is remarkable and even quite inexpensive plotters will show your boat moored neatly alongside the exact pontoon in a marina.

Most compact plotters use the excellent Navionics electronic cartography, while most computer-based systems use the familiar Admiralty charts or sometimes Imray charts. Many navigators have laptops or notebooks on board for Admiralty or Imray chart systems, and Admiralty charts can also be downloaded as apps onto iPhones and iPads. High definition laptop screens give you the best viewing, but even large screens don't show you the overall picture as well as a full-sized paper chart, and in practice it's not always easy to judge, from the screen alone, whether a waypoint you have entered so easily is in the best or safest position for the passage as a whole.

With compact chart plotters in particular, whose cartography, while certainly impressive, is not so clear or familiar as a large display of an Admiralty chart, it can be all too easy to join two waypoints to form a neat looking track that passes unintentionally close to some charted but difficult-to-spot danger. You also need to be sure that, at the end of one passage leg, you are in a safe position to set off on the following leg and are not starting from somewhere that gives a tricky angle on your next target waypoint.

Even when using plotters or PC systems, I like to choose my waypoints with reference to Admiralty charts of the area concerned. In compiling this guide, I have considered routes and passages to and from all directions, and potentially undertaken in a wide range of weather and tidal conditions. I have selected waypoints that I use myself and would be happy to rely on under most

conceivable circumstances. If you regularly use a chart plotter to find your way about, this Guide will provide an ideal source of waypoints for passage planning and landfalls in the English Channel cruising area.

## Enter and edit

While it's now very easy to move a cursor on a plotter screen to enter a waypoint, or with some systems just touch the screen where you'd like to place a waypoint, you usually find the initial waypoint position is not quite what you'd have marked on a paper chart with a pencil and the benefit of the clear overview that such a chart provides. Moving a cursor across a small screen is not a particularly precise business and you often find that a waypoint selected in this way is not quite the right distance off a headland or perhaps doesn't give the best turning-point between two successive legs in a route.

While you don't want to pass precariously close to a reef or sandbank, there's also no point in rounding such dangers too far off. Strangely enough, waypoint routes entered directly onto a screen often pass much further away from given buoys, headlands or dangers than you'd want to in practice.

So once you have entered waypoints into a plotter system by clicking on cursor positions, you can easily edit them using this Guide, fine-tuning the numbers of latitude and longitude so that you'll be happy with each waypoint position not just for the passage in hand, but also for future passages that may use that particular waypoint. A navigator must be confident that stored waypoints are 'quality waypoints' that will serve him safely in future passages if he clicks them into a different route, or perhaps sets them as a destination in slightly stressful conditions of heavy weather or poor visibility. The waypoints in this Guide have been carefully specified with that important long-term criterion in mind.

## Waypoint naming

As anyone who uses computer systems quickly discovers, it doesn't take long to build up large directories of material, whether you are talking about documents and folders in a PC or waypoints and routes in a navigation system. As you accumulate more and more waypoints in different cruising areas, it's vital to be certain, not only that you are saving good quality data, but that you label this data clearly to make it unambiguously identifiable when you come to use it much later.

Compact chart plotters only allow limited fields for waypoint names, so you may find it convenient to use the waypoint reference numbers in this Guide as identifiers in a plotter database. PC or laptop based navigation systems allow more generous 'comment' space for waypoint descriptions, so with these you can easily enter the 'Waypoint names and positions' that are given in the second column of the waypoint tables in this guide.

And always remember, as with any vital data punched into a computer, to check and double-check the result, to make sure that the latitudes and longitudes you have entered, stored and will later rely on are exactly correct.

## DATUM OF CHARTED POSITIONS

The latitudes and longitudes of all waypoints in this Guide are referred to WGS 84 datum (World Geodetic System 1984), the current international standard for chart cartography.

If you still have (as I do) some older, perhaps favourite paper charts based on earlier datum systems, WGS 84 waypoints plotted on these charts will not appear in exactly the positions intended by this Guide – may, for example, appear closer to or further from a buoy or headland, or sometimes even turn up the wrong side of a buoy. So be very careful when physically plotting WGS 84 waypoints on older charts without making the necessary datum corrections.

Most older Admiralty charts of UK waters were based on datum OSGB 36 (Ordnance Survey of Great Britain 1936), while those covering French and Channel Island waters were generally referred to ED 50 (European Datum 1950). Unless they are extremely old, such charts will contain a note near their title giving the small latitude and longitude corrections to be made either when plotting WGS 84 waypoints on a chart with a different datum or, in the other direction, entering waypoint positions taken from an older chart into a WGS 84 GPS or plotter system. In most cases and in most conditions these small differences will not have much practical effect on safe navigation, either because there's plenty of room for manoeuvre or because you'll naturally steer the right side of a buoy or beacon once you have spotted and identified it. In poor visibility, however, homing towards a slightly misplaced waypoint could have more serious consequences.

## A CAUTIONARY TALE

I have commented earlier that small plotter screens are poor at showing the overall context in which routing decisions are made. Even laptop sized screens give a very limited feel of a sea area when the chart is zoomed out, and once you start zooming in you quickly lose the sense of perspective by which safe routes are worked out. A large paper chart, on the other hand, conveys not just navigational detail but also the clear relationship between all the marks, dangers and stretches of coast. When you are working out passage legs, there's nothing to beat paper charts for a strategic overview and for choosing more or less where to set waypoints, even if their precise positions are then specified on the screen.

When a plotter screen is well zoomed in, it's easy for buoys or beacons to be confused with each other, which is exactly what happened in this example when a semi-displacement motor yacht, *Lucky Break*, was making a passage between St Peter Port in Guernsey and the 'French Channel Islands' Iles Chausey. *Lucky Break* is just under 40ft long with a cruising speed of around 17 knots.

On the morning in question conditions were quiet and there was nothing problematic about making this passage. However, the original plan had been to head for St Helier and spend a night there before going on down to Granville or Chausey next morning. It was only as *Lucky Break* was approaching the southwest corner of Jersey that her owner decided to press on for Iles Chausey directly and stay there for a lazy afternoon before continuing to Granville in the evening. Because this change was made on the spur of the moment, the passage legs between La Corbière and Chausey were worked out quickly on the plotter.

Figure 3 shows *Lucky Break*'s revised passage direct to Chausey. From a clearing waypoint west of La Corbière, the new

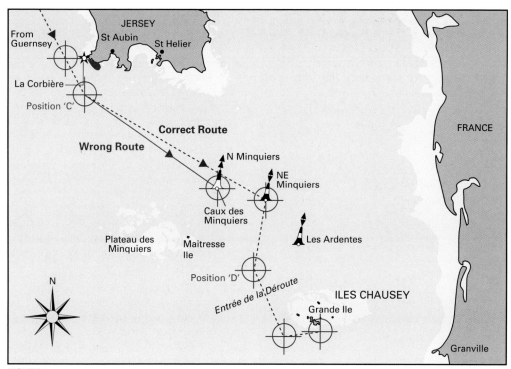

**FIGURE 3**

route continued on the same track for three miles to clear the dangers off Jersey's south coast. At position 'C', *Lucky Break* would turn more easterly towards the NE Minquiers E-cardinal buoy, and from here head just west of south for five miles until Les Ardentes reef had been safely passed, and then SSE towards the southwest corner of the Chausey plateau.

These new waypoints hadn't been considered in advance and were set up simply by using the plotter cursor and clicking positions onto the screen. But when scrolling the plotter across to the NE Minquiers buoy, the chart must have been well zoomed in and the skipper actually clicked the cursor at the **North Minquiers** buoy, merrily setting off for this waypoint by mistake.

Because the track to North Minquiers would barely be 5° different from the correct route, the problem wouldn't be obvious from the new 'course to steer'. However, perusing the Admiralty 2669 paper chart would have revealed the error, because the NE Minquiers is a good three miles further from position 'C'.

It's also puzzling that the mistake wasn't spotted as *Lucky Break* reached a north-cardinal buoy rather than the east-cardinal the skipper should have been expecting. However the vis was fairly hazy, the sun more or less ahead and I suppose the crew saw what they expected to see. Off the North Minquiers, the skipper clicked onto a new waypoint, position 'D', which he'd chosen as a suitable leg from the **NE Minquiers** for clearing Les Ardentes reef before turning towards Chausey.

Chillingly, heading for 'D' from the North Minquiers buoy would lead *Lucky Break* straight towards one of the shallowest dangers of the Caux des Minquiers which the NE Minquiers buoy is there to guard! Above half-tide this wouldn't be a problem, but the tide was now well down with this 2m drying head at a dangerous stage, not far below the surface. Thank goodness the skipper wasn't completely asleep. After only a few minutes on the new track, he realised they should have been steering SSW towards 'D', but the plotter was leading them *east* of south. He quickly pulled both engines back to neutral and they lay idling while he worked out what was wrong.

At 17 knots, the boat had already travelled over a mile from the North Minquiers buoy and the skipper now noticed that Maîtresse Ile and its islets seemed closer than they should have been. Then, as *Lucky Break* rolled slightly in the gentle swell, he saw an eerie patch of lazily breaking water not far to the southeast, probably the lurking reef they might soon have hit.

It was a sight to give any navigator the shivers in this rock-strewn area. The skipper turned the boat in her length and headed slowly back towards the buoy they'd just passed. When he saw the north-cardinal cones and read the name he felt pretty guilty about making such a slip. It was certainly careless, but also a lesson for all of us in the dangers of clicking waypoints directly onto a plotter screen when you can't see the big picture. Your paper chart should always be there beside you, providing that crucial overview.

## GENERAL CAUTION

All the waypoints in this Guide have been chosen and specified with great care, to be safe, suitable and convenient when used in conjunction with GPS, either for making a landfall on the relevant section of coast or for cruising between sections. However, it is never necessarily safe to approach any waypoint from all directions. Navigators must always refer to the appropriate large-scale Admiralty charts when planning landfalls or passages in any of the areas covered by this Guide.

On the question of published accuracy, it is also important to remember that, while the marked positions of all waypoints and the accuracy of their latitudes and longitudes have been exhaustively checked before publication, the small risk of errors can never be eliminated entirely. This Waypoint Guide is presented in good faith as a considerable aid and convenience to navigators, but neither the Author nor the Publishers can hold themselves responsible for any accident or misadventure allegedly attributable, wholly or partly, to the use of any waypoint contained herein, whether or not there was any Author's or Publisher's error in specifying or printing the waypoint positions or their latitudes and longitudes.

All navigators at sea are ultimately responsible for their own safety and must assure themselves of the accuracy and relevance of published information before acting upon it. In particular, any published waypoint from whatever source must always be used in a seamanlike manner, and its accuracy and suitability for a specific navigational purpose verified by reference to the largest scale Admiralty charts of the area.

# Cross-Channel routes – West Channel area

| ⊕ Waypoint name and position | Route |
|---|---|
| WCH01 Falmouth to L'Aberwrac'h | WCR01–WCR05 |
| WCH02 Falmouth to the Chenal du Four | WCR01–WCR03 |
| WCH03 Fowey to L'Aberwrac'h | WCR02–WCR05 |
| WCH04 Fowey to the Chenal du Four | WCR02–WCR03 |
| WCH05 Plymouth to L'Aberwrac'h | WCR09–WCR05 |
| WCH06 Plymouth to the Chenal du Four | WCR09–WCR04–WCR03 |
| WCH07 Plymouth to Morlaix | WCR09–WCR07–WCR06 |
| WCH08 Salcombe to Morlaix | WCR20–WCR06 |
| WCH09 Plymouth to Trébeurden | WCR09–WCR08–WCR11–WCR10 |
| WCH10 Salcombe to Trébeurden west of Les Triagoz | WCR20–WCR08–WCR11–WCR10 |
| WCH11 Salcombe to Trébeurden or Perros-Guirec | WCR20–WCR12 |
| WCH12 Dartmouth to Trébeurden or Perros-Guirec | WCR24–WCR12 |
| WCH13 Dartmouth to Tréguier | WCR24–WCR13 |
| WCH14 Dartmouth to Lézardrieux | WCR24–WCR17–WCR15 |
| WCH15 Tor Bay to Tréguier | WCR25–WCR13 |
| WCH16 Tor Bay to Lézardrieux | WCR25–WCR17–WCR15 |
| WCH17 Guernsey to Tréguier | WCR21–WCR14–WCR13 |
| WCH18 Guernsey to Lézardrieux west of Roches Douvres | WCR21–WCR14–WCR16–WCR15 |
| WCH19 Guernsey to Lézardrieux east of Roches Douvres | WCR21–WCR18–WCR17–WCR15 |
| WCH20 Guernsey to St Quay or Binic | WCR21–WCR19 |
| WCH21 Salcombe to Les Hanois | WCR20–WCR22 |
| WCH22 Dartmouth to Les Hanois | WCR24–WCR22 |
| WCH23 Tor Bay to Les Hanois | WCR25–WCR22 |
| WCH24 Dartmouth to the Little Russel | WCR24–WCR23–WCR26 |
| WCH25 Tor Bay to the Little Russel | WCR25–WCR23–WCR26 |
| WCH26 West Shambles to the Little Russel | WCR30–WCR29–WCR28–WCR27–WCR26 |
| WCH27 East Shambles to the Little Russel | WCR31–WCR29–WCR28–WCR27–WCR26 |

# Cross-Channel routes – Central Channel area

| ⊕ | Waypoint name and position | Route |
|---|---|---|
| CCH01 | West Shambles to Alderney | CCR01–CCR10 |
| CCH02 | East Shambles to Alderney | CCR02–CCR10 |
| CCH03 | Poole to Guernsey via Alderney race | CCR03–CCR09–CCR08–CCR07 |
| CCH04 | Poole to Cherbourg west entrance | CCR03–CCR11 |
| CCH05 | Needles to Guernsey via Alderney race | CCR04–CCR09–CCR08–CCR07 |
| CCH06 | Needles to Cherbourg west entrance | CCR04–CCR11 |
| CCH07 | Needles to St Vaast-la-Hougue | CCR04–CCR13–CCR14–CCR15 |
| CCH08 | East Solent (West Princessa) to Cherbourg east entrance | CCR05–CCR12 |
| CCH09 | East Solent (Nab Tower west) to Cherbourg east entrance | CCR06–CCR12 |
| CCH10 | East Solent (West Princessa) to St Vaast-la-Hougue | CCR05–CCR14–CCR15 |
| CCH11 | East Solent (Nab Tower west) to St Vaast-la-Hougue | CCR06–CCR14–CCR15 |

# Cross-Channel routes – East Channel area

| ⊕ | Waypoint name and position | Route |
|---|---|---|
| ECH01 | East Solent (Bembridge Ledge) to Courseulles-sur-Mer | ECR01–ECR04 |
| ECH02 | East Solent (Nab Tower west) to Ouistreham | ECR02–ECR05 |
| ECH03 | East Solent (Nab Tower east) to Le Havre | ECR03–ECR06–ECR07 |
| ECH04 | Brighton to Le Havre, Deauville or the Seine | ECR08–ECR09–ECR10–ECR07 |
| ECH05 | Newhaven to Le Havre, Deauville or the Seine | ECR11–ECR12–ECR07 |
| ECH06 | Brighton to Fécamp | ECR08–ECR13–ECR14–ECR15 |
| ECH07 | Newhaven to Fécamp | ECR11–ECR13–ECR14–ECR15 |
| ECH08 | Brighton to St Valery-en-Caux | ECR08–ECR16–ECR17–ECR18 |
| ECH09 | Newhaven to St Valery-en-Caux | ECR11–ECR16–ECR17–ECR18 |
| ECH10 | Newhaven to Dieppe | ECR11–ECR19–ECR20–ECR21 |
| ECH11 | Eastbourne to Dieppe | ECR22–ECR19–ECR20–ECR21 |
| ECH12 | Eastbourne to St Valery-sur-Somme | ECR22–ECR23 |
| ECH13 | Dover to Boulogne | ECR24–ECR25–ECR26–ECR27–ECR28 |
| ECH14 | Dover to Calais | ECR24–ECR29–ECR30–ECR31–ECR32–ECR33 |

# West Channel Route Waypoints

| ⊕ | Waypoint name and position | Latitude | Longitude |
|---|---|---|---|
| WCR01 | Falmouth entrance, 4ca SW of St Anthony Head lighthouse | 50°08.184'N | 005°01.410'W |
| WCR02 | Fowey entrance, 0.16M 130°T from Fowey lighthouse | 50°19.527'N | 004°38.641'W |
| WCR03 | Le Four west clearing, 1M due W of Le Four lighthouse | 48°31.380'N | 004°49.835'W |
| WCR04 | Grande Basse de Portsall, 1¼M due W of W-card buoy | 48°36.701'N | 004°48.010'W |
| WCR05 | L'Aberwrac'h N approach, 1.2M 348°T from Le Libenter buoy | 48°38.628'N | 004°38.830'W |
| WCR06 | Stolvezen, 2ca NW of Stolvezen red buoy | 48°42.789'N | 003°53.623'W |
| WCR07 | Grand Chenal outer, 2ca NE of Pot de Fer E-card buoy | 48°44.370'N | 003°53.800'W |
| WCR08 | Les Triagoz west clearing, 5M due W of Triagoz lighthouse | 48°52.281'N | 003°46.392'W |
| WCR09 | Plymouth W entrance, 2ca W of breakwater W lighthouse | 50°20.070'N | 004°09.837'W |
| WCR10 | Trébeurden approach, 150m S of Ar Gourédec S-card buoy | 48°46.332'N | 003°36.595'W |
| WCR11 | Le Crapaud S, 1.3M S of Le Crapaud W-card buoy | 48°45.370'N | 003°40.590'W |
| WCR12 | Les Sept Îles west, 2¼M W of Île aux Moines lighthouse | 48°52.723'N | 003°32.816'W |
| WCR13 | Tréguier outer, 3ca 287°T from Basse Crublent red buoy | 48°54.380'N | 003°11.600'W |
| WCR14 | Roches Douvres west clearing, 3M WNW of lighthouse | 49°07.431'N | 002°53.071'W |
| WCR15 | Grand Chenal inner, 3ca NNW of Rosédo white pyramid | 48°51.770'N | 003°00.930'W |
| WCR16 | Chenal de Bréhat N, 1¾M 021°T from Le Paon lighthouse | 48°53.554'N | 002°58.207'W |
| WCR17 | Grand Chenal approach, 8ca NW of Nord Horaine buoy | 48°55.002'N | 002°56.020'W |
| WCR18 | Barnouic E clearing, 2½M SE of Barnouic E-card tower | 48°59.764'N | 002°45.789'W |
| WCR19 | St Quay N approach, 6ca WNW of Madeux beacon | 48°40.620'N | 002°49.661'W |
| WCR20 | Salcombe approach, 4ca SE of Bolt Head | 50°12.369'N | 003°46.672'W |
| WCR21 | Little Russel south, 6ca ESE of St Martin's lighthouse | 49°25.100'N | 002°30.840'W |
| WCR22 | Les Hanois W clearing, 2M west of lighthouse | 49°26.100'N | 002°45.205'W |
| WCR23 | Casquets TSS SW clearing, off SW corner of TSS | 49°46.090'N | 002°50.726'W |
| WCR24 | Dartmouth approach, 1ca W of Castle Ledge green buoy | 50°19.999'N | 003°33.274'W |
| WCR25 | Berry Head clearing, ½M due E of lighthouse | 50°23.977'N | 003°28.234'W |
| WCR26 | Little Russel north, 9ca 067°T from Platte Fougère lighthouse | 49°31.183'N | 002°27.866'W |
| WCR27 | Casquets west clearing, 2M due W of Casquets lighthouse | 49°43.320'N | 002°25.698'W |
| WCR28 | Casquets TSS SE, 7.9M 006°T from Casquets lighthouse | 49°51.264'N | 002°21.407'W |
| WCR29 | Casquets TSS east, 3¾M 115°T from East Channel buoy | 49°57.131'N | 002°23.746'W |
| WCR30 | West Shambles, 1ca due W of W-card buoy | 50°29.785'N | 002°24.572'W |
| WCR31 | East Shambles, 1ca due E of E-card buoy | 50°30.783'N | 002°19.924'W |

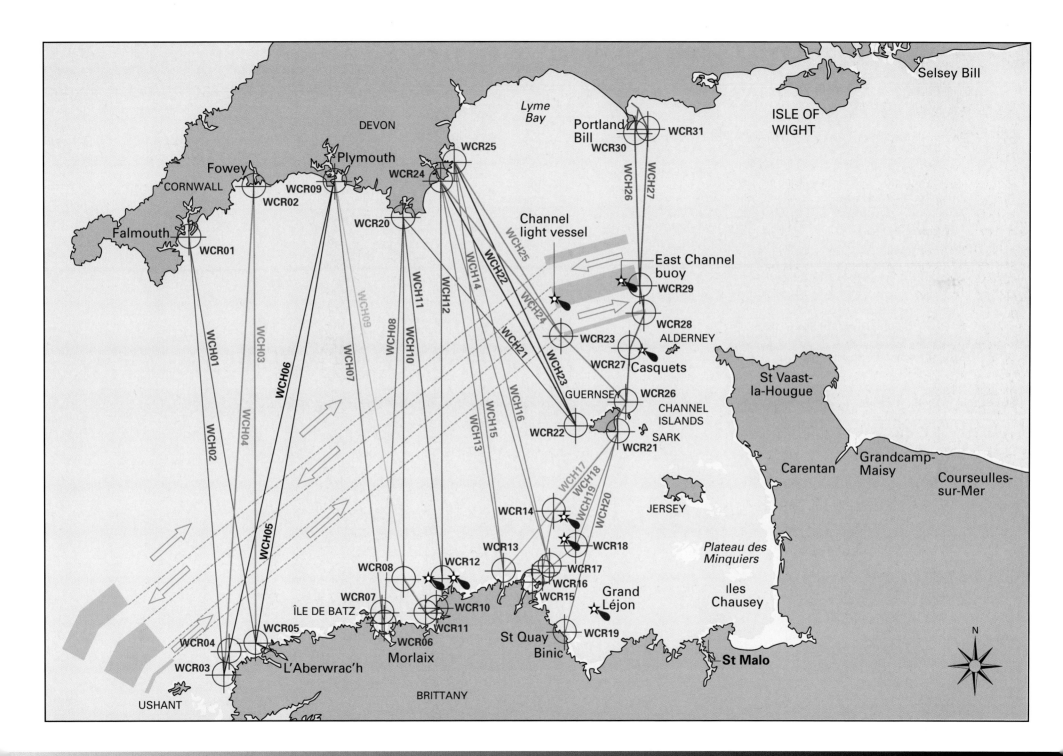

# Central Channel Route Waypoints

| ⊕ | Waypoint name and position | Latitude | Longitude |
|---|---|---|---|
| CCR01 | West Shambles, 1ca due W of W-card buoy | 50°29.785'N | 002°24.572'W |
| CCR02 | East Shambles, 1ca due E of E-card buoy | 50°30.783'N | 002°19.924'W |
| CCR03 | Poole outer approach, 7ca E of Old Harry | 50°38.550'N | 001°54.256'W |
| CCR04 | Needles outer, ½ca W of Bridge W-card buoy | 50°39.630'N | 001°36.976'W |
| CCR05 | West Princessa, ½ca W of Princessa W-cardinal buoy | 50°40.155'N | 001°03.744'W |
| CCR06 | Nab Tower west clearing, 2M W of Nab Tower | 50°40.076'N | 000°00.290'W |
| CCR07 | Little Russel north, 9ca 067°T from Platte Fougère lighthouse | 49°31.183'N | 002°27.866'W |
| CCR08 | Alderney Race south, 3½M S of old Telegraph Tower | 49°38.779'N | 002°13.268'W |
| CCR09 | Alderney Race north inner, 4M due E of Alderney lighthouse | 49°43.785'N | 002°03.724'W |
| CCR10 | Alderney outer approach, 6½ca N of Château à l'Étoc lighthouse | 49°44.585'N | 002°10.631'W |
| CCR11 | Cherbourg west entrance, 1½ca W of Fort de l'Ouest | 49°40.450'N | 001°39.090'W |
| CCR12 | Cherbourg east entrance, 6ca 025°T from Fort de l'Est | 49°40.824'N | 001°35.544'W |
| CCR13 | Barfleur NE clearing, 3M 063°T from Barfleur lighthouse | 49°43.120'N | 001°11.820'W |
| CCR14 | Pointe de Saire clearing, 1¾M E of Pointe de Saire lighthouse | 49°36.366'N | 001°11.083'W |
| CCR15 | Le Gavendest clearing, 1ca SE of Le Gavendest S-card buoy | 49°34.300'N | 001°13.780'W |

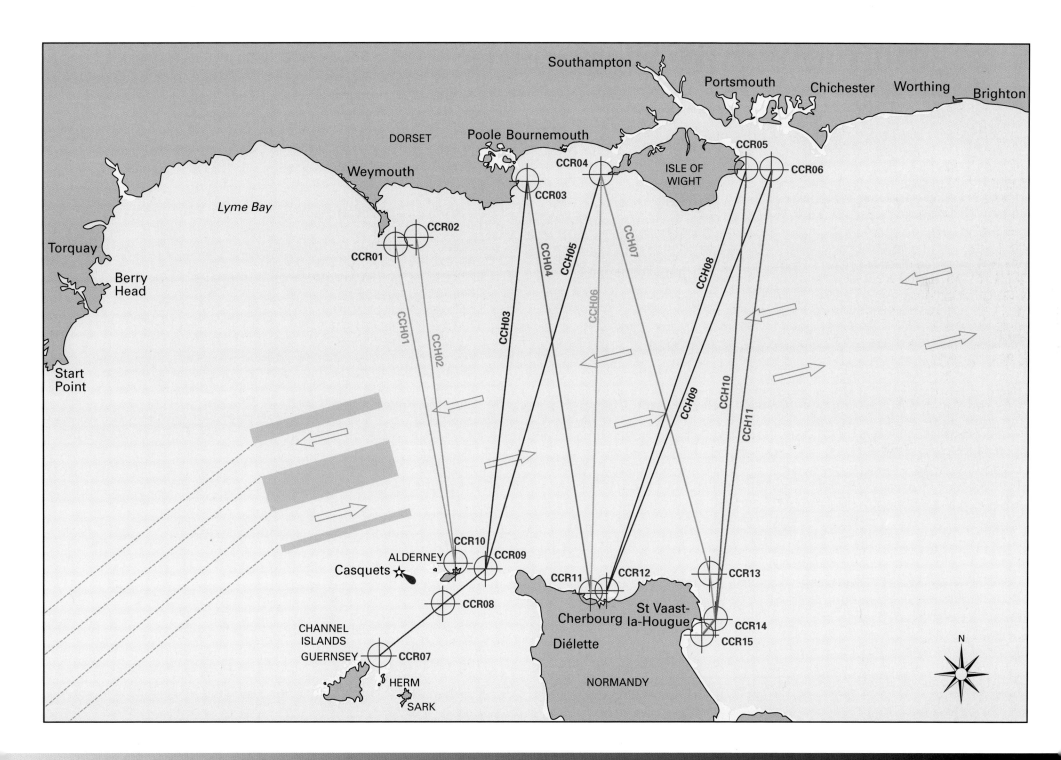

# East Channel Route Waypoints

| ⊕ | Waypoint name and position | Latitude | Longitude |
|---|---|---|---|
| ECR01 | Bembridge Ledge, 1ca east of E-card buoy | 50°41.151'N | 001°02.658'W |
| ECR02 | Nab Tower west clearing, 2M W of Nab Tower | 50°40.076'N | 001°00.290'W |
| ECR03 | Nab Tower east clearing, 1¾M E of Nab Tower | 50°40.076'N | 000°54.410'W |
| ECR04 | Courseulles offing, 3M due N of Courseulles E pierhead | 49°23.260'N | 000°27.680'W |
| ECR05 | Ouistreham outer, 2ca E of Ouistreham E-card buoy | 49°20.420'N | 000°14.510'W |
| ECR06 | Position ¼M due W of 'A5' W-card buoy | 49°45.878'N | 000°17.876'W |
| ECR07 | Le Havre approach channel, close E of LH7 green buoy | 49°30.250'N | 000°00.700'W |
| ECR08 | Brighton entrance, close SE of west breakwater head | 50°48.473'N | 000°06.345'W |
| ECR09 | Position 3M due west of CS1 yellow shipping lane buoy | 50°33.702'N | 000°08.615'W |
| ECR10 | Dover Strait TSS, SW clearing and crossing waypoint | 50°15.534'N | 000°01.177'W |
| ECR11 | Newhaven entrance, 1ca SE of outer breakwater head | 50°46.488'N | 000°03.612'E |
| ECR12 | Dover Strait TSS, SW separation zone crossing waypoint | 50°17.033'N | 000°15.576'E |
| ECR13 | Dover Strait TSS, NW separation zone crossing waypoint | 50°35.411'N | 000°01.434'E |
| ECR14 | Dover Strait TSS, SW separation zone crossing waypoint | 50°15.708'N | 000°09.538'E |
| ECR15 | Fécamp entrance, 2ca due W of outer pierheads | 49°45.920'N | 000°21.500'E |
| ECR16 | Dover Strait TSS, NW separation zone crossing waypoint | 50°36.934'N | 000°13.346'E |
| ECR17 | Dover Strait TSS, SW separation zone crossing waypoint | 50°18.217'N | 000°21.179'E |
| ECR18 | St Valery-en-Caux entrance, 250m N of west pierhead | 49°52.535'N | 000°42.540'E |
| ECR19 | Dover Strait TSS, NW separation zone crossing waypoint | 50°37.937'N | 000°21.016'E |
| ECR20 | Dover Strait TSS, SW separation zone crossing waypoint | 50°19.820'N | 000°28.740'E |
| ECR21 | Dieppe entrance, 1ca NNE of west breakwater head | 49°56.350'N | 001°05.000'E |
| ECR22 | Eastbourne entrance, near Sovereign Harbour fairway buoy | 50°47.400'N | 000°20.710'E |
| ECR23 | Somme estuary, AT-SO fairway buoy, actual position | 50°14.000'N | 001°28.080'E |
| ECR24 | Dover west entrance, 1½ca 120°T from Admiralty pierhead | 51°06.613'N | 001°19.863'E |
| ECR25 | Dover Strait TSS, SE separation zone crossing waypoint | 50°56.591'N | 001°35.076'E |
| ECR26 | Cap Gris-Nez clearing, 1.2M 300°T of Cap Gris-Nez lighthouse | 50°52.678'N | 001°33.339'E |
| ECR27 | Bassure de Baas inner, ½M E of N-cardinal buoy | 50°48.534'N | 001°33.821'E |
| ECR28 | Boulogne entrance, 2ca NW of south breakwater head | 50°44.599'N | 001°33.866'E |
| ECR29 | Dover Strait TSS, northwest side joining waypoint | 51°05.569'N | 001°27.671'E |
| ECR30 | Dover Strait TSS, southeast side joining waypoint | 50°58.644'N | 001°38.383'E |
| ECR31 | Calais channel outer, 8ca 320°T from Sangatte lighthouse | 50°57.809'N | 001°45.711'E |
| ECR32 | Calais channel inner, 0.33M 265°T from west pierhead | 50°58.214'N | 001°49.885'E |
| ECR33 | Calais entrance, near Calais west pierhead | 50°58.344'N | 001°50.357'E |

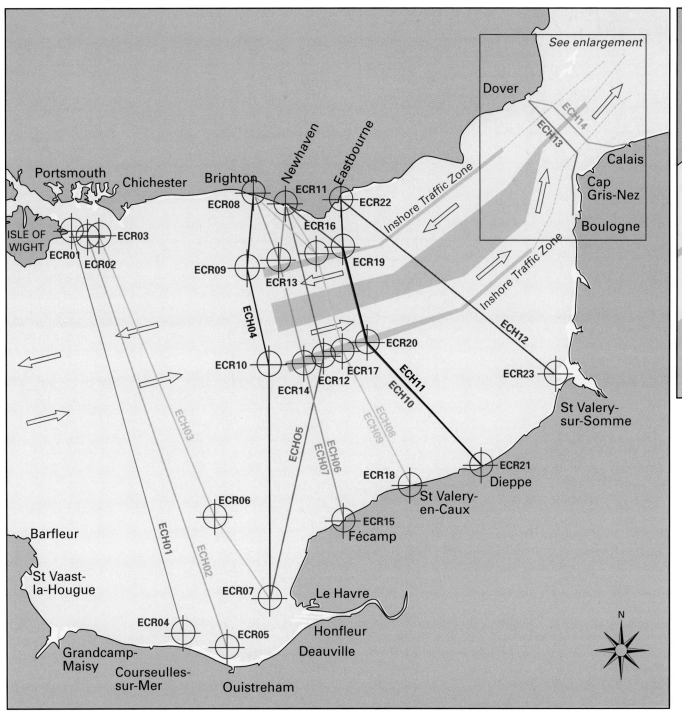

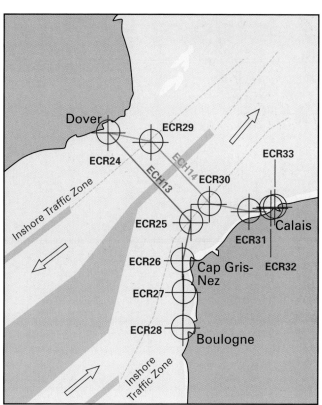

# 1 Isles of Scilly North

| ⊕ | | Waypoint name and position | Latitude | Longitude |
|---|---|---|---|---|
| 1 | 1 | Crow Sound approach, 1M due E of Tolls Island | 49°55.720'N | 006°15.040'W |
| 1 | 2 | Crow Sound inner, close SW of Hats S-card buoy | 49°56.200'N | 006°17.160'W |
| 1 | 3 | Crow Bar, 4½ca 296°T from Hats S-card buoy | 49°56.405'N | 006°17.756'W |
| 1 | 4 | Tresco South, 1½ca due E of Nut Rock | 49°55.882'N | 006°19.963'W |
| 1 | 5 | Hugh Town approach, 4ca 285°T from breakwater head | 49°55.210'N | 006°19.600'W |
| 1 | 6 | Hugh Town entrance, ½ca due N of breakwater head | 49°55.160'N | 006°18.990'W |
| 1 | 7 | North Channel outer, 1.33M W of Biggal Rock on leading line | 49°55.865'N | 006°25.486'W |
| 1 | 8 | Maiden Bower clearing, ¾M W of Maiden Bower summit | 49°56.817'N | 006°24.735'W |
| 1 | 9 | New Grimsby outer, 4ca NW of Kettle Rock | 49°58.440'N | 006°21.550'W |
| 1 | 10 | New Grimsby entrance, 1ca NE of Shipman Head | 49°58.110'N | 006°21.420'W |
| 1 | 11 | Old Grimsby outer, ½M NW of Golden Ball | 49°58.810'N | 006°20.920'W |
| 1 | 12 | Old Grimsby entrance, 3ca SSW of Golden Ball | 49°58.170'N | 006°20.560'W |
| 1 | 13 | Round Island clearing, 6ca due N of lighthouse | 49°59.350'N | 006°19.400'W |
| 1 | 14 | White Island clearing, 6ca NE of Baker Rock | 49°59.299'N | 006°16.711'W |
| 1 | 15 | St Martin's northeast, 1M NE of St Martin's daymark | 49°58.696'N | 006°14.901'W |
| 1 | 16 | St Martin's east, 1½M E of St Martin's daymark | 49°57.990'N | 006°13.640'W |
| 1 | 17 | Eastern Isles clearing, 6ca E of Mouls Rock | 49°57.160'N | 006°13.640'W |

**Refer to Charts**
Admiralty charts 34, 883
Imray C7, 2400.1, 2400.3, 2400.14

## COASTAL DANGERS
The Isles of Scilly are littered with rocks and ledges, so great care is needed both when approaching the archipelago and when piloting the channels between the islands. There are too many dangers to list here, but the following are particularly important to watch on a normal cruise to the islands.

## Eastern rocks
Approaching Crow Sound from off Land's End or the Lizard, take care not to make a landfall north of the Eastern Isles. Various drying hazards lie up to ¾ mile east and southeast of St Martin's Head, dangerous if you were approaching this stretch in a mist of summer haze.

## The Hats
The Hats ledge lies across Crow Sound as you approach the north end of St Mary's island from eastward. Be sure to pass close south and west of Hats S-cardinal buoy before skirting round Bar Point.

## Crow Bar
This shallow and partly drying sandbank lies north and a shade west of Bar Point. The shallowest parts dry at chart datum from between 0.5m and 0.8m. For passing the bar, much depends on the swell and sea state. In quiet weather, some yachts and motorboats will be able to creep over 1½–2 hours after a mean low water, but with any swell strangers should wait until half-flood or later. Some three cables southwest of Crow Bar, Crow Rock isolated danger beacon may be passed fairly close either side.

## Steeple Rock
This head (0.1m over it) needs watching near LW in the North Channel. Steeple Rock lies seven cables southwest of the highest point of Mincarlo islet and is cleared by the North Channel leading line – St Agnes old lighthouse in transit with the gap between the two summits of Great Smith Rocks bearing 130°T.

## Kettle Bottom Rocks
This ledge of drying rocks extends two cables northwest of Kettle Point, the northwest tip of Tresco; it needs watching when entering New Grimsby Sound from northward. The leading marks for New Grimsby can be tricky to make out (Star Castle Hotel on St Mary's in transit with the west side of Hangman Island bearing 157°T)

so it is simplest to keep fairly close to Shipman Head when coming into New Grimsby from the northwest.

## Deep Ledges
Deep Ledges and Tide Rock lie within four cables ENE and east of Round Island and jut out beyond a direct line struck between the north tip of Round Island and the outer Lion Rock; ¾ mile just east of north from Round Island. These dangers are important for boats skirting close round the north or for those entering St Helen's Pool through the Gap.

## St Martin's Head
This distinctive headland, marked by a prominent red-and-white daymark, has Deep Ledge (0.9m over it) not quite ½ mile to the north; the Chapel Rocks and Little Ledge close on its northeast side; Flat Ledge ½ mile east by north of the daymark; and the various Eastern Rocks – up to ¾ mile east of the Head.

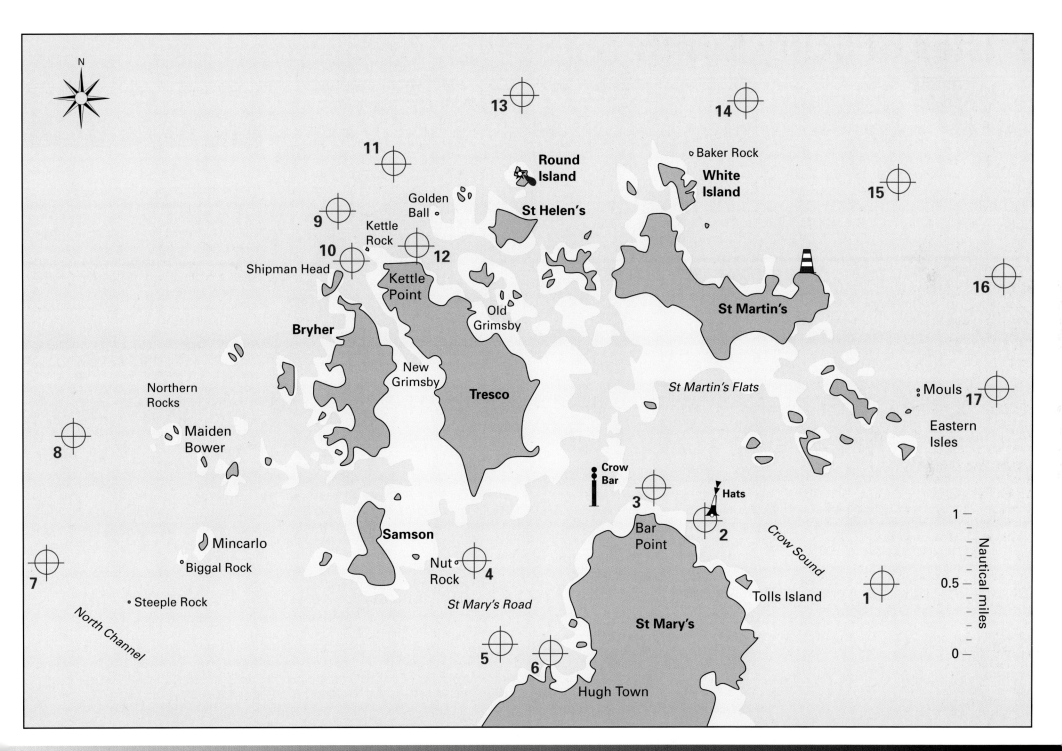

N

13

14

11

Round
Island

Baker Rock

White
Island

15

Golden
Ball

St Helen's

9

Kettle
Rock

10

12

Shipman Head

Kettle
Point

St Martin's

16

Bryher

Old
Grimsby

New
Grimsby

Tresco

St Martin's Flats

Mouls

17

Northern
Rocks

Eastern
Isles

8

Maiden
Bower

Crow
Bar

Samson

3

Hats

Mincarlo

Bar
Point

2

Crow Sound

Biggal Rock

Nut
Rock

4

1

7

Tolls Island

Steeple Rock

St Mary's Road

0.5

North Channel

5

6

St Mary's

1

Nautical miles

0.5

0

Hugh Town

| ⊕ | | Waypoint name and position | Latitude | Longitude |
|---|---|---|---|---|
| 2 | 1 | Crow Sound approach, 1M due E of Tolls Island | 49°55.720'N | 006°15.040'W |
| 2 | 2 | St Mary's Sound outer, 4ca due S of Peninnis Head lighthouse | 49°53.881'N | 006°18.218'W |
| 2 | 3 | Porth Cressa entrance, 1ca due E of Biggal Rock | 49°54.364'N | 006°18.777'W |
| 2 | 4 | Porth Conger South, ¼M due S of The Hoe | 49°53.070'N | 006°19.760'W |
| 2 | 5 | Smith Sound South, 4½ca due E of Flat Carn Rock | 49°52.541'N | 006°21.366'W |
| 2 | 6 | Western Rocks South, ¾M due S of Black Rock | 49°51.120'N | 006°23.930'W |
| 2 | 7 | Bishop Rock clearing, 1M SW of Bishop Rock lighthouse | 49°51.670'N | 006°27.840'W |
| 2 | 8 | Broad Sound outer, 4ca NW of Bishop Rock lighthouse | 49°52.650'N | 006°27.180'W |
| 2 | 9 | Crim Rocks clearing, ¾M due W of the Peaked Rock | 49°53.790'N | 006°28.510'W |
| 2 | 10 | North Channel outer, 1.33M W of Biggal Rock on leading line | 49°55.865'N | 006°25.486'W |
| 2 | 11 | Broad Sound middle, 1½ca S of Gunner S-card buoy | 49°53.490'N | 006°25.080'W |
| 2 | 12 | Broad Sound inner, ½ca NW of Old Wreck N-card buoy | 49°54.310'N | 006°22.880'W |
| 2 | 13 | North Channel inner, 4ca NE of Old Wreck N-card buoy | 49°54.540'N | 006°22.380'W |
| 2 | 14 | Smith Sound North, ¼M NW of Great Smith Rock | 49°54.310'N | 006°22.060'W |
| 2 | 15 | Porth Conger North, 1ca NNW of The Cow Rock | 49°53.980'N | 006°20.500'W |
| 2 | 16 | St Mary's Sound inner, 1ca 325°T of N Bartholomew red buoy | 49°54.570'N | 006°20.080'W |
| 2 | 17 | Hugh Town approach, 4ca 284°T from breakwater head | 49°55.210'N | 006°19.600'W |
| 2 | 18 | Hugh Town entrance, ½ca due N of breakwater head | 49°55.160'N | 006°18.990'W |
| 2 | 19 | Tresco South, 1½ca due E of Nut Rock | 49°55.882'N | 006°19.963'W |

**Refer to Charts**
Admiralty charts 34, 883
Imray C7, 2400.1, 2400.3, 2400.14

## COASTAL DANGERS

### Spanish Ledges

In St Mary's Sound, the south approach round St Mary's island, the Spanish Ledges lie about ½ mile southwest of Peninnis Head, marked on their east side by an E-cardinal bell buoy. Coming into St Mary's Sound from seaward, it is important to pass between Peninnis Head and the Spanish Ledge buoy; then, continuing northwest, leave the Bartholomew red buoy to port as you round the southwest corner of St Mary's.

### Western Rocks

This far southwestern group of reefs and islets, about 1½ miles east of the Bishop Rock, have numerous dangers around them and unpredictable tidal streams running through them. On a circumnavigation of the archipelago, keep a good ¾ mile south of the group.

### The Bishop Rock

This famous, prominent lighthouse on the southwest edge of the Isles of Scilly is easily recognised. However, boats rounding this southwest corner should avoid the area of overfalls which can extend nearly ½ mile south of the Bishop. There are also overfalls close north of the Bishop, and on the north side of Broad Sound over Flemming's Ledge.

### Crim Rocks

The most westerly dangers of the Isles of Scilly, the Crim Rocks, are unmarked except by their position about 1½ miles north and a shade west of Bishop Rock lighthouse, and by the only above-water head known as the Peaked Rock (2m high). Boats approaching the islands from westward or making a circumnavigation of the group must take great care to avoid the Crim Rocks. The whole area around these reefs is uneasy with breaking swell and overfalls.

### Gunners Ledge

The Gunners Rock and Gunners Ledge lie not quite 1½ miles east of the Crim Peaked Rock, marked on their south side by the Gunner S-cardinal buoy. Coming into Broad Sound from the southwest, passing four cables or so to the northwest of Bishop Rock lighthouse, be sure to pass between Gunner S-cardinal and Round Rock N-cardinal buoys; be careful, as it is easy to confuse the two from a distance.

### Jeffrey Rock

Along the inner end of Broad Sound, passing to the north of Annet island, steer to leave the Old Wreck N-cardinal buoy fairly close to the southeast and so avoid Jeffrey Rock (with only 0.9m over it) which lurks four cables west of the Old Wreck buoy.

### Steeple Rock

This head (0.1m over it) needs watching near LW in the North Channel. Steeple Rock lies seven cables southwest of the highest point of Mincarlo islet and is cleared by the North Channel leading line – St Agnes old lighthouse in transit with the gap between the two summits of Great Smith rocks bearing 130°T.

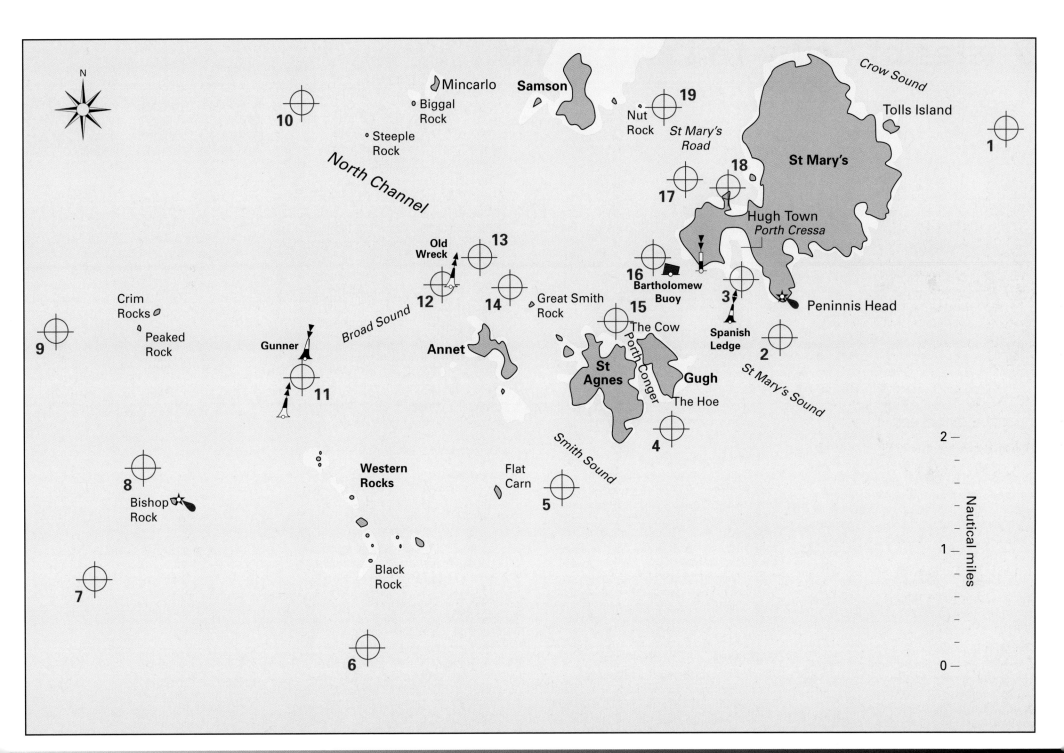

N

**10**

**Samson** **19**
Mincarlo
Nut
Rock
Biggal
Rock
*St Mary's*
*Road*

Steeple
Rock

**18**

**17**

**St Mary's**

Crow Sound

Tolls Island

**1**

North Channel

Old
Wreck **13**

**12**

**14**

Great Smith
Rock

**15**

**16**
**Bartholomew**
**Buoy**

Hugh Town
*Porth Cressa*

**3**

Peninnis Head

Crim
Rocks

Peaked
Rock

**9**

Gunner

Broad Sound

The Cow

**Annet**

Porth Conger

Spanish
Ledge

**2**

*St Mary's Sound*

**11**

**St**
**Agnes**

**Gugh**

The Hoe

**4**

Smith Sound

**Western**
**Rocks**

Flat
Carn

**5**

**8**

Bishop
Rock

**7**

Black
Rock

**6**

2 —

1 —

0 —

*Nautical miles*

# 3 Isles of Scilly to Land's End

**Refer to Charts**
Admiralty charts 1148, 2565
Imray C7, 2400.1, 2400.2

| ⊕ | | Waypoint name and position | Latitude | Longitude |
|---|---|---|---|---|
| 3 | 1 | Crow Sound approach, 1M due E of Tolls Island | 49°55.720'N | 006°15.040'W |
| 3 | 2 | St Mary's Sound outer, 4ca due S of Peninnis Head lighthouse | 49°53.881'N | 006°18.218'W |
| 3 | 3 | Porth Conger South, ¼M due S of The Hoe | 49°53.070'N | 006°19.760'W |
| 3 | 4 | Round Island clearing, 6ca due N of lighthouse | 49°59.350'N | 006°19.400'W |
| 3 | 5 | White Island clearing, 6ca NE of Baker Rock | 49°59.299'N | 006°16.711'W |
| 3 | 6 | St Martin's northeast, 1M NE of St Martin's daymark | 49°58.696'N | 006°14.901'W |
| 3 | 7 | St Martin's east, 1½M E of St Martin's daymark | 49°57.990'N | 006°13.640'W |
| 3 | 8 | Eastern Isles clearing, 6ca E of Mouls Rock | 49°57.160'N | 006°13.640'W |
| 3 | 9 | Seven Stones North, 4M due N of light-float | 50°07.620'N | 006°04.340'W |
| 3 | 10 | Seven Stones light-float, ½M due E of float position | 50°03.620'N | 006°03.560'W |
| 3 | 11 | Seven Stones South, 4M due S of light-float | 49°59.620'N | 006°04.340'W |
| 3 | 12 | Wolf Rock North, 2M due N of lighthouse | 49°58.740'N | 005°48.560'W |
| 3 | 13 | Wolf Rock South, 2M due S of lighthouse | 49°54.740'N | 005°48.560'W |
| 3 | 14 | Pendeen clearing, 2½M 300°T from lighthouse | 50°11.138'N | 005°43.643'W |
| 3 | 15 | Cape Cornwall clearing, 2M due W of old chimney | 50°07.633'N | 005°45.622'W |
| 3 | 16 | Longships clearing, ¾M due W of lighthouse | 50°04.040'N | 005°45.950'W |
| 3 | 17 | Runnel Stone SW, ½M SW of S-card buoy | 50°00.816'N | 005°40.916'W |

## COASTAL DANGERS

### Seven Stones reef

This notorious reef lies 6–7 miles northeast of St Martin's Head, and is marked on its northeast side by the Seven Stones light-float. Boats approaching the Isles of Scilly from the south coast of England would not normally stray near the Seven Stones, but those on passage to and from the southwest coast of Ireland need to be aware of the Seven Stones. In particular, boats making for the Isles of Scilly direct from Ireland need to watch their longitude carefully as they approach the Scillies.

### Eastern Rocks

Approaching Crow Sound from off Land's End or the Lizard, take care not to make a landfall north of the Eastern Isles. Various drying hazards lie up to ¾ mile east and southeast of St Martin's Head, dangerous if you were approaching this stretch in a mist of summer haze.

### St Martin's Head

This distinctive headland, marked by a prominent red-and-white daymark, has Deep Ledge (0.9m over it) not quite ½ mile to the north; the Chapel Rocks and Little Ledge close on its northeast side; Flat Ledge ½ mile east by north of the daymark; and the various Eastern Rocks – Hard Lewis Rocks, Polreath, Southward Ledge – up to ¾ mile east of the Head. All these dangers must be given a wide berth when skirting this northeast corner of the Scillies archipelago.

### Wolf Rock

The Wolf is not so much a danger as a signpost, and the lighthouse is a useful mark if bound directly between the Lizard and the Isles of Scilly. The Wolf Rock lies just over seven miles southwest of Gwennap Head, the southern tip of the Land's End peninsula, and is fairly steep-to on all sides.

### The Longships

The Longships Rocks extend just over one mile west from Land's End. The westernmost rock is marked by the famous lighthouse, which can be passed fairly close on its west side. There is a passage inside the Longships in quiet weather, by keeping close to the Land's End shore.

### Runnel Stone

This nasty drying rock lies about ¾ mile south of Gwennap Head and is marked on its south side by the Runnel Stone S-cardinal whistle buoy. This buoy is a convenient point of departure for the Isles of Scilly if you are leaving from Penzance or Newlyn.

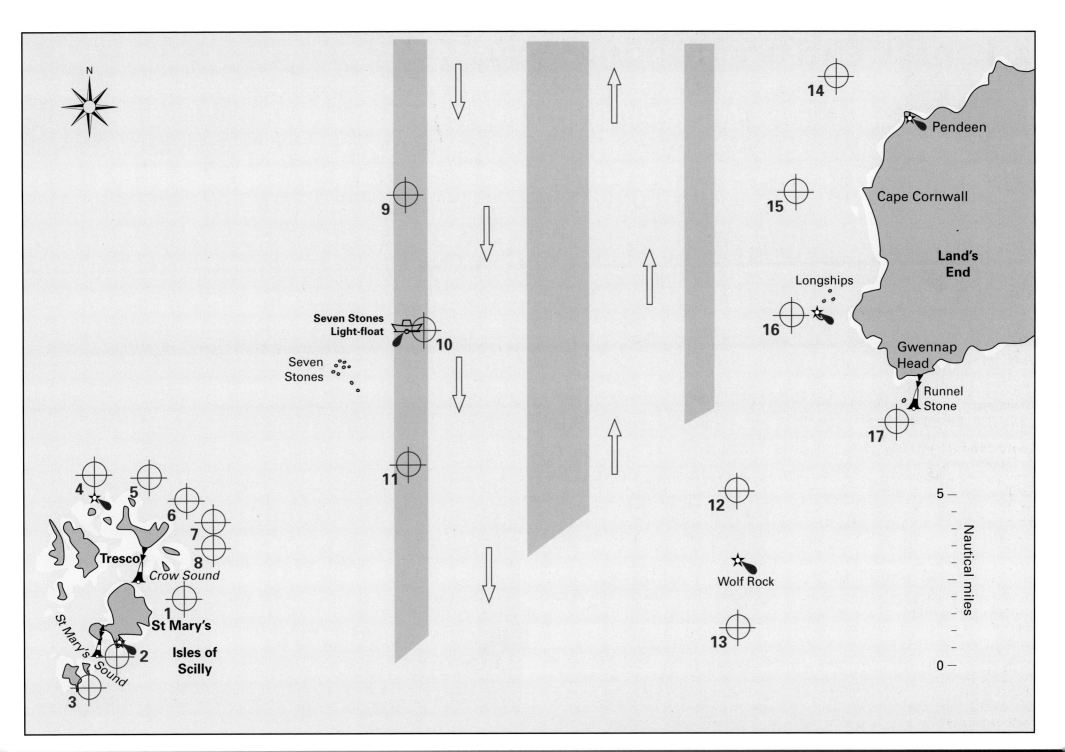

N

14

Pendeen

Cape Cornwall

15

**Land's End**

Longships

9

16

Gwennap Head

**Seven Stones Light-float**

10

Runnel Stone

Seven Stones

17

4

5

6

7

**Tresco**

8

11

5

*Crow Sound*

12

Wolf Rock

1

**St Mary's**

Nautical miles

*St Mary's Sound*

2

**Isles of Scilly**

13

3

0

# 4 Land's End and Mounts Bay

| ⊕ | | Waypoint name and position | Latitude | Longitude |
|---|---|---|---|---|
| 4 | 1 | Cape Cornwall clearing, 2M due W of old chimney | 50°07.633′N | 005°45.622′W |
| 4 | 2 | Longships clearing, ¾M due W of lighthouse | 50°04.040′N | 005°45.950′W |
| 4 | 3 | Runnel Stone SW, ½M SW of S-card buoy | 50°00.816′N | 005°40.916′W |
| 4 | 4 | Mount's Bay SW, 1M SE of Carn-Du headland | 50°02.910′N | 005°32.150′W |
| 4 | 5 | Low Lee East, ¼M due E of E-card buoy | 50°05.556′N | 005°30.996′W |
| 4 | 6 | Newlyn approach, ½M 100°T from S pierhead | 50°06.098′N | 005°31.801′W |
| 4 | 7 | Newlyn entrance, close NE of S pierhead | 50°06.204′N | 005°32.539′W |
| 4 | 8 | Penzance approach, 6ca SE of S pierhead | 50°06.644′N | 005°31.027′W |
| 4 | 9 | Penzance entrance, close NE of S pierhead | 50°07.093′N | 005°31.638′W |
| 4 | 10 | St Michael's Mount approach, 4ca 260°T from tower | 50°06.923′N | 005°29.297′W |
| 4 | 11 | Mountamopus, ½M SW of S-card buoy | 50°04.351′N | 005°26.886′W |

**Refer to Charts**
Admiralty chart 777, 2345
Imray C7, 2400.1, 2400.10

## COASTAL DANGERS

### The Longships
The Longships Rocks extend just over one mile west from Land's End. The westernmost rock is marked by the famous lighthouse, which can be passed fairly close on its west side. There is a passage inside the Longships in quiet weather, by keeping close to the Land's End shore.

### Runnel Stone
This nasty drying rock lies about ¾ mile south of Gwennap Head and is marked on its south side by the Runnel Stone S-cardinal whistle buoy. This buoy is a convenient point of departure for the Isles of Scilly if you are leaving from Penzance or Newlyn.

### Newlyn and Penzance approaches
The Low Lee shoal (with 1.1m over it) lies 3½ cables ENE of Penlee Point, marked on its northeast side by an E-cardinal buoy. Most boats will prefer to pass outside this buoy when approaching Newlyn from the south or southeast. The Carn Base shoal (with 1.8m over it) lies just over three cables northwest of the Low Lee E-cardinal buoy, but has plenty of water over it for most craft except near low springs.

If rounding Battery Rocks between Penzance and Newlyn, pass outside Gear Rock isolated danger beacon, which stands not quite ½ mile south of Penzance south pierhead.

### St Michael's Mount
If approaching St Michael's Mount from Penzance harbour, keep the tower bearing due east true from Penzance until you are within four cables of the Mount. This will clear the various rocky ledges fringing the bay between Penzance and the Mount, including the Outer Penzeath Rock (awash at chart datum) which lies ½ mile due west from St Michael's harbour west pierhead.

### Mountamopus
The Mountamopus shoal (with 1.8m over it) lies on the north side of Mount's Bay, about ¾ mile south of Cudden Point. The shoal is marked on its southwest side by a S-cardinal buoy, which makes a useful mark when approaching Penzance from the Lizard.

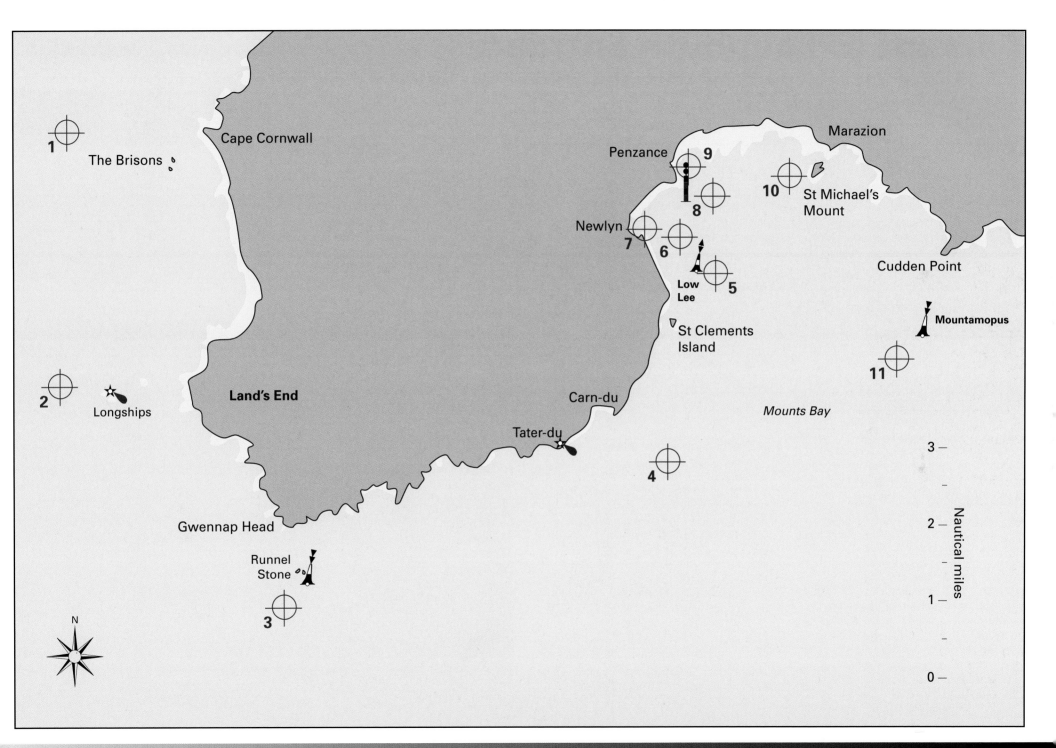

**1**

The Brisons ₀

Cape Cornwall

Marazion

Penzance **9**

**10** St Michael's Mount

Newlyn **8**

**7**

**6**

Cudden Point

Low Lee **5**

**2**
Longships

**Land's End**

St Clements Island

Mountamopus

**11**

Carn-du

Mounts Bay

Tater-du

**4**

Gwennap Head

Runnel Stone

**3**

N

Nautical miles

3 —

2 —

1 —

0 —

# 5 Lizard to Falmouth Entrance

| ⊕ | | Waypoint name and position | Latitude | Longitude |
|---|---|---|---|---|
| 5 | 1 | Porthleven approach, 4ca 240°T from S breakwater light | 50°04.633'N | 005°19.554'W |
| 5 | 2 | Mullion approach, 2ca NW of N tip of Mullion Island | 50°00.935'N | 005°16.234'W |
| 5 | 3 | Porth Mellin anchorage, 150m WSW of harbour entrance | 50°00.860'N | 005°15.666'W |
| 5 | 4 | Boa West, 4M due W of Lizard lighthouse | 49°57.620'N | 005°18.290'W |
| 5 | 5 | Lizard clearing, 3M due S of lighthouse | 49°54.620'N | 005°12.140'W |
| 5 | 6 | Lizard inner (calm weather), 1½M due S of lighthouse | 49°56.120'N | 005°12.140'W |
| 5 | 7 | Black Head clearing, 1½M SE of headland | 49°59.190'N | 005°04.450'W |
| 5 | 8 | Manacles clearing, ½M due E of E-card buoy | 50°02.800'N | 005°01.144'W |
| 5 | 9 | Helford River approach, ½M 020°T from Nare Point | 50°05.594'N | 005°04.340'W |
| 5 | 10 | Helford River entrance, 300m due S of Toll Point | 50°05.824'N | 005°06.084'W |
| 5 | 11 | Falmouth entrance, 4ca SW of St Anthony Head lighthouse | 50°08.184'N | 005°01.410'W |

**Refer to Charts**
Admiralty charts 154, 777
Imray C6, C7, 2400.9, 2400.11, 2400.12

## COASTAL DANGERS

### The Boa

The Boa rocky shoals lie three miles or so west of Lizard lighthouse and have plenty of water over them, but there are overfalls in this area during the strongest hours of the tide, especially when the stream is weather-going. Unless conditions are very quiet, it is worth giving the shoals a wide berth using the Boa West clearing waypoint in the table.

### Lizard Point

The Lizard has drying rocks extending ½ mile seaward, and a potentially dangerous race which is at its worst when the Channel ebb is running hard against a strong westerly or southwesterly. The race is cleared by staying three miles off the Point, although in quiet weather you can cut in closer using the Lizard inner waypoint in the table.

### The Manacles

Approaching Falmouth or the Helford River from the south, keep well east of the Manacles Rocks which lurk up to ¾ mile east and southeast from Manacle Point. These dangers are guarded by an E-cardinal bell buoy.

### Helford River approaches

Approaching the Helford River from the direction of the Manacles, Nare Point should be given at least ¼ mile clearance since rocky ledges extend east and northeast from the end of the promontory for about one cable. On the north side of the Helford estuary, the August Rock (dries 1.4m) lurks about four cables south of Rosemullion Head. During the summer this Rock is marked on its southeast side by a small green buoy which is not always easy to spot.

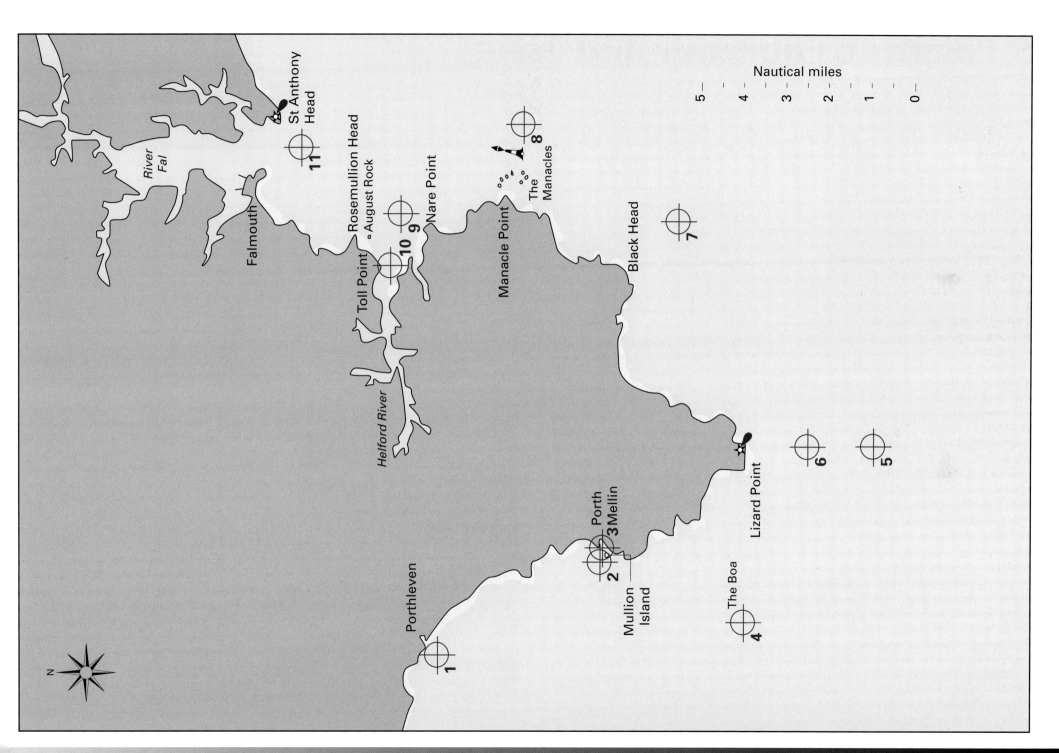

Nautical miles

River Fal

St Anthony Head

11

Rosemullion Head

August Rock

Nare Point

The Manacles

8

Falmouth

Toll Point

10

9

Manacle Point

Black Head

7

Helford River

Lizard Point

6

5

Porthleven

Porth
Mellin

3

2

The Boa

4

Mullion
Island

1

N

# 6 Falmouth Harbour and River

| ⊕ | | Waypoint name and position | Latitude | Longitude |
|---|---|---|---|---|
| 6 | 1 | Falmouth entrance, 4ca SW of St Anthony Head lighthouse | 50°08.184′N | 005°01.410′W |
| 6 | 2 | Black Rock east, 100m due E of E-card buoy | 50°08.678′N | 005°01.660′W |
| 6 | 3 | Pendennis Point, 1½ca due E of E tip of headland | 50°08.647′N | 005°02.273′W |
| 6 | 4 | The Governor, 100m due E of Governor E-card buoy | 50°09.151′N | 005°02.319′W |
| 6 | 5 | Falmouth Eastern breakwater, 150m due N of pierhead | 50°09.425′N | 005°02.957′W |
| 6 | 6 | Falmouth inner harbour, 300m NW of Queen's Jetty head | 50°09.506′N | 005°03.704′W |
| 6 | 7 | St Mawes entrance, 100m due S of St Mawes S-card buoy | 50°09.049′N | 005°01.416′W |
| 6 | 8 | St Mawes harbour, 1½ca 170°T from St Mawes pierhead | 50°09.347′N | 005°00.812′W |
| 6 | 9 | Narrows gap, midway between East and West Narrows buoys | 50°09.410′N | 005°01.981′W |
| 6 | 10 | Carrick Road, 100m due W of Vilt green conical buoy | 50°09.990′N | 005°02.360′W |
| 6 | 11 | St Just Pool, 100m 100°T from St Just red can buoy | 50°10.426′N | 005°01.640′W |
| 6 | 12 | St Just entrance, 300m 200°T from Messack Point | 50°10.760′N | 005°01.550′W |
| 6 | 13 | Mylor approach, midway between red and green fairway buoys | 50°10.764′N | 005°02.690′W |
| 6 | 14 | Carick Carlys, 100m 260°T from Carick green buoy | 50°11.577′N | 005°02.818′W |
| 6 | 15 | Restronguet entrance, 150m SE of Restronguet Pt SE tip | 50°11.542′N | 005°03.448′W |
| 6 | 16 | Turnaware approach, 250m 110°T from Pill Point | 50°12.146′N | 005°02.444′W |

## Refer to Charts
Admiralty chart 32
Imray Y58, 2400.12

## COASTAL DANGERS

### Lugo Rock
This rocky shoal (with 0.6m over it) lies 1½ cables south of Castle Point, just opposite St Mawes Castle. Lugo is marked on its south side by St Mawes S-cardinal buoy. Do not be tempted to cut inside this buoy except above half-tide.

### St Just to Turnaware Point
Above St Just, the buoyed channel is about 250m wide, with shallow flats on both sides of the river having soundings close to chart datum in parts. Most boats can stray outside the buoys above half-tide, when it is safe to approach Restronguet Creek and moor in the deeper area near the mouth. Further upstream, a drying spit extends some 250m northwest from Turnaware Point, marked at its northwest tip by an unlit green buoy.

### St Mawes Bank
This broad shoal on the east side of Carrick Road can catch you out near low water if you are tacking upstream and not paying full attention to the buoys. In particular, there is a 1.2m patch just outside the southernmost of the yellow buoys that are laid in this area during the summer to mark off a water-skiing area.

### Mylor approaches
Above Carrick Road, the main river channel trends over to the east shore past Carclase Point and St Just. The west side of the river is very shallow opposite Mylor Creek and between Mylor and Restronguet Creeks. Most boats may cross this area above half-tide, but within a couple of hours of low water deeper draught yachts and motor boats can easily find themselves aground if they stray out of the buoyed channel.

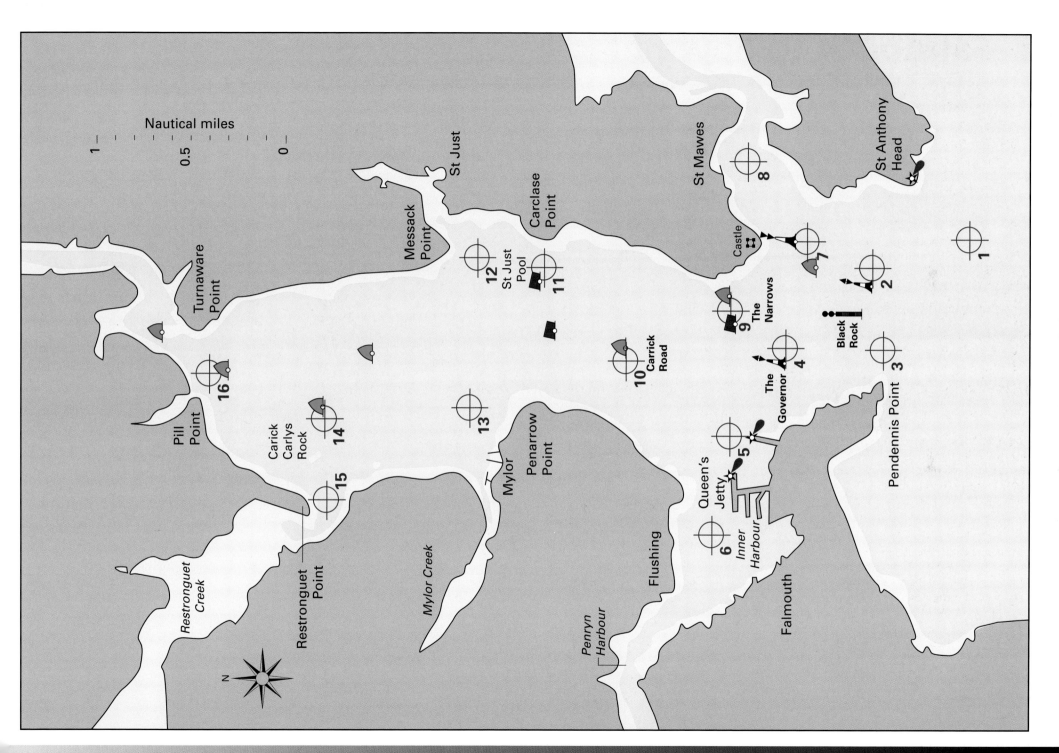

Nautical miles

1    0.5    0

St Just

St Mawes

St Anthony Head

Messack Point

Carclase Point

Castle

8

7

1

2

Turnaware Point

St Just Pool

12

11

The Narrows

9

Black Rock

Carrick Road

10

4

Pendennis Point

3

Pill Point

Carick Carlys Rock

16

14

13

Penarrow Point

The Governor

Queen's Jetty

5

Mylor

15

Restronguet Point

Mylor Creek

Flushing

Inner Harbour

6

Restronguet Creek

Penryn Harbour

Falmouth

N

# 7 Falmouth to Fowey

| ⊕ | | Waypoint name and position | Latitude | Longitude |
|---|---|---|---|---|
| 7 | 1 | Falmouth entrance, 4ca SW of St Anthony Head lighthouse | 50°08.184'N | 005°01.410'W |
| 7 | 2 | St Anthony approach, ¾M due S of Zone Point | 50°07.607'N | 005°00.609'W |
| 7 | 3 | Porthscatho anchorage, 2ca due S of Pednvadan | 50°10.931'N | 004°58.103'W |
| 7 | 4 | Gull Rock clearing, ¾M SE of Gull Rock | 50°11.220'N | 004°53.470'W |
| 7 | 5 | Dodman clearing, 1½M SE of Dodman Point cross | 50°12.153'N | 004°46.547'W |
| 7 | 6 | Gwineas clearing, ½M SE of Gwineas buoy | 50°14.146'N | 004°44.829'W |
| 7 | 7 | Chapel Point, ¾M due E of headland | 50°15.418'N | 004°44.818'W |
| 7 | 8 | Mevagissey entrance, 1ca NE of south pierhead | 50°16.223'N | 004°46.807'W |
| 7 | 9 | Charlestown dock, 1ca SE of pierheads gap | 50°19.765'N | 004°45.236'W |
| 7 | 10 | Polkerris anchorage, 1½ca 260°T from pierhead | 50°20.220'N | 004°41.165'W |
| 7 | 11 | Gribbin Head, 8ca 145°T from daymark | 50°18.367'N | 004°39.673'W |
| 7 | 12 | Fowey entrance, 0.16M 130°T from Fowey lighthouse | 50°19.527'N | 004°38.641'W |

## Refer to Charts

Admiralty charts 31, 147, 148, 154, 1267
Imray C6, 2400.8, 2400.9

## COASTAL DANGERS

### The Whelps

If coasting between Falmouth and Fowey, you need to stay outside The Whelps rocks (drying 4.6m) which extend south of Gull Rock (38m high) for 3½ cables. Gull Rock is a distinctive islet just over ½ mile east of Nare Head, between Gerrans Bay and Veryan Bay.

### Dodman Point

Dodman Point has a race extending ½ mile southward, while the Gwineas Rocks, marked by an E-cardinal buoy, lie two miles to the northeast. When approaching Fowey from SSW, bear in mind that the Dodman is unlit, as is most of the coast between Falmouth and Fowey.

### Cannis Rock

Cannis Rock (dries 4.6m) lies not quite ¼ mile southeast of Gribbin Head, on the west side of the approaches to Fowey. Gribbin Head has a large distinctive daymark with red-and-white horizontal stripes and the Cannis Rock is marked on its southeast side by a S-cardinal buoy.

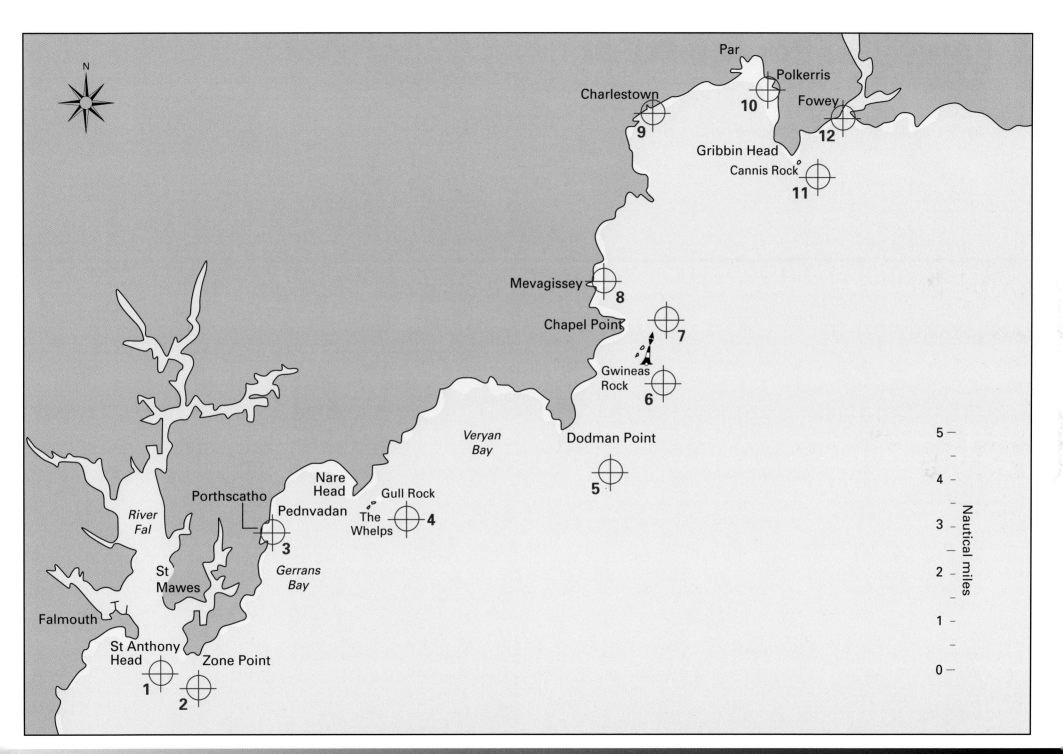

N

Par

Polkerris

Charlestown

**10**

Fowey

**9**

Gribbin Head

**12**

Cannis Rock

**11**

Mevagissey

**8**

Chapel Point

**7**

Gwineas
Rock

**6**

*Veryan
Bay*

Dodman Point

**5**

Nare
Head

Gull Rock

Porthscatho

**4**

Pednvadan

The
Whelps

*River
Fal*

**3**

St
Mawes

*Gerrans
Bay*

Falmouth

St Anthony
Head

Zone Point

**1**

**2**

5 —

4 —

Nautical miles

3 —

2 —

1 —

0 —

| ⊕ | | Waypoint name and position | Latitude | Longitude |
|---|---|---|---|---|
| 8 | 1 | Gribbin Head, 8ca 145°T from daymark | 50°18.367'N | 004°39.673'W |
| 8 | 2 | Fowey entrance, 0.16M 130°T from Fowey lighthouse | 50°19.527'N | 004°38.641'W |
| 8 | 3 | Polperro approach, ¼M S of Polperro west headland | 50°19.555'N | 004°30.934'W |
| 8 | 4 | Looe Island south, 1M S of Looe Island spot height | 50°19.234'N | 004°27.083'W |
| 8 | 5 | Looe approach, 1½M SE of Looe Banjo pierhead | 50°19.992'N | 004°25.417'W |
| 8 | 6 | Looe entrance, 100m 120°T from Looe Banjo pierhead | 50°21.034'N | 004°26.997'W |
| 8 | 7 | Eddystone north clearing, 1½M N of lighthouse | 50°12.342'N | 004°15.935'W |
| 8 | 8 | Eddystone south clearing, 1½M S of lighthouse | 50°09.342'N | 004°15.935'W |
| 8 | 9 | Rame Head clearing, 1M S of ruined chapel | 50°17.834'N | 004°13.381'W |
| 8 | 10 | Penlee Point clearing, 1M S of SE tip of headland | 50°18.066'N | 004°11.311'W |

**Refer to Charts**
Admiralty charts 30, 148, 1267, 1613, 1900
Imray C6, C14, 2400.8, 2400.13

## COASTAL DANGERS

### Cannis Rock
Cannis Rock (dries 4.6m) lies not quite ¼ mile southeast of Gribbin Head, on the west side of the approaches to Fowey. Gribbin Head has a large distinctive daymark with red-and-white horizontal stripes and the Cannis Rock is marked on its southeast side by a S-cardinal buoy.

### Udder Rock
Between Fowey harbour entrance and Polperro, Udder Rock (dries 0.6m) lies ½ mile offshore opposite a white obelisk between Pencarrow Head and Nealand Point. Udder Rock is marked on its south side by an unlit S-cardinal buoy, and the white obelisk in transit with a white painted mark on the shore provides a striking mark for the Rock.

### St George's or Looe Island
Looe Island, which lies ¾ mile south of Looe harbour entrance, is fringed by a drying rocky shore and has a drying tail of reefs known as the Rennies (drying 4.6m) extending a good three cables to the southeast. Any boats bound between Looe and further west should round Looe Island by ¾ mile to keep well clear of the Rennies.

### Eddystone Rocks
The Eddystone Rocks, marked by a tall lighthouse, lie nine miles SSW of Plymouth Sound and should be given a wide berth in heavy weather or poor visibility.

© Neil Harrison | Dreamstime.com

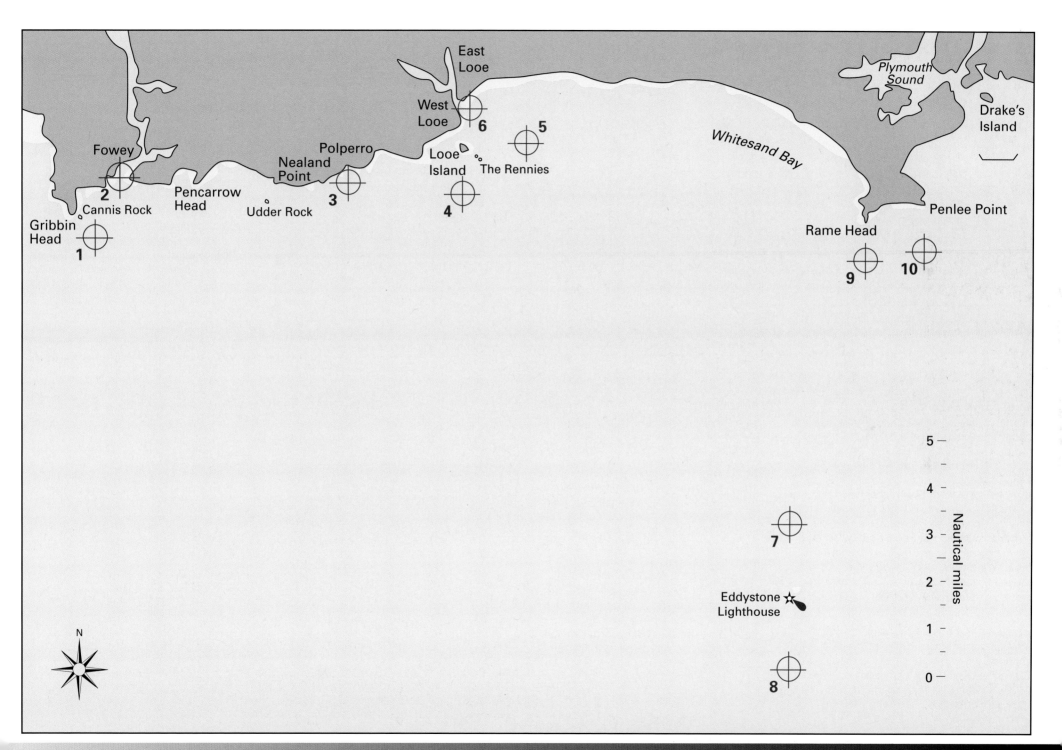

East
Looe

Plymouth
Sound

Drake's
Island

West
Looe

**6**

**5**

Whitesand Bay

Fowey

Polperro

**2**

Nealland
Point

Looe
Island

The Rennies

Cannis Rock

Pencarrow
Head

**3**

Penlee Point

Gribbin
Head

Udder Rock

**4**

Rame Head

**1**

**9**

**10**

5 —

–

4 —

–

**7**

3 —

Nautical miles

–

2 —

Eddystone ☆
Lighthouse

–

1 —

–

N

0 —

**8**

# 9 Plymouth Sound

| ⊕ | | Waypoint name and position | Latitude | Longitude |
|---|---|---|---|---|
| 9 | 1 | Rame Head clearing, 1M S of ruined chapel | 50°17.834'N | 004°13.381'W |
| 9 | 2 | Penlee Point clearing, 1M S of SE tip of headland | 50°18.066'N | 004°11.311'W |
| 9 | 3 | Plymouth SE approach, 1M W of Great Mewstone summit | 50°18.452'N | 004°07.985'W |
| 9 | 4 | Great Mewstone SW, 6ca SW of Great Mewstone summit | 50°18.029'N | 004°07.081'W |
| 9 | 5 | Cawsand anchorage, 1½ca due E of Pemberknowse Point | 50°19.916'N | 004°11.789'W |
| 9 | 6 | Plymouth W entrance, 2ca W of breakwater W lighthouse | 50°20.070'N | 004°09.837'W |
| 9 | 7 | Plymouth E entrance, 1½ca E of breakwater E lighthouse | 50°20.015'N | 004°08.004'W |
| 9 | 8 | Melampus, 100m due E of Melampus red can buoy | 50°21.153'N | 004°08.642'W |
| 9 | 9 | Smeaton Pass South, 100m SW of South Mallard S-card buoy | 50°21.481'N | 004°08.349'W |
| 9 | 10 | Smeaton Pass North, 1ca due W of Mallard light-tower | 50°21.605'N | 004°08.482'W |
| 9 | 11 | Sutton approach, 50m SE of Fisher's Nose lighthouse | 50°21.786'N | 004°07.991'W |
| 9 | 12 | Millbay approach, 1ca due S of Millbay pierhead | 50°21.652'N | 004°09.171'W |
| 9 | 13 | Drake Channel, 75m NW of NW Drake's Island red buoy | 50°21.454'N | 004°09.549'W |
| 9 | 14 | West Vanguard, 75m SW of West Vanguard green buoy | 50°21.463'N | 004°10.019'W |
| 9 | 15 | Mayflower Marina approach, 250m 340°T from Devil's Pt | 50°21.732'N | 004°10.129'W |

## Refer to Charts
Admiralty charts 30, 148, 1900, 1967
Imray C6, C14, 2400.8, 2400.13

## The Bridge
The Bridge is that narrow neck of shoals and drying rocks which separates Drake's Island from the Mount Edgcumbe shore on the west side of the estuary. It makes a useful short-cut for boats bound up the Tamar, even if only as far as the Mayflower Marina. The narrow channel across the Bridge is marked by red and green post beacons and carries a least depth of 2m, although the fairway is very fine near low water. The Bridge should only be taken in reasonable visibility when you can pick up the marks safely, but with a couple of hours rise of tide it is perfectly straightforward.

## COASTAL DANGERS
Plymouth Sound is one of the most easily and safely accessible natural harbours along the south coast, which is why it became such an important naval base in the days of sail. Cawsand Bay, opposite the breakwater on the west side of the Sound, has been a strategic passage anchorage since the times when large unwieldy ships of war could only just work against the wind, and it was not always possible to get in or out of harbour unless conditions were favourable. Cawsand, with its gently shelving bottom and easy access, was a natural holding anchorage for the port of Plymouth.

Because the estuary is so straightforward, boats should stay out of the buoyed channels when possible, leaving them clear for ferries, naval ships and coasters. There are few estuary dangers to mention in Plymouth Sound, but the following are worth watching.

## Penlee Point
This headland should not be shaved too close, since it has a small off-lying patch, drying 3.4m, within one cable due south.

## Shagstone
On the east side of the estuary, a drying tail ending at the Shagstone extends west from the Renney Rocks for about two cables. This ledge needs avoiding if you are approaching Plymouth Sound from the east round the Great Mewstone and are planning to use the Eastern Channel past the breakwater. Keep a good offing passing the Mewstone and then make towards the East Tinker E-cardinal buoy until the east end of the breakwater bears north true. Then it should be safe to alter a shade to starboard for the Eastern Channel.

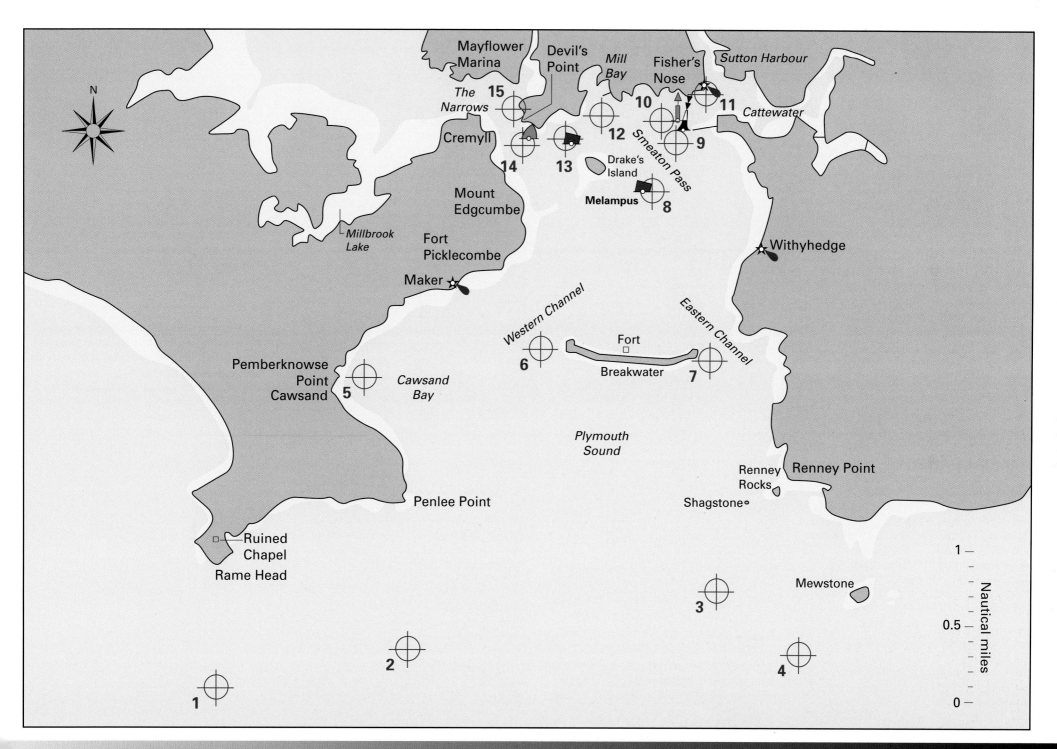

N

Mayflower
Marina

Devil's
Point

Mill
Bay

Fisher's
Nose

Sutton Harbour

*The Narrows*

**15**

Cattewater

Cremyll

**10**

**11**

*Smeaton Pass*

**12**

**9**

**14**

**13**

Drake's
Island

Mount
Edgcumbe

**Melampus**

**8**

*Millbrook
Lake*

Fort
Picklecombe

Withyhedge

Maker

*Western Channel*

*Eastern Channel*

Pemberknowse
Point
Cawsand

Fort

**6**

**7**

**5**

*Cawsand
Bay*

Breakwater

*Plymouth
Sound*

Renney
Rocks

Renney Point

Penlee Point

Shagstone

Ruined
Chapel

Rame Head

Mewstone

**3**

1

Nautical miles

**2**

0.5

**4**

**1**

0

# 10 Yealm River to Salcombe

| ⊕ | | Waypoint name and position | Latitude | Longitude |
|---|---|---|---|---|
| 10 | 1 | Plymouth SE approach, 1M W of Great Mewstone summit | 50°18.452'N | 004°07.985'W |
| 10 | 2 | Great Mewstone SW, 6ca SW of Great Mewstone summit | 50°18.029'N | 004°07.081'W |
| 10 | 3 | Yealm River approach, 6ca SE of Great Mewstone SE shore | 50°17.977'N | 004°05.700'W |
| 10 | 4 | Yealm entrance, 6ca 200°T from Wembury church spire | 50°18.510'N | 004°05.280'W |
| 10 | 5 | Yealm bar, 1½ca 205°T of Season Pt SW tip, on leading line | 50°18.600'N | 004°04.260'W |
| 10 | 6 | Ebb Rocks clearing, ½M 240°T from Gara Point | 50°17.950'N | 004°05.150'W |
| 10 | 7 | Hilsea Point clearing, 7ca due S of Hilsea Point | 50°16.980'N | 004°03.040'W |
| 10 | 8 | R Erme approach, ½M SW of Battisborough Island SW tip | 50°17.850'N | 003°58.290'W |
| 10 | 9 | R Erme entrance, 140m SE of Battisborough Island SW tip | 50°18.180'N | 003°57.640'W |
| 10 | 10 | Burgh Island, 3ca S of SW tip of island | 50°16.410'N | 003°54.060'W |
| 10 | 11 | Hope Cove outer, 2ca NW of Bolt Tail NW tip | 50°14.700'N | 003°52.460'W |
| 10 | 12 | Hope Cove entrance, 2ca NE of Bolt Tail NW tip | 50°14.700'N | 003°51.970'W |
| 10 | 13 | Bolt Tail west, ½M W of Bolt Tail SW tip | 50°14.460'N | 003°52.990'W |
| 10 | 14 | Bolt Tail south, 1¼M S of Bolt Tail SW tip | 50°13.210'N | 003°52.210'W |
| 10 | 15 | Ham Stone clearing, 6ca 190°T from Ham Stone | 50°12.511'N | 003°49.999'W |
| 10 | 16 | Bolt Head south, 6ca due S of Bolt Head SE tip | 50°12.050'N | 003°47.080'W |
| 10 | 17 | Salcombe approach, 4ca SE of Bolt Head on leading line | 50°12.369'N | 003°46.672'W |
| 10 | 18 | Salcombe entrance, ½ca S of Poundstone on leading line turn | 50°13.586'N | 003°46.668'W |
| 10 | 19 | Prawle Point clearing, ½M due S of headland | 50°11.620'N | 003°43.210'W |

## Refer to Charts
Admiralty charts 28, 30, 1613
Imray C6, 2400.5, 2400.6, 2400.8

## Salcombe bar
Salcombe entrance has a sand bar extending roughly NE–SW across the estuary from Limebury Point on the east side towards the steep cliffs on the west side. The bar is widest off Limebury and narrowest on the leading line. The shallowest soundings are about a metre at chart datum, with a hump of about 1.3m as you cross the bar on the leading line.

In offshore winds and most moderate weather, the bar is no problem to boats except towards low springs. But in fresh or heavy weather from between southwest and southeast, seas can break steeply and unexpectedly over the bar, especially during a spring ebb. In heavy onshore weather, boats should avoid Salcombe if possible, or at least try to enter well above half-flood.

## COASTAL DANGERS

### Great Mewstone dangers
The prominent Great Mewstone, on the west side of the approaches to the Yealm River, has various dangers around it which need avoiding. On the southwest side of the Great Mewstone, the Little Mewstone ledges extend underwater for a cable or so, so you should not cut this islet too close on this side.

Two drying patches known as the Outer and Inner Slimers lurk a couple of cables from the east side of the Great Mewstone, drying 1.5m and 0.3m respectively. These heads are only a problem if you arrive a bit early for the Yealm – it is best to approach the estuary at least a couple of hours after low water.

On the east side of the estuary, within three cables of Gara Point at the southwest tip of Yealm Head, the Western Ebb and Eastern Ebb Rocks are both awash at chart datum. To the north of the Great Mewstone is the narrow neck across Wembury Ledge, which should only be used with local knowledge within a couple of hours of high water.

### Hilsea Point Rock
Not usually a practical problem, Hilsea Point Rock (with 2.1m over it) lies ¼ mile offshore, just under four cables southeast of Hilsea Point opposite an old coastguard lookout.

### Wells Rock
Wells Rock (with only 1.2m over it) lies about one mile southeast of the estuary of the River Erme and ½ mile south by east from Beacon Point. In practice, it is only a potential danger for any boat coasting close inshore in Bigbury Bay, between Burgh Island and the Erme.

### Greystone Ledge, Ham Stone and Gregory Rocks
Between Bolt Tail and Bolt Head, you should keep at least ½ mile off the cliffs, to clear these various ledges and above-water rocks.

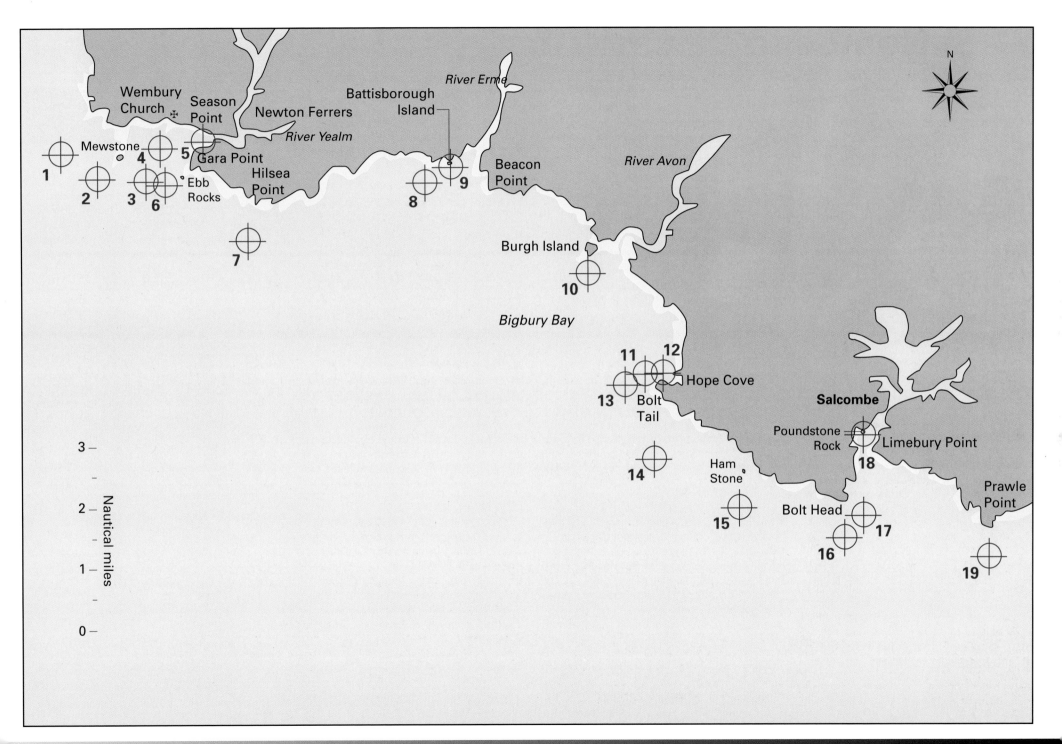

N

Wembury
Church ⴲ

Season
Point

Newton Ferrers

*River Yealm*

Battisborough
Island

*River Erme*

Mewstone

*River Avon*

Gara Point

Hilsea
Point

Ebb
Rocks

Beacon
Point

1

2

3

4

5

6

7

8

9

Burgh Island

10

*Bigbury Bay*

11

12

13

Hope Cove

Bolt
Tail

**Salcombe**

Poundstone
Rock

Limebury Point

18

Ham
Stone

14

Prawle
Point

Bolt Head

15

16

17

19

3 —

–

2 —

Nautical miles

–

1 —

–

0 —

# 11 Salcombe to Dartmouth

| ⊕ | Waypoint name and position | Latitude | Longitude |
|---|---|---|---|
| 11 1 | Salcombe approach, 4ca SE of Bolt Head on leading line | 50°12.369'N | 003°46.672'W |
| 11 2 | Salcombe entrance, ½ca S of Poundstone on leading line turn | 50°13.586'N | 003°46.668'W |
| 11 3 | Prawle Point clearing, ½M due S of headland | 50°11.620'N | 003°43.210'W |
| 11 4 | Start Point outer, 2M SE of lighthouse | 50°11.930'N | 003°36.340'W |
| 11 5 | Start Point inner, 6ca SE of lighthouse | 50°12.930'N | 003°37.890'W |
| 11 6 | Hallsands anchorage, close off the village | 50°14.140'N | 003°39.440'W |
| 11 7 | Skerries buoy, actual position | 50°16.320'N | 003°33.770'W |
| 11 8 | Blackpool Sands anchorage, 1ca off the beach | 50°19.040'N | 003°36.480'W |
| 11 9 | Dartmouth approach, 1ca W of Castle Ledge green buoy | 50°19.999'N | 003°33.274'W |
| 11 10 | Dart entrance, between Dartmouth Castle and Kettle Point | 50°20.548'N | 003°33.831'W |
| 11 11 | West Rock clearing, ½ca due S of West Rock S-card buoy | 50°19.810'N | 003°32.470'W |
| 11 12 | Mew Stone clearing, ½ca SE of Mew Stone S-card buoy | 50°19.888'N | 003°31.841'W |
| 11 13 | Eastern Blackstone clearing, 2ca SE of eastern rock | 50°20.060'N | 003°30.970'W |

## Refer to Charts

Admiralty chart 1634, 2253
Imray C5, 2300.1, 2300.7, 2300.9, 2400.5

### Eastern Blackstone

This two-pronged above-water rock, ½ mile east by north from the Mew Stone, is sometimes difficult to spot from a distance when seen against the coast or the Mew Stone. The Eastern Blackstone is fairly steep-to and can be passed either side, although you can easily be carried closer than intended by a strong spring tide.

## COASTAL DANGERS

### Salcombe Bar

Salcombe entrance has a sand bar extending roughly NE–SW across the estuary from Limebury Point on the east side towards the steep cliffs on the west side. The bar is widest off Limebury and narrowest on the leading line. The shallowest soundings are about a metre at chart datum, with a hump of about 1.3m as you cross the bar on the leading line.

In offshore winds and most moderate weather, the bar is no problem to boats except towards low springs. But in fresh or heavy weather from between southwest and southeast, seas can break steeply and unexpectedly over the bar, especially during a spring ebb. In heavy onshore weather, boats should avoid Salcombe if possible, or at least try to enter well above half-flood.

### Start Point Race

A race extends up to 1½ miles SE of Start Point, although its position and severity depend on wind and tide. In moderate weather you can round Start close in, keeping ¼ mile south of the Black Stone to avoid Cherrick Rocks. In fresh wind-over-tide conditions, stay a good two miles offshore.

### The Skerries Bank

Lying towards the south end of Start Bay, the Skerries Bank is only a danger in strong wind-over-tide conditions, or in strong southeasterlies, when steep breaking seas can build up, especially over the southern tail of the bank. In offshore or quiet weather, boats with normal draught can sail safely over the bank.

### Combe Rocks

Half a mile west of Dartmouth entrance, this straggling area of drying and above-water rocks juts seaward off Combe Point for well over one cable. Boats coasting inshore towards Dartmouth from near Blackpool Sands should give this promontory a wide berth, keeping at least one cable off the pinnacle of Old Combe Rock (3m high).

### The Mew Stone

This prominent islet (35m high) off the east side of Dartmouth entrance has a tail of shoals and drying rocks extending more than ¼ mile from its west face. Boats coasting towards Dartmouth from the direction of Tor Bay should keep south of Mew Stone and West Rock S-cardinal buoys before turning in towards the Castle Ledge green buoy.

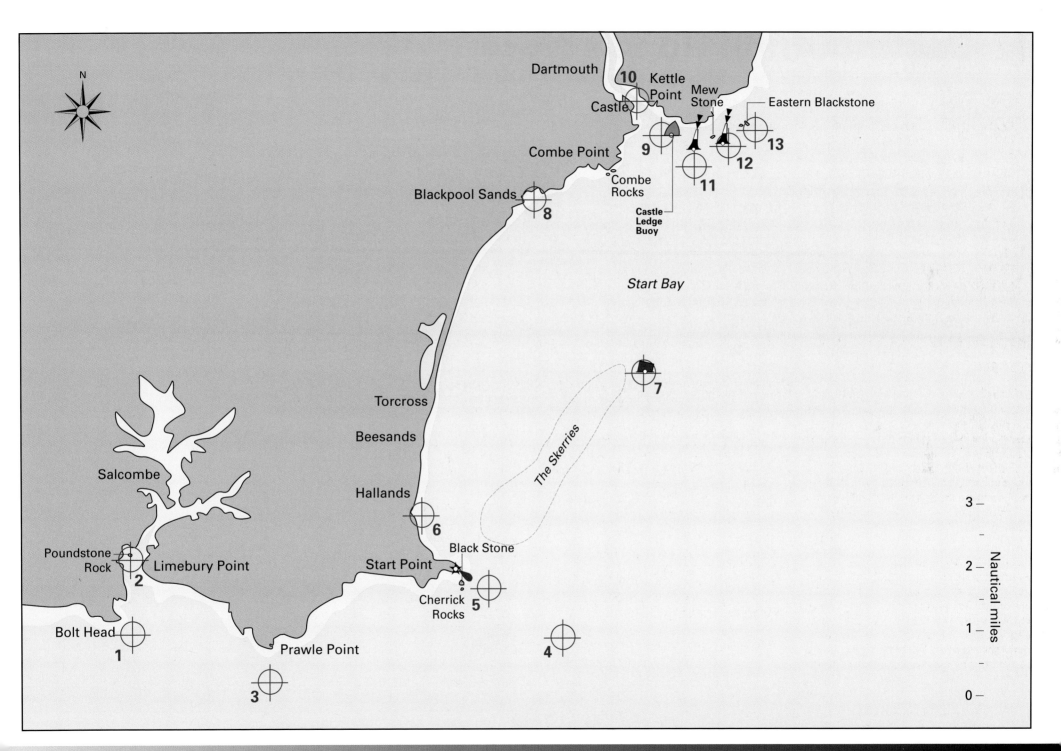

N

Dartmouth

**10** Kettle Point

Castle

Mew Stone

Eastern Blackstone

**9**

**13**

**12**

Combe Point

**11**

Combe Rocks

**Castle Ledge Buoy**

Blackpool Sands

**8**

*Start Bay*

Torcross

**7**

Beesands

*The Skerries*

Salcombe

Hallands

**6**

3 —

Poundstone Rock

Limebury Point

Black Stone

Start Point

**2**

**5**

— 2

Cherrick Rocks

Bolt Head

**4**

**1**

1 —

Prawle Point

**3**

Nautical miles

0 —

# 12 Dartmouth to Hope's Nose

| ⊕ | | Waypoint name and position | Latitude | Longitude |
|---|---|---|---|---|
| 12 | 1 | Dart entrance, between Dartmouth Castle and Kettle Point | 50°20.548′N | 003°33.831′W |
| 12 | 2 | Dartmouth approach, 1ca W of Castle Ledge green buoy | 50°19.999′N | 003°33.274′W |
| 12 | 3 | West Rock clearing, ½ca due S of West Rock S-card buoy | 50°19.810′N | 003°32.470′W |
| 12 | 4 | Mew Stone clearing, ½ca SE of Mew Stone S-card buoy | 50°19.888′N | 003°31.841′W |
| 12 | 5 | Eastern Blackstone clearing, 2ca SE of eastern rock | 50°20.060′N | 003°30.970′W |
| 12 | 6 | Nimble Rock clearing, 8ca 050°T from Eastern Blackstone | 50°20.707′N | 003°30.256′W |
| 12 | 7 | Sharkham Point clearing, ½M SE of Sharkham Point | 50°22.550′N | 003°29.220′W |
| 12 | 8 | Berry Head clearing, ½M due E of lighthouse | 50°23.977′N | 003°28.234′W |
| 12 | 9 | Berry Head north, 3ca due N of lighthouse | 50°24.272′N | 003°29.010′W |
| 12 | 10 | Brixham approach, 1½ca NW of breakwater head | 50°24.440′N | 003°30.943′W |
| 12 | 11 | Brixham inner, 100m due N of north fish quay | 50°24.027′N | 003°30.698′W |
| 12 | 12 | Torquay approach, 50m due S of green entrance buoy | 50°27.397′N | 003°31.803′W |
| 12 | 13 | West Shag clearing, 3ca due S of West Shag rock | 50°26.934′N | 003°30.787′W |
| 12 | 14 | Thatcher Rock clearing, 3ca due S of south face | 50°26.995′N | 003°29.380′W |
| 12 | 15 | Ore Stone south, 4ca due S of south face | 50°27.000′N | 003°28.300′W |
| 12 | 16 | Ore Stone east, ½M due E of east face | 50°27.439′N | 003°27.466′W |
| 12 | 17 | Hope's Nose clearing, ¾M 080°T from NE tip of headland | 50°27.970′N | 003°27.700′W |

### Refer to Charts
Admiralty chart 26, 1613, 1634, 2253
Imray C5, 2300.1, 2300.7, 2300.8

### Morris Rogue
Approaching Torquay harbour along the north side of Tor Bay from the direction of the Ore Stone, you need to stay at least ½ mile offshore to the west of Thatcher Rock, in order to clear Morris Rogue (with 0.8m over it).

## COASTAL DANGERS

### The Mew Stone
This prominent islet (35m high) off the east side of Dartmouth entrance has a tail of shoals and drying rocks extending more than ¼ mile from its west face. Boats coasting towards Dartmouth from the direction of Tor Bay should keep south of Mew Stone and West Rock S-cardinal buoys before turning in towards the Castle Ledge green buoy.

### Eastern Blackstone
This two-pronged above-water rock, ½ mile east by north from the Mew Stone, is sometimes difficult to spot from a distance when seen against the coast or the Mew Stone. The Eastern Blackstone is fairly steep-to and can be passed either side, although you can easily be carried closer than intended by a strong spring tide.

### Nimble Rock
This isolated head, with less than 1m over it, lies about ½ mile southeast of Scabbacombe Head. To clear Nimble Rock, keep Start Point lighthouse open either side of the Eastern Blackstone. A striking mark is the cliff summit behind Scabbacombe Bay in transit with Scabbacombe Head bearing 330°T.

### Mag Rock
Mag Rock, which dries 3.8m, extends up to 1½ cables east of Sharkham Point. This ledge is only a problem if you are coasting close inshore past the bays and coves between Dartmouth and Berry Head.

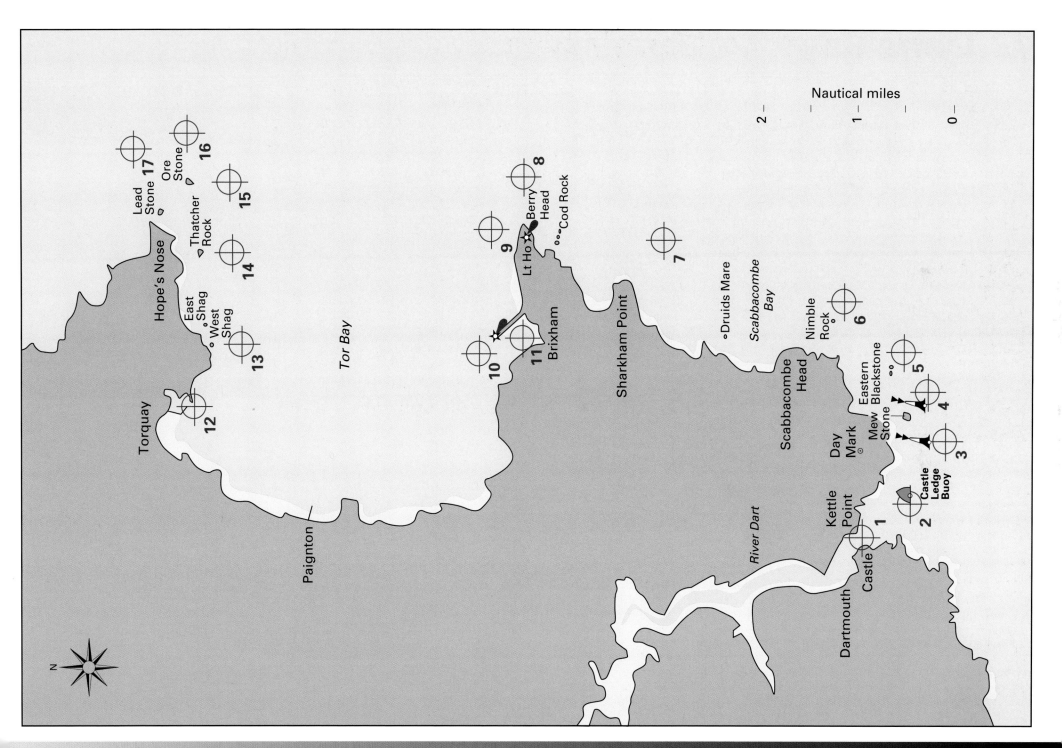

Nautical miles

2    1    0

17 Lead Stone
Ore Stone 16
Thatcher Rock
15
14
Hope's Nose
East Shag
West Shag
13
Torquay
12
Paignton

Tor Bay

8 Berry Head
°°°Cod Rock
9 Lt Ho
10    11 Brixham

7

Druids Mare
Scabbacombe Bay
Nimble Rock
6
Sharkham Point
Scabbacombe Head
Eastern Blackstone
5
Mew Stone
Day Mark
4
Kettle Point
3
1
2 Castle Ledge Buoy
Dartmouth Castle

River Dart

N

# 13 Lyme Bay

| ⊕ | | Waypoint name and position | Latitude | Longitude |
|---|---|---|---|---|
| 13 | 1 | Mew Stone clearing, ½ca SE of Mew Stone S-card buoy | 50°19.888'N | 003°31.841'W |
| 13 | 2 | Berry Head east, ½M due E of lighthouse | 50°23.977'N | 003°28.234'W |
| 13 | 3 | Berry Head north, 3ca due N of lighthouse | 50°24.272'N | 003°29.010'W |
| 13 | 4 | Ore Stone south, 4ca due S of south face | 50°27.000'N | 003°28.300'W |
| 13 | 5 | Ore Stone east, ½M due E of east face | 50°27.439'N | 003°27.466'W |
| 13 | 6 | Hope's Nose clearing, ¾M 080°T from NE tip of headland | 50°27.970'N | 003°27.700'W |
| 13 | 7 | Babbacombe Bay, ½M 321°T from Long Quarry Point | 50°28.967'N | 003°30.346'W |
| 13 | 8 | Teignmouth approach, 2ca SE of the Ness east tip | 50°32.119'N | 003°29.540'W |
| 13 | 9 | Exe approach, 1ca due E of Exe E-card buoy | 50°36.001'N | 003°22.213'W |
| 13 | 10 | Beer haven anchorage, 1ca off the beach | 50°41.638'N | 003°05.332'W |
| 13 | 11 | River Axe entrance, 3ca due S of mouth | 50°41.839'N | 003°03.302'W |
| 13 | 12 | Lyme Regis approach, ½M 116°T from pierhead on leading line | 50°42.973'N | 002°55.475'W |
| 13 | 13 | Bridport approach, ½M 190°T from W pierhead on leading line | 50°42.335'N | 002°45.687'W |
| 13 | 14 | Portland inner west approach, 1M NW of lighthouse | 50°31.550'N | 002°28.480'W |
| 13 | 15 | Portland clearing, 2½M due S of lighthouse | 50°28.348'N | 002°27.378'W |
| 13 | 16 | Portland outer clearing, 3½M due S of lighthouse | 50°27.348'N | 002°27.378'W |
| 13 | 17 | West Shambles, 1ca W of W-card buoy | 50°29.785'N | 002°24.572'W |

**Refer to Charts**
Admiralty chart 26, 2290, 3315
Imray C5, 2300.1, 2300.4, 2300.6, 2300.8

## COASTAL DANGERS

### Teignmouth approaches

Teignmouth is an interesting and unspoilt harbour, but the bar at the river mouth requires some care. It is no problem in any winds from a westerly quarter, when strangers should enter above half-tide. In any winds from the east, strangers should stay clear and make for Torquay or Brixham instead.

### River Exe approaches

The Exe is one of the most unspoilt estuaries in the West Country, although its bar and shifting sands at the entrance help to keep it so. Strangers should only approach in offshore winds, making for the Exe E-cardinal buoy, not long after low water ideally, when most of the drying banks are visible and should provide some lee in the fairway. Although the channel is lit, you should not attempt the Exe entrance at night unless you have been in a couple of times in daylight.

### Portland Race

The worst of Portland Race extends 1½–2 miles south of the Bill. Keep a good 3–3½ miles off the Bill if passing outside, or within ¼ mile if passing inside. If making for the inner passage from Dartmouth or Torbay, use the Portland inner west approach waypoint in order to close the Bill safely north of the Race. Then shave close to the Bill all the way round to the east side, watching out for crab-pot floats all the time.

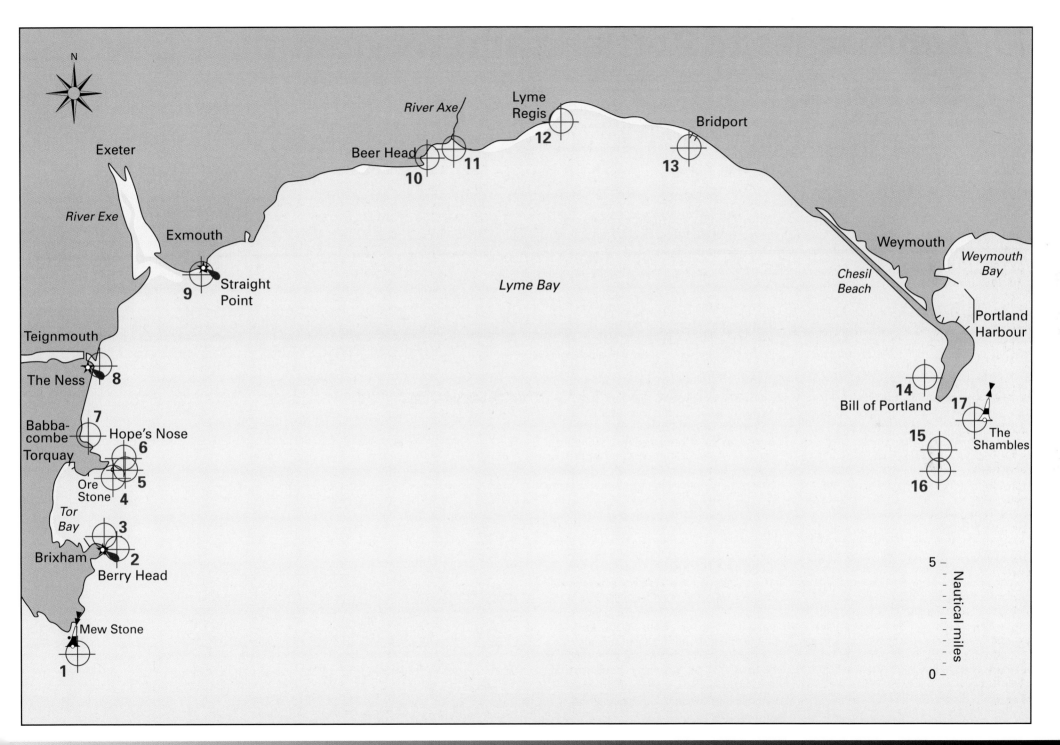

N

Exeter

River Exe

River Axe

Lyme Regis

Bridport

Exmouth

Beer Head

**11**

**12**

**13**

**10**

Straight Point

**9**

Weymouth

Weymouth Bay

Lyme Bay

Chesil Beach

Portland Harbour

Teignmouth

The Ness

**8**

**14**

Bill of Portland

**17**

Babba- combe

**7**

Hope's Nose

**15**

The Shambles

Torquay

**6**

**5**

**16**

Ore Stone

**4**

Tor Bay

**3**

Brixham

**2**

Berry Head

Mew Stone

**1**

5

Nautical miles

0

# 14 Approaches to Portland and Weymouth

| ⊕ | Waypoint name and position | Latitude | Longitude |
|---|---|---|---|
| 14 1 | Portland inner west approach, 1M NW of lighthouse | 50°31.550'N | 002°28.480'W |
| 14 2 | Portland inner east approach, ½M E of Old Low lighthouse | 50°31.176'N | 002°26.288'W |
| 14 3 | Portland clearing, 2½M due S of lighthouse | 50°28.348'N | 002°27.378'W |
| 14 4 | Portland outer clearing, 3½M due S of lighthouse | 50°27.348'N | 002°27.378'W |
| 14 5 | West Shambles, 1ca due W of W-card buoy | 50°29.785'N | 002°24.572'W |
| 14 6 | East Shambles, 1ca due E of E-card buoy | 50°30.783'N | 002°19.924'W |
| 14 7 | Grove Point clearing, ½M due E of outer rock | 50°32.970'N | 002°24.070'W |
| 14 8 | Portland Harbour, ½M 080°T from outer breakwater north head | 50°35.196'N | 002°24.079'W |
| 14 9 | Weymouth approach, ¼M due E of South pierhead | 50°36.580'N | 002°26.090'W |

### Refer to Charts
Admiralty chart 2255, 2610
Imray C4, 2300.3

### Tides round Portland Bill
The tides are strong round the Bill, whether you are taking the inner or the offshore passage. With the inner passage, it is usually best to go through near slack water just as the stream is starting to run in your favour. If you are staying well offshore, carrying a fair tide round the Bill will take you past and away as quickly as possible.

## COASTAL DANGERS

### Portland Race
The worst of Portland Race extends 1½–2 miles south of the Bill. Keep a good 3–3½ miles off the Bill if passing outside, or within ¼ mile if passing inside. If making for the inner passage from Dartmouth or Torbay, use the Portland inner west approach waypoint in order to close the Bill safely north of the Race. Then shave close to the Bill all the way round to the east side, watching out for crab-pot floats all the time.

### The Shambles
The Shambles Bank lies from 2½–4 miles E by S of Portland Bill, extending roughly ENE/WSW and marked at either end by the East Shambles E-cardinal buoy and the West Shambles W-cardinal buoy. The lowest soundings are 3.4m and local yachts and fishing boats pass over the bank in quiet weather, but it does not take much wind and tide to turn the area into a hostile maelstrom of dangerous white water.

On the east-going stream, the worst of Portland Race lies SSE of the Bill, almost within one mile of the West Shambles buoy. Boats coming from the west outside the Race and bound for Weymouth therefore have to be careful if turning in to pass between Portland and the Shambles. Passing east-about the Shambles is usually easier and safer, but adds another three miles into Weymouth if coming from the west. In reasonable weather, by far the most efficient route into Weymouth from the west is to take the inner passage round the Bill (see note under Portland Race above). The important tactic in this case is to make your landfall on the Bill well north of the lighthouse and the Race.

### Crab-pot buoys
There are numerous crab-pot buoys in the vicinity of Portland Bill, especially close inshore through the inner passage. Take special care to watch out for these buoys, many of which are small and can be pulled half underwater by the tide. With the Race close on one side and the rocky shore of the Bill on the other, a rope snarled round a propeller or rudder could have serious consequences.

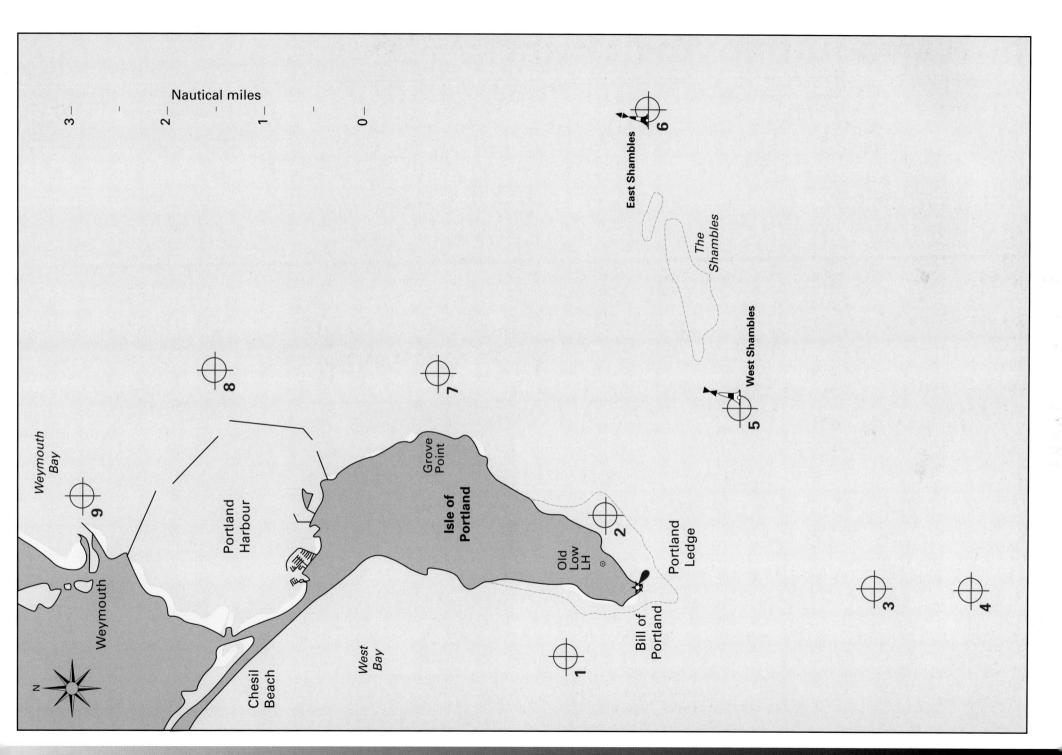

Nautical miles

3   2   1   0

East Shambles

6

The Shambles

West Shambles

5

8

7

Weymouth Bay

9

Portland Harbour

Grove Point

Isle of Portland

2

N

Weymouth

Old Low LH

Portland Ledge

West Bay

3

Chesil Beach

Bill of Portland

1

4

# 15 Weymouth to Anvil Point

| ⊕ | Waypoint name and position | Latitude | Longitude |
|---|---|---|---|
| 15 1 | Weymouth approach, ¼M due E of South pierhead | 50°36.580'N | 002°26.090'W |
| 15 2 | Portland Harbour, ½M 080°T from outer breakwater north head | 50°35.196'N | 002°24.079'W |
| 15 3 | Grove Point clearing, ½M due E of outer rock | 50°32.970'N | 002°24.070'W |
| 15 4 | East Shambles, 1ca due E of E-card buoy | 50°30.783'N | 002°19.924'W |
| 15 5 | Lulworth Cove approach, 2ca S of east headland tip | 50°36.810'N | 002°14.770'W |
| 15 6 | Worbarrow Bay west, ¾M SE of Bindon Hill occas. light | 50°36.810'N | 002°12.820'W |
| 15 7 | Worbarrow Bay east, 3ca SW of the Tout outer tip | 50°36.680'N | 002°11.580'W |
| 15 8 | Chapman's Pool approach, 6ca 300°T from St Alban's light | 50°35.043'N | 002°04.209'W |
| 15 9 | St Alban's inner, 1ca due S of St Alban's Head | 50°34.490'N | 002°03.300'W |
| 15 10 | St Alban's Ledge clearing, 5M SW of St Alban's light | 50°31.246'N | 002°08.924'W |
| 15 11 | St Alban's Head clearing, 4M due S of St Alban's Head | 50°30.590'N | 002°03.300'W |
| 15 12 | Anvil Point clearing, 1M SE of Durlston Head | 50°34.970'N | 001°55.930'W |
| 15 13 | Peveril Point outer, 1.1M E of Peveril Point | 50°36.440'N | 001°54.920'W |
| 15 14 | Peveril Point inner, 1ca E of Peveril Ledge red buoy | 50°36.415'N | 001°55.938'W |

## Refer to Charts

Admiralty chart 2172, 2255, 2610
Imray C4, 2300.3

## Anvil Point Race

There is a much smaller race on the southwest-going stream between Anvil Point and Durlston Head, extending up to ¾ mile offshore and sometimes quite boisterous with wind-over-tide. Waypoint 15–12 keeps you one mile southeast of Durlston Head, although you can cut much closer inshore in quiet conditions.

## COASTAL DANGERS

### The Shambles

The Shambles Bank lies from 2½–4 miles E by S of Portland Bill, extending roughly ENE/WSW and marked at either end by the East Shambles E-cardinal buoy and the West Shambles W-cardinal buoy. The lowest soundings are 3.4m and local yachts and fishing boats pass over the bank in quiet weather, but it does not take much wind and tide to turn the area into a hostile maelstrom of dangerous white water.

### Lulworth Gunnery Ranges

The military practice ranges off Lulworth are used during the week throughout the year except in August, but are only active on a few selected weekends. The planned firing times are published well in advance and the schedule distributed to Harbourmasters and Yacht Clubs in the area. During firing, the range area is patrolled by the well-known blue-hulled Range Safety Boats, which work on VHF Ch 18.

### St Alban's Ledge and Race

St Alban's Ledge extends southwest from St Alban's Head for a good four miles. The Ledge has plenty of depth over it, with soundings between about 10–18m compared with 25–30m in the deeper water on either side. The danger for boats is the overfalls caused by the Ledge, which can be savage at springs with a weather-going stream. The tide can reach four knots along this stretch of coast, sometimes more locally over St Alban's Ledge where the flow is squeezed vertically. You need to stay a good four miles south of St Alban's Head to avoid the worst of the race (see ⊕15–10 and 15–11 in the table).

In moderate weather you can take the inner passage close inshore under St Alban's, although there will often be some uneasy water even here (see ⊕15–9 in the table). You have to shave very close to St Alban's to avoid overfalls altogether, although it is certainly a steep-to headland with no dangers to within about 50m of the shore.

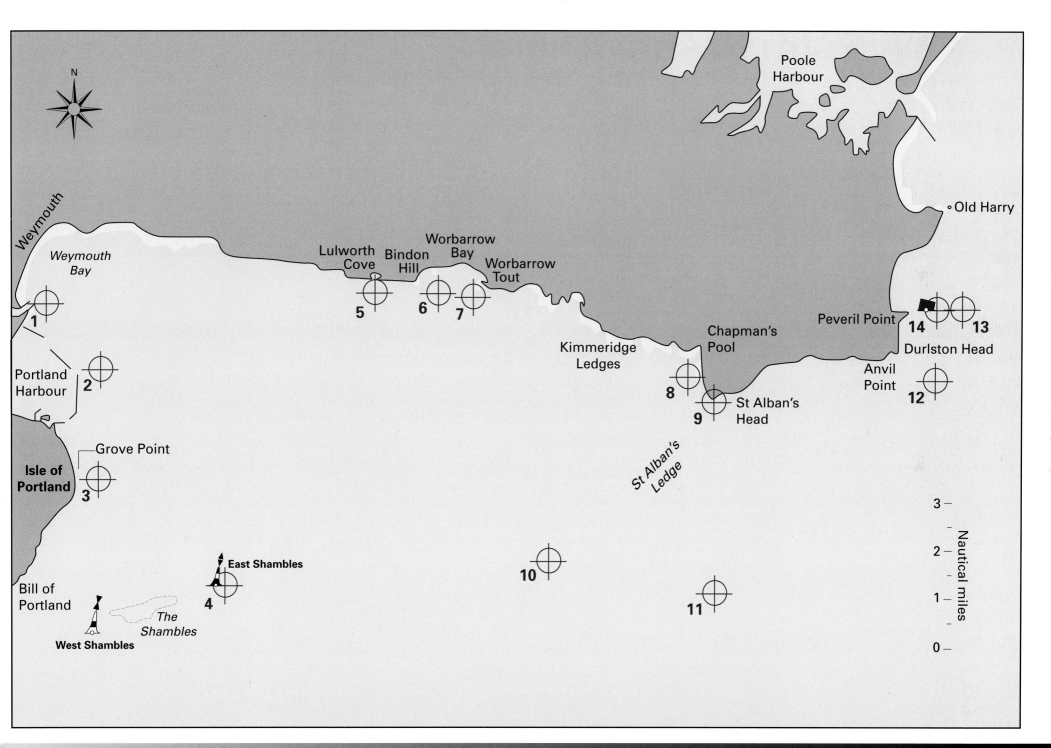

Poole Harbour

N

Weymouth

Weymouth Bay

° Old Harry

Worbarrow Bay

Lulworth Cove

Bindon Hill

Worbarrow Tout

5

6

7

1

Peveril Point

14

13

Chapman's Pool

Kimmeridge Ledges

Durlston Head

Portland Harbour

2

8

Anvil Point

12

9

St Alban's Head

Grove Point

Isle of Portland

3

St Alban's Ledge

East Shambles

4

10

Bill of Portland

The Shambles

11

West Shambles

3 —

— 
2 —

Nautical miles

1 —

— 
0 —

| ⊕ | Waypoint name and position | Latitude | Longitude |
|---|---|---|---|
| 16 1 | Anvil Point clearing, 1M SE of Durlston Head | 50°34.970'N | 001°55.930'W |
| 16 2 | Peveril Point outer, 1.1M E of Peveril Point | 50°36.440'N | 001°54.920'W |
| 16 3 | Peveril Point inner, 1ca E of Peveril Ledge red buoy | 50°36.415'N | 001°55.938'W |
| 16 4 | Poole outer approach, 7ca E of Old Harry | 50°38.550'N | 001°54.256'W |
| 16 5 | Swash Channel entrance, 100m due S of Poole Bar buoy | 50°39.232'N | 001°55.145'W |
| 16 6 | East Looe approach, 6½ca 070°T from Haven Hotel | 50°41.212'N | 001°55.883'W |
| 16 7 | Christchurch approach, 6ca 075°T from Haven House Inn | 50°43.604'N | 001°43.594'W |
| 16 8 | Christchurch Ledge SE clearing, 3M 130°T from Hengistbury Head | 50°40.815'N | 001°41.358'W |

**Refer to Charts**
Admiralty charts 2172, 2611, 2615
Imray C4, 2300.2

## COASTAL DANGERS

### Tidal races between Anvil Point and Handfast Point

There is quite a localised race on the southwest-going stream between Anvil Point and Durlston Head, extending up to ¾ mile offshore and sometimes quite boisterous with wind-over-tide. Waypoint 16–1 keeps you one mile southeast of Durlston Head, although you can cut much closer inshore in quiet conditions.

A mile or so further north, the race off Peveril Point, although fairly localised, can be quite savage on the ebb. The tide curving out of Swanage Bay swirls round Peveril Point and across Peveril Ledge, meeting at an angle the main SSW-going stream coming down from Poole Bay. Smaller yachts and motor boats can take a dusting through Peveril race, so give this corner a wide berth during the ebb.

Further north again, there are areas of overfalls on the ebb off Ballard Point and Handfast Point (Old Harry), although at neaps and in quiet weather these areas represent only a slight agitation within a fairly small area.

### Hook Sand

The main Swash Channel into Poole Harbour has a long training wall on the west side and the shoals of the Hook Sand on the east. The Swash Channel is well buoyed, but the Hook Sand needs treating with respect, especially by boats working west across Poole Bay towards Poole entrance, perhaps tacking close inshore towards Boscombe and Bournemouth before working out again towards the Poole fairway buoy and the Swash Channel entrance. Craft approaching or skirting the east side of the Hook Sand must always be careful not to stray inside the seaward red buoy and put themselves aground on the *outside edge* of the bank.

### Christchurch Ledge

The rocky shoals of Christchurch Ledge extend southeast from Hengistbury Head for almost three miles, although the shallowest finger of the ledge (with only 3.8m over it) reaches out for 1½ miles. The seas over the ledge can be dangerous in heavy onshore weather, when boats making for the North Channel should stay in the deep water between Christchurch Ledge and the Dolphin Bank. During the summer, a yellow buoy moored not quite 2½ miles southeast of Hengistbury Head gives a useful guide to the outer end of Christchurch Ledge.

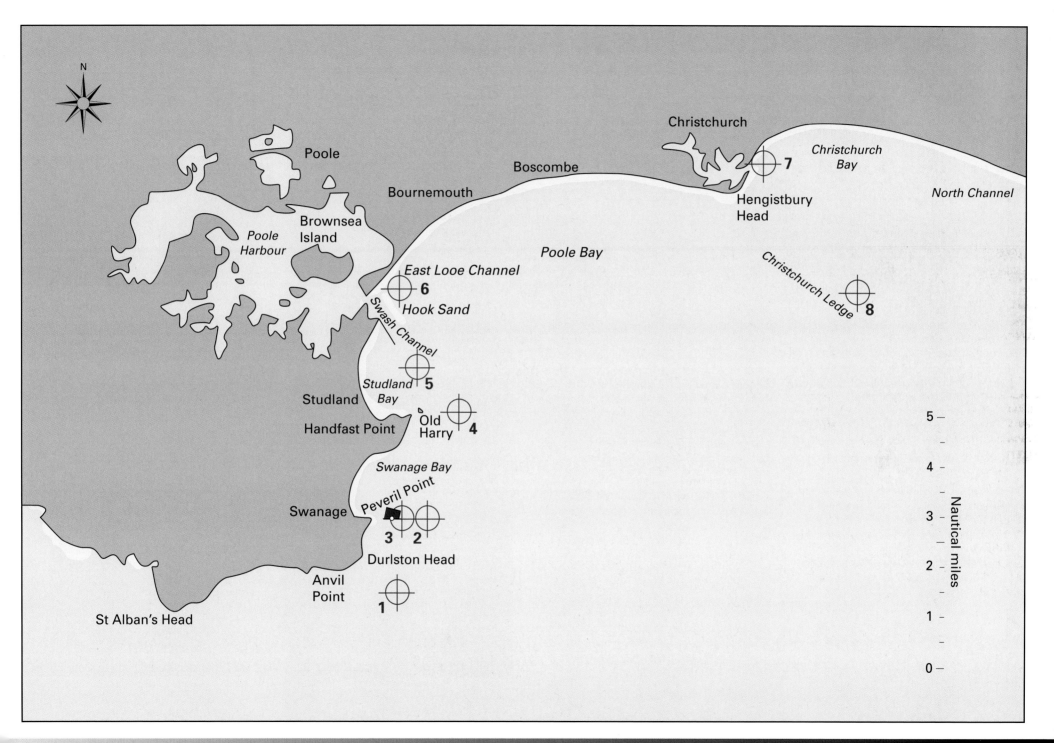

N

Poole

Brownsea Island

Poole Harbour

Christchurch

Christchurch Bay

Boscombe

Bournemouth

North Channel

East Looe Channel
6

Hook Sand

Poole Bay

Hengistbury Head

Swash Channel

Christchurch Ledge
8

5

Studland Bay

Studland

Old Harry
4

Handfast Point

Swanage Bay

Peveril Point

Swanage

3  2

Durlston Head

Anvil Point

1

St Alban's Head

5 —

4 —

3 —

Nautical miles

2 —

1 —

0 —

| ⊕ | Waypoint name and position | Latitude | Longitude |
|---|---|---|---|
| 17 1 | Christchurch approach, 6ca 075°T from Haven House Inn | 50°43.604'N | 001°43.594'W |
| 17 2 | Christchurch Ledge SE clearing, 3M 130°T from Hengistbury Head | 50°40.815'N | 001°41.358'W |
| 17 3 | North Channel outer, summer buoy actual position | 50°42.959'N | 001°37.912'W |
| 17 4 | North Channel approach, 1ca W of North Head green buoy | 50°42.690'N | 001°35.670'W |
| 17 5 | North Channel inner, 6ca 260°T of Hurst Light | 50°42.374'N | 001°33.952'W |
| 17 6 | Needles fairway buoy, actual position | 50°38.240'N | 001°38.980'W |
| 17 7 | Needles outer, ½ca W of Bridge W-card buoy | 50°39.630'N | 001°36.976'W |
| 17 8 | Mid Shingles, 1½ca SE of red buoy | 50°41.109'N | 001°34.501'W |
| 17 9 | Warden clearing, 100m NW of Warden green bell buoy | 50°41.520'N | 001°33.600'W |
| 17 10 | Hurst Point, 3½ca SE of Hurst Light | 50°42.230'N | 001°32.650'W |

**Refer to Charts**
Admiralty chart 2035, 2615
Imray C4, 2200.1, 2200.2, 2200.8

© Bortescristian I Dreamstime.com

## COASTAL DANGERS

### The Needles Channel

The Needles Channel is rough with wind over tide, especially in a southwesterly over the ebb, when the North Channel is quieter. In heavy weather, seas can break dangerously between the Needles and Hurst Point. Remember that the tide sets across the Shingles bank, so that the ebb through the Needles will be trying to set you west towards the Shingles.

The Bridge Ledge, which extends westward from the Needles lighthouse for almost one mile, has overfalls over it with wind over tide, and is dangerous in heavy onshore weather. In such conditions, you should stay in the Needles Channel entrance between the Bridge W-cardinal buoy and the SW Shingles red buoy.

### The North Channel

The North Channel into and out of the Solent can be a quieter and safer passage than the Needles Channel in heavy onshore weather. However, approaching the North Channel under these conditions requires care, partly to stay in the deep water between Christchurch Ledge and the Dolphin, and then to pick up the North Head green buoy without straying too close either to the Shingles bank on the south side or the lee shore on the north side.

### Alum, Totland and Colwell Bays

Boats tacking through the Needles Channel should obviously take care of the Shingles Bank on the northwest side, but also be wary of tacking too close into the bays on the southeast side between the Needles and Fort Albert. Alum, Totland and Colwell Bays all have rocky shoal areas, especially Colwell Bay, the most northerly of the three. The dangerous Warden ledge, between Totland and Colwell Bays, extends a good four cables northwest towards the Needles Channel from Warden Point.

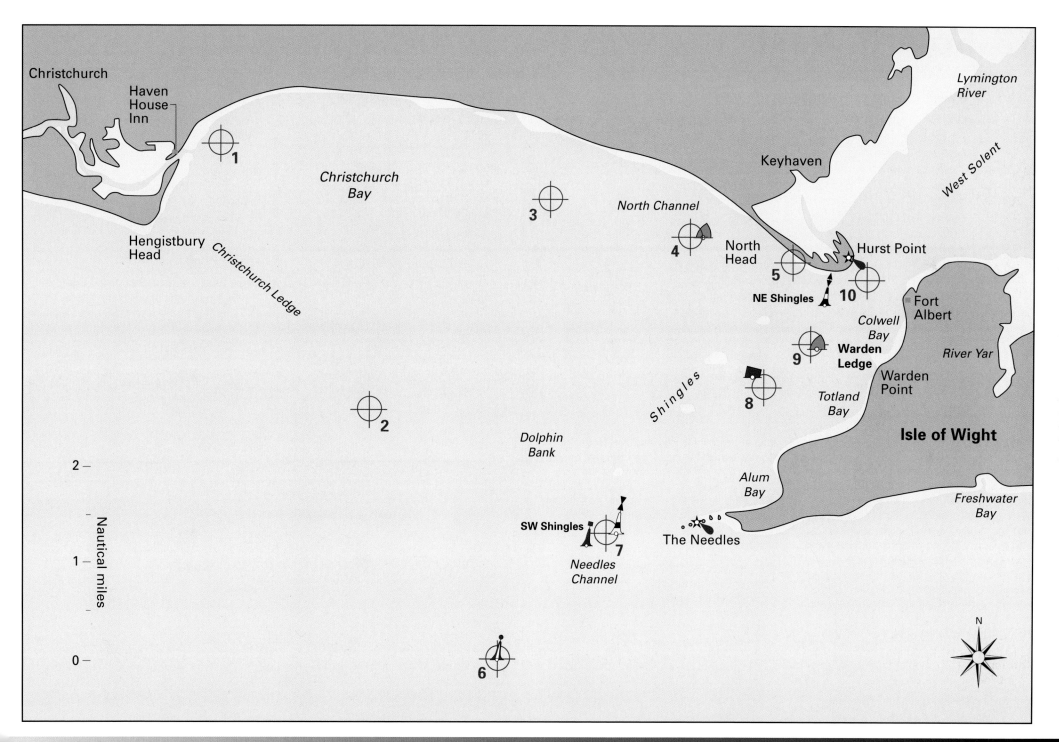

Christchurch

Haven
House
Inn

**1**

Christchurch
Bay

Hengistbury
Head

Christchurch Ledge

**3**

North Channel

Keyhaven

**4**

North
Head

Hurst Point

**5**

NE Shingles

**10**

Fort
Albert

Colwell
Bay

**9**

Warden
Ledge

River Yar

Warden
Point

Shingles

**8**

Totland
Bay

**Isle of Wight**

**2**

Dolphin
Bank

Alum
Bay

Freshwater
Bay

SW Shingles

**7**

The Needles

Needles
Channel

**6**

2 —

1 —

0 —

Nautical miles

N

# 18 Solent West

## Refer to Charts

Admiralty charts 2021, 2035, 2036
Imray C15, 2200.1, 2200.8

¾ mile just north of west from the Newtown River entrance.
Between the Newtown River and Gurnard Head, the coast within about ½ mile of the Isle of Wight is relatively shallow, with the Salt Mead Ledges marked by Salt Mead green buoy and Thorness Bay awaiting the unwary who tack in too close.

### Lepe Middle and Beaulieu Spit

The approaches to the Beaulieu River are also shallow, and boats making towards Beaulieu entrance from Lymington have to keep out into the Solent a little near low water. The outer mark for Beaulieu entrance is the East Lepe red buoy which provides a fairway position for the final approaches to the Beaulieu River.

## COASTAL DANGERS

### Yarmouth approaches

When approaching Yarmouth from the Needles Channel, stay outside the Black Rock green conical buoy before dropping south of east towards the harbour entrance. The tides are strong off Yarmouth entrance, with overfalls between the Black Rock buoy and the pierhead at springs on a weather-going stream. Because of the strong tides, turn in towards the harbour in good time, allowing for the cross-set as you crab towards the ferry terminal past the pier.

### Lymington Flats

The approaches to Lymington are shallow, with wide drying flats on either side of the entrance between Hurst and Pitts Deep.

Tacking up towards Lymington from Hurst against a northeasterly, you have to be careful not to stray too far inshore off Pennington Spit and Pennington Marshes. A direct line from Hurst Point towards the Jack in the Basket beacon lies just outside the shoal areas where soundings are down to less than 1m.

### Newtown approaches

The approaches to the Newtown River are shallow. Arriving from the west, you need to pick up the W-cardinal buoy from a position somewhere near Hamstead Ledge green buoy, which lies about

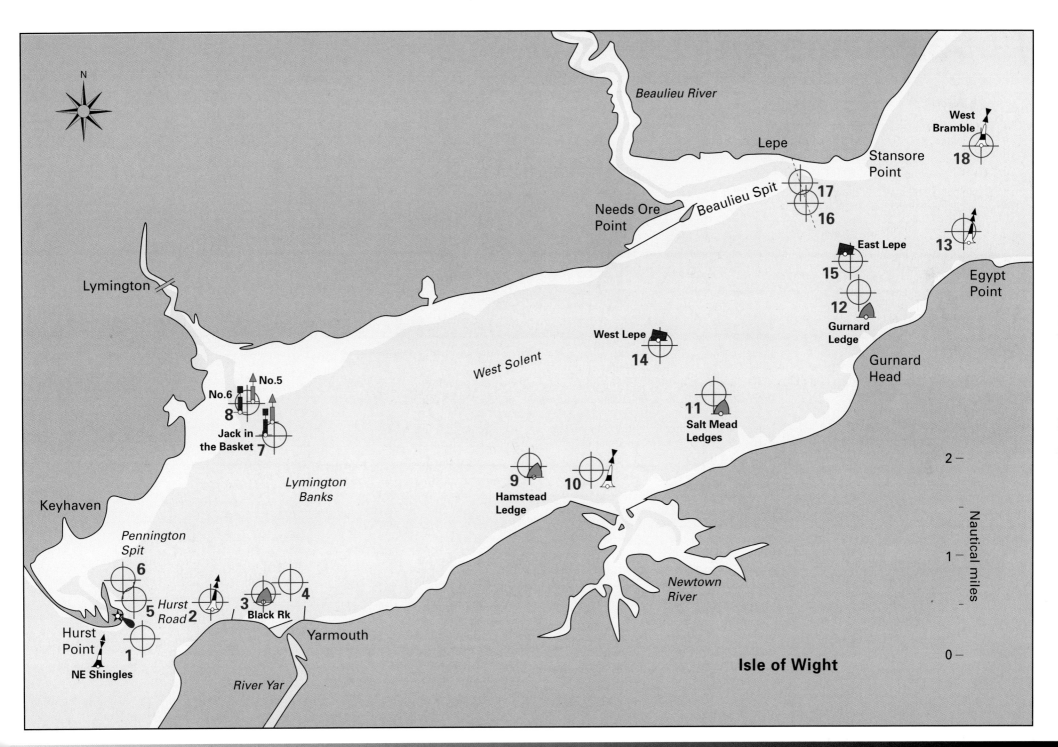

N

*Beaulieu River*

West
Bramble

**18**

Lepe

Stansore
Point

Needs Ore
Point

*Beaulieu Spit*

**17**

**16**

**13**

East Lepe

**15**

Egypt
Point

**12**

Gurnard
Ledge

Lymington

Gurnard
Head

*West Solent*

West Lepe

**14**

No.5

No.6

**11**

Salt Mead
Ledges

**8**

Jack in
the Basket **7**

Hamstead
Ledge

**9**

**10**

*Lymington
Banks*

*Newtown
River*

Keyhaven

2 —

*Pennington
Spit*

**6**

**5** Hurst
Road **2**

**4**

**3** Black Rk

1 —

Nautical miles

Hurst
Point

**1**

Yarmouth

**Isle of Wight**

0 —

**NE Shingles**

*River Yar*

# 19 Southampton Water

| ⊕ | Waypoint name and position | Latitude | Longitude |
|---|---|---|---|
| 19 1 | Calshot Spit, 50m SE of light-float | 50°48.335'N | 001°17.626'W |
| 19 2 | Calshot Reach, 50m SW of Reach green buoy | 50°49.034'N | 001°17.687'W |
| 19 3 | Hamble Point, 50m S of Hamble Point S-card buoy | 50°50.127'N | 001°18.662'W |
| 19 4 | Hound inner, 50m NE of Hound green buoy | 50°51.714'N | 001°21.512'W |
| 19 5 | NW Netley inner, 50m NE of NW Netley green buoy | 50°52.323'N | 001°22.719'W |
| 19 6 | Hythe Marina approach, 1ca NE of Hythe E-card beacon | 50°52.704'N | 001°23.767'W |
| 19 7 | Itchen approach, 1½ca SE of QEII terminal SW tip | 50°52.886'N | 001°23.551'W |
| 19 8 | Test approach, 150m SW of QEII terminal SW tip | 50°52.933'N | 001°23.806'W |
| 19 9 | Ocean Village entrance, ½ca 150°T from N pierhead SE tip | 50°53.689'N | 001°23.250'W |
| 19 10 | Town Quay approach, 1ca 150°T from pierhead FG lights | 50°53.464'N | 001°24.257'W |

**Refer to Charts**
Admiralty charts 2035, 2036, 2041
Imray C15, 2200.1, 2200.7, 2200.10

## COASTAL DANGERS

### Bramble Bank

The Bramble Bank is a broad area of shoals, part of which dry, between the south end of Southampton Water and the north corner of the Solent. The Bramble is well marked and straightforward to circumvent, either by the Thorn Channel from the southwest or the North Channel from the southeast. The main significance of the Bramble for boats is that it concentrates shipping bound in or out of Southampton Water into a narrow fairway – the Thorn Channel – which forces ships to make tight turns off Calshot Spit and off the West Bramble buoy.

Yachts and motorboats should therefore navigate the Thorn Channel with great circumspection, following any directions given by the harbour control launches and staying, as far as possible, just outside the marked channel on the 'wrong' side of the buoys.

### Fast ferries

Between the West Bramble buoy and Southampton, you are liable to meet fast hydrofoils and catamaran ferries, which are normally very careful to pick their way through the traffic but which can be thrown by sudden changes of course. When a fast hydrofoil or catamaran is approaching, try to maintain a more or less constant course and speed until they have passed.

### Ashlett Creek flats

On the west side of Southampton Water, between Calshot Castle and Esso oil terminal off Fawley, the estuary is very shallow within ½ mile of the shore. Care must be taken in this area if you are tacking up or downstream and tending to hold onto your course at the end of each tack.

### Hamble Spit

The approaches to the Hamble River are shallow on both sides, with the Hamble Spit on the west side of the fairway and the banks off Warsash on the east side. Yachts coming up Southampton Water from Calshot will normally pick up the Hamble Point S-cardinal buoy and then follow the channel past the red and green posts; however, boats arriving from further up Southampton Water must resist the temptation to cut the corner inside the Hamble Point buoy.

### Deans Lake

The upper west side of Southampton Water is also shallow, between the Esso oil terminal and the approaches to Hythe Marina Village. Yachts tacking across the estuary must be wary about holding on beyond the channel buoys and beacons on the west side.

### Weston Shelf

In the upper reaches of Southampton Water, as you approach the junction between the River Test and the River Itchen, beware of the shallows on the northeast side of the river above Netley. Cutting the corner towards Ocean Village inside the Moorhead and Weston Shelf green buoys can result in a considerable delay.

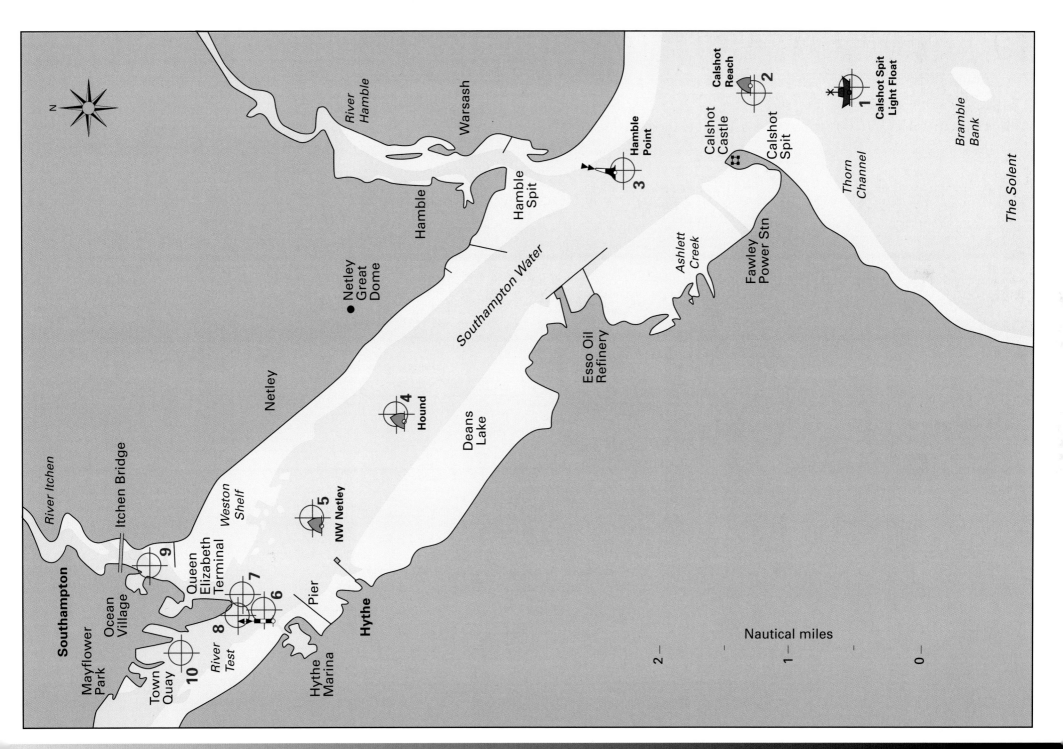

N

*River Hamble*

Warsash

*River Hamble*

Hamble

Hamble Spit

**2** Calshot Reach

Calshot Castle

**1** Calshot Spit Light Float

*Bramble Bank*

*Thorn Channel*

Calshot Spit

*The Solent*

**3** Hamble Point

Ashlett Creek

Fawley Power Stn

Southampton Water

Esso Oil Refinery

● Netley Great Dome

Deans Lake

Netley

**4** Hound

*River Itchen*

Itchen Bridge

*Weston Shelf*

**5** NW Netley

**9**

Southampton

Mayflower Park

Ocean Village

Queen Elizabeth Terminal

**7**

**6**

Pier

Hythe

Town Quay

**8**

*River Test*

**10**

Hythe Marina

Nautical miles

2 — — 1 — 0

| ⊕ | Waypoint name and position | Latitude | Longitude |
|---|---|---|---|
| 20 **1** | Calshot Reach, 50m SW of Reach green buoy | 50°49.034'N | 001°17.687'W |
| 20 **2** | Calshot Spit, 50m SE of light-float | 50°48.335'N | 001°17.626'W |
| 20 **3** | Calshot East, 50m W of Calshot N-card bell buoy | 50°48.420'N | 001°17.090'W |
| 20 **4** | North Channel NW, 1ca SW of summer yellow buoy | 50°48.560'N | 001°16.770'W |
| 20 **5** | North Channel SE, ½ca NE of East Bramble E-card buoy | 50°47.274'N | 001°13.581'W |
| 20 **6** | West Bramble, actual position of W-card buoy | 50°47.200'N | 001°18.650'W |
| 20 **7** | Egypt Point, 1½ca 340°T from Gurnard N-card buoy | 50°46.352'N | 001°18.926'W |
| 20 **8** | Cowes approach, 3ca 255°T from Prince Consort N-card buoy | 50°46.339'N | 001°18.007'W |
| 20 **9** | Old Castle Point, ½M E of Prince Consort N-card buoy | 50°46.418'N | 001°16.773'W |
| 20 **10** | SE Ryde Middle, 1ca S of S-card buoy | 50°45.839'N | 001°12.093'W |
| 20 **11** | Wootton Creek entrance, 100m N of Wootton beacon | 50°44.587'N | 001°12.129'W |
| 20 **12** | Ryde Sand clearing, ½M 160°T from Sturbridge N-card buoy | 50°44.875'N | 001°07.974'W |
| 20 **13** | Sturbridge clearing, 1ca N of N-card buoy | 50°45.440'N | 001°08.240'W |
| 20 **14** | No Man's Land, ¼M N of No Man's Land Fort north edge | 50°44.660'N | 001°05.690'W |
| 20 **15** | Horse Sand, 4ca SW of Horse Sand Fort SW edge | 50°44.706'N | 001°04.768'W |
| 20 **16** | Portsmouth approach, 100m SE of Outer Spit S-card buoy | 50°45.549'N | 001°05.437'W |
| 20 **17** | Southsea Castle, ¼M SW of castle lighthouse | 50°46.550'N | 001°05.655'W |

**Refer to Charts**
Admiralty charts 1905, 2036, 2037
Imray C15, 2200.1, 2200.3, 2200.5, 2200.6

southwest towards the Isle of Wight. Strangers should always keep north of No Man's Land, although to the east of the fort you can start nudging back inshore towards St Helen's Fort and the entrance to Bembridge Harbour.

## Horse Sand Fort

This northeastern partner of the two Spithead forts guards the east side of the approach channel for Portsmouth Harbour. Horse Sand Fort stands about 1¾ miles off the Southsea shore and marks the south end of a dangerous submerged barrier across the shallowest part of Horse and Dean Sand. This barrier, a relic of the Second World War, is marked at intervals by yellow posts with x topmarks. There is a narrow navigable gap through the centre of this barrier, marked by a concrete dolphin and a spar beacon. This passage should only be taken above half-tide, and then only in quiet conditions unless you know the area well.

## COASTAL DANGERS

### Bramble Bank

The Bramble Bank is a wide triangular area of shoals, some of which dry, in the three-way junction between the south end of Southampton Water and the north corner of the Solent. The Bramble is well marked and straightforward to circumvent, either by the Thorn Channel from the southwest or the North Channel from the southeast.

However, the main significance of the Bramble for boats is that it concentrates shipping bound in or out of Southampton Water into a narrow fairway – the Thorn Channel – which forces ships to make tight turns off Calshot Spit and off the West Bramble buoy. Yachts should therefore navigate the Thorn Channel with great care, following any directions given by the

harbour control launches and staying, as far as possible, just outside the marked channel on the 'wrong' side of the buoys.

### Mother Bank

Between Osborne Bay and Ryde off the northeast side of the Isle of Wight, the south side of the Solent is very shallow with one or two patches that dry at chart datum. This broad shoal area is marked on its north side by several red can buoys and boats straying inside these buoys near low water are prone to be brought up short.

### Ryde Sands

Opposite and to the east of Ryde Pier, an extensive shoal area of drying sand and mud stretches north of the Isle of Wight coast for over one mile. These flats are marked on their north side by red post beacons more or less opposite the Sturbridge Shoal N-cardinal buoy.

### No Man's Land

To the east of Ryde Sands, No Man's Land Fort stands on the edge of the continuing shoal area opposite Nettlestone Point, with an underwater obstruction stretching back

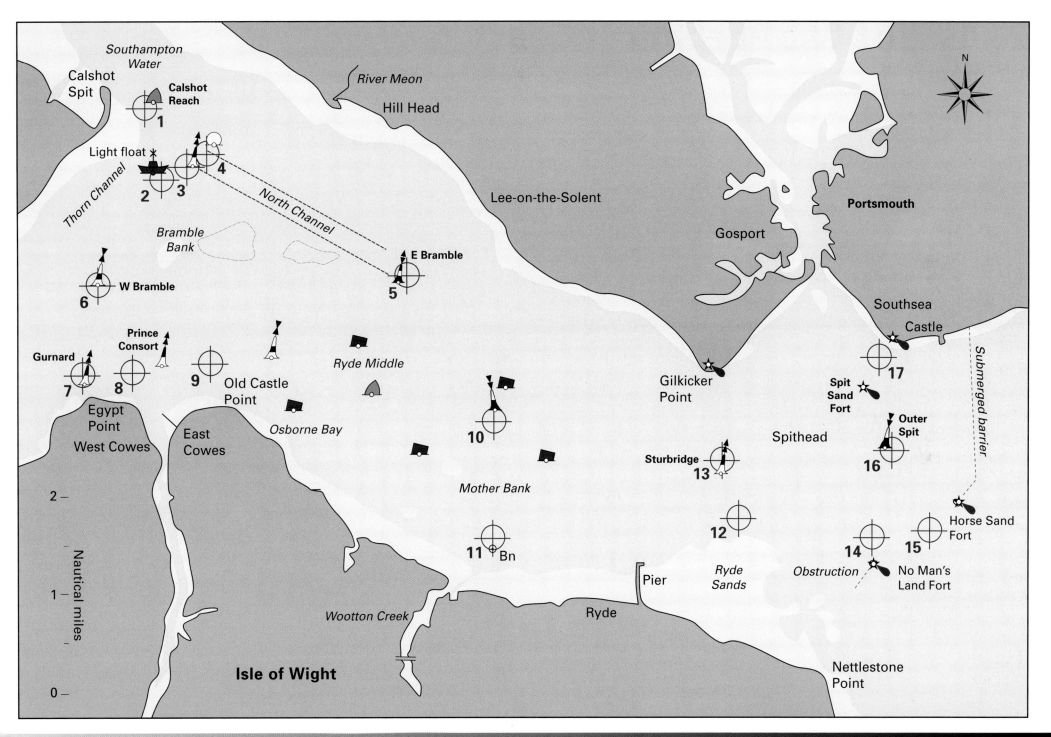

Southampton Water

Calshot Spit

Calshot Reach

**1**

River Meon

Hill Head

Light float

**2**   **3**   **4**

Thorn Channel

North Channel

Lee-on-the-Solent

Portsmouth

Bramble Bank

E Bramble

**5**

Gosport

W Bramble

**6**

Southsea Castle

**17**

Prince Consort

Gurnard

**7**   **8**   **9**

Old Castle Point

Ryde Middle

Gilkicker Point

Spit Sand Fort

Spithead

Outer Spit

**16**

Egypt Point

West Cowes

East Cowes

Osborne Bay

**10**

Mother Bank

Sturbridge

**13**

Submerged barrier

**2 —**

Nautical miles

**11**   Bn

**12**

Ryde Sands

**14**   **15**

Horse Sand Fort

Obstruction

No Man's Land Fort

**1 —**

Pier

**Isle of Wight**

Wootton Creek

Ryde

Nettlestone Point

**0 —**

| ⊕ | Waypoint name and position | Latitude | Longitude |
|---|---|---|---|
| 21 1 | Warden clearing, 100m NW of Warden green bell buoy | 50°41.520'N | 001°33.600'W |
| 21 2 | Mid Shingles, 1½ca SE of red buoy | 50°41.109'N | 001°34.501'W |
| 21 3 | Needles outer, ½ca W of Bridge W-card buoy | 50°39.630'N | 001°36.976'W |
| 21 4 | Needles fairway buoy, actual position | 50°38.240'N | 001°38.980'W |
| 21 5 | Freshwater Bay, 4ca 160°T from conspicuous hotel | 50°39.815'N | 001°30.514'W |
| 21 6 | St Catherine's inner, 1½M due S of lighthouse | 50°33.050'N | 001°17.890'W |
| 21 7 | St Catherine's outer, 5M due S of lighthouse | 50°29.550'N | 001°17.890'W |
| 21 8 | Dunnose inner, 2½M SE of main radar scanner | 50°34.513'N | 001°08.810'W |
| 21 9 | Dunnose outer, 5M SE of main radar scanner | 50°32.775'N | 001°06.032'W |
| 21 10 | Nab Tower west clearing, 2M W of Nab Tower | 50°40.076'N | 001°00.290'W |
| 21 11 | West Princessa, ½ca W of Princessa W-card buoy | 50°40.155'N | 001°03.744'W |
| 21 12 | Bembridge Ledge, 1ca E of E-card buoy | 50°41.151'N | 001°02.658'W |
| 21 13 | Nab Tower east clearing, 1¾M E of Nab Tower | 50°40.076'N | 000°54.410'W |

### Refer to Charts
Admiralty charts 2037, 2045
Imray C3, 2200.1

### East Solent approach
Foreland Point, the extreme east tip of the Isle of Wight, has Bembridge Ledge extending ¾ mile due east, with a wide area of drying ledges up to three cables offshore on the southeast side. Keep outside the Bembridge Ledge E-cardinal buoy when rounding the Foreland since the Cole Rock, inside the buoy, dries 0.2m at chart datum.

## COASTAL DANGERS

### The Needles Channel
The Needles Channel is rough with wind over tide, especially in a southwesterly over the ebb, when the North Channel is quieter. In heavy weather, seas can break dangerously between the Needles and Hurst Point. Remember that the tide sets across the Shingles bank, so that the ebb through the Needles will be trying to set you west towards the Shingles.

The Bridge Ledge, which extends westward from the Needles lighthouse for almost one mile, has overfalls over it with wind over tide, and is dangerous in heavy onshore weather. In such conditions, you should stay in the Needles Channel entrance between the Bridge W-cardinal buoy and the SW Shingles red buoy.

### The North Channel
The North Channel into and out of the Solent can be a quieter and safer passage than the Needles Channel in heavy onshore weather. However, approaching the North Channel under these conditions requires care, partly to stay in the deep water between Christchurch Ledge and the Dolphin, and then to pick up the North Head green buoy without straying too close either to the Shingles bank on the south side or the lee shore on the north side.

### St Catherine's Point
Overfalls extend up to 1½ miles southwest and southeast of St Catherine's Point, which are steep with a strong wind over tide and dangerous in gales. In heavy weather, the whole area up to at least five miles seaward of St Catherine's Point and Dunnose Head can be dangerously rough, partly because of the uneven seabed south of St Catherine's and partly because of the strong tides around the south of the Isle of Wight.

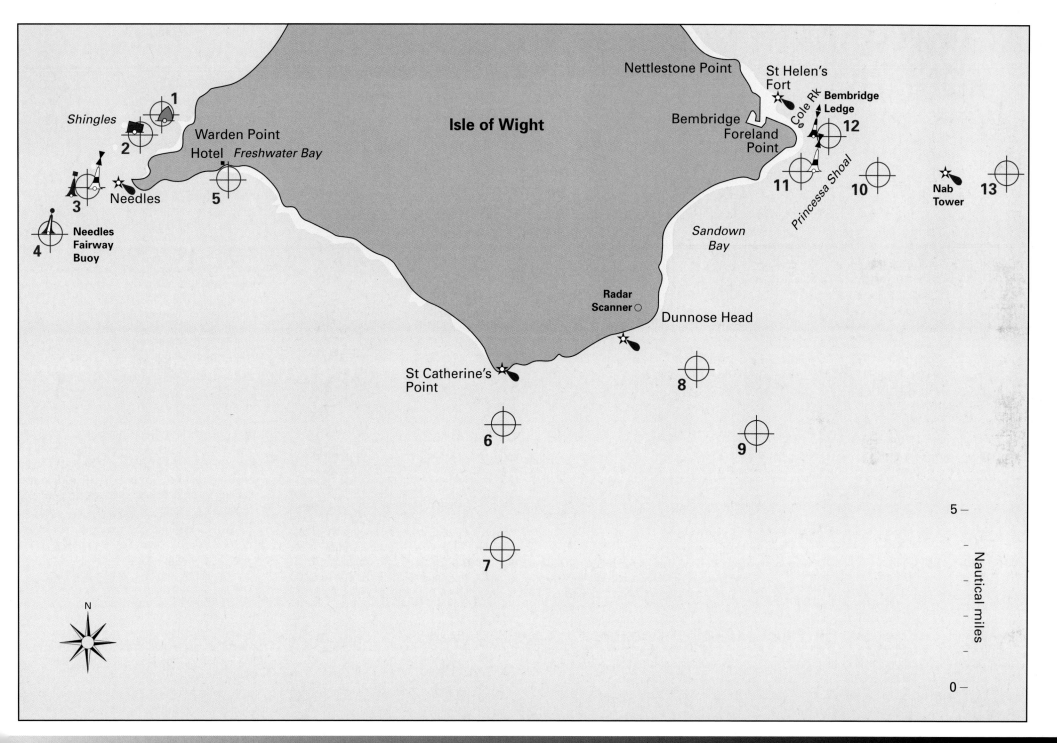

Shingles

Isle of Wight

Nettlestone Point

St Helen's Fort

Cole Rk

Bembridge Ledge

12

1

2

Warden Point Hotel

Freshwater Bay

Bembridge Foreland Point

11

Princessa Shoal

10

Nab Tower

13

3

Needles

5

4

Needles Fairway Buoy

Sandown Bay

Radar Scanner ○

Dunnose Head

8

St Catherine's Point

6

9

7

N

5 —

Nautical miles

0 —

| ⊕ | | Waypoint name and position | Latitude | Longitude |
|---|---|---|---|---|
| 22 | 1 | Ryde Sand clearing, ½M 160°T from Sturbridge N-card buoy | 50°44.875'N | 001°07.974'W |
| 22 | 2 | Sturbridge clearing, 1ca N of N-card buoy | 50°45.440'N | 001°08.240'W |
| 22 | 3 | No Man's Land, ¼M N of No Man's Land Fort north edge | 50°44.660'N | 001°05.690'W |
| 22 | 4 | Horse Sand, 4ca SW of Horse Sand Fort SW edge | 50°44.706'N | 001°04.768'W |
| 22 | 5 | Portsmouth approach, 100m SE of Outer Spit S-card buoy | 50°45.549'N | 001°05.437'W |
| 22 | 6 | Southsea Castle, ¼M SW of castle lighthouse | 50°46.550'N | 001°05.655'W |
| 22 | 7 | Bembridge approach, 3ca 025°T from St Helen's Fort | 50°42.572'N | 001°04.847'W |
| 22 | 8 | Bembridge channel, 2ca NW of St Helen's Fort | 50°42.447'N | 001°05.263'W |
| 22 | 9 | St Helen's Road, 3ca 340°T from lifeboat house | 50°41.692'N | 001°04.396'W |
| 22 | 10 | Bembridge Ledge, 1ca E of E-card buoy | 50°41.151'N | 001°02.658'W |
| 22 | 11 | West Princessa, ½ca W of W-card buoy | 50°40.155'N | 001°03.744'W |
| 22 | 12 | Nab Tower west clearing, 2M W of Nab Tower | 50°40.076'N | 001°00.290'W |
| 22 | 13 | Nab Tower east clearing, 1¾M E of Nab Tower | 50°40.076'N | 000°54.410'W |
| 22 | 14 | Langstone approach, 1M 190°T from fairway buoy | 50°45.341'N | 001°01.630'W |
| 22 | 15 | Langstone fairway, actual position of fairway buoy | 50°46.320'N | 001°01.360'W |
| 22 | 16 | Langstone narrows, 100m E of QR entrance light | 50°47.235'N | 001°01.604'W |
| 22 | 17 | Chichester approach, 4ca 195°T from West Pole beacon | 50°45.326'N | 000°56.651'W |
| 22 | 18 | Chichester entrance, 50m E of bar beacon | 50°45.922'N | 000°56.424'W |
| 22 | 19 | Medmery Bank clearing, 3M 245°T from Selsey CG Tower | 50°42.580'N | 000°52.490'W |
| 22 | 20 | Looe Channel west, 1ca NW of Boulder green buoy | 50°41.640'N | 000°49.230'W |
| 22 | 21 | Looe Channel east, 1M SE of The Mixon red beacon | 50°41.676'N | 000°45.217'W |
| 22 | 22 | Selsey anchorage, 1ca due S of lifeboat house | 50°43.480'N | 000°46.740'W |
| 22 | 23 | Owers clearing, 1ca due S of Owers S-card buoy | 50°38.497'N | 000°41.088'W |
| 22 | 24 | Outer Owers, 1½M due S of Owers S-card buoy | 50°37.096'N | 000°41.088'W |

**Refer to Charts**
Admiralty charts 2036, 2037, 2045, 3418
Imray C3, C9, 2200.1, 2200.3, 2200.4, 2200.5

## Selsey Bill

For anyone approaching the Solent from the east along the Sussex coast, the low promontory of Selsey Bill, with its dangerous off-lying banks and shoals, is always an uneasy obstacle before the last clear stretch towards the Spithead forts. If you are making a cross-Channel landfall near the Nab Tower in fresh weather, Selsey is lurking not far to starboard, a nasty lee shore in a southwesterly and barely seven miles from the Nab.

The main danger area stretches south from Selsey Bill for about three miles to the Boulder, Pullar and Middle Ground banks, and southeast for six miles to the southern tip of the Outer Owers. The inshore areas of drying rock and sand lie up to 1½ miles from the Bill, from the Mixon off to the SSE, past the Dries and the Grounds to the southwest and then the Streets to the west.

The narrow Looe channel runs between these inner dangers and the outer banks, a useful short-cut round Selsey in daylight and reasonable weather. But tide is a critical factor around the Bill. The streams run strongly through the narrow west end of the Looe and play funny tricks near the banks. Although the Looe channel is easier these days with GPS, you still have to be careful in a summer haze when the buoys can be difficult to pick up and the coast invisible as you go round.

## COASTAL DANGERS

### East Solent approach

Foreland Point, the extreme east tip of the Isle of Wight, has Bembridge Ledge extending ¾ mile due east, with a wide area of drying ledges up to three cables offshore on the southeast side. Keep outside the Bembridge Ledge E-cardinal buoy when rounding the Foreland since the Cole Rock, inside the buoy, dries 0.2m at chart datum.

### Horse Sand Fort

This northeastern partner of the two Spithead forts guards the east side of the approach channel for Portsmouth Harbour. Horse Sand Fort stands about 1¾ miles off the Southsea shore and marks the south end of a dangerous submerged barrier across the shallowest part of Horse and Dean Sand. This barrier, a relic of the Second World War, is marked at intervals by yellow posts with x topmarks.

There is a narrow navigable gap through the centre of the barrier, marked by a concrete dolphin and a spar beacon. This passage should only be taken above half-tide, and then only in quiet conditions unless you know the area well.

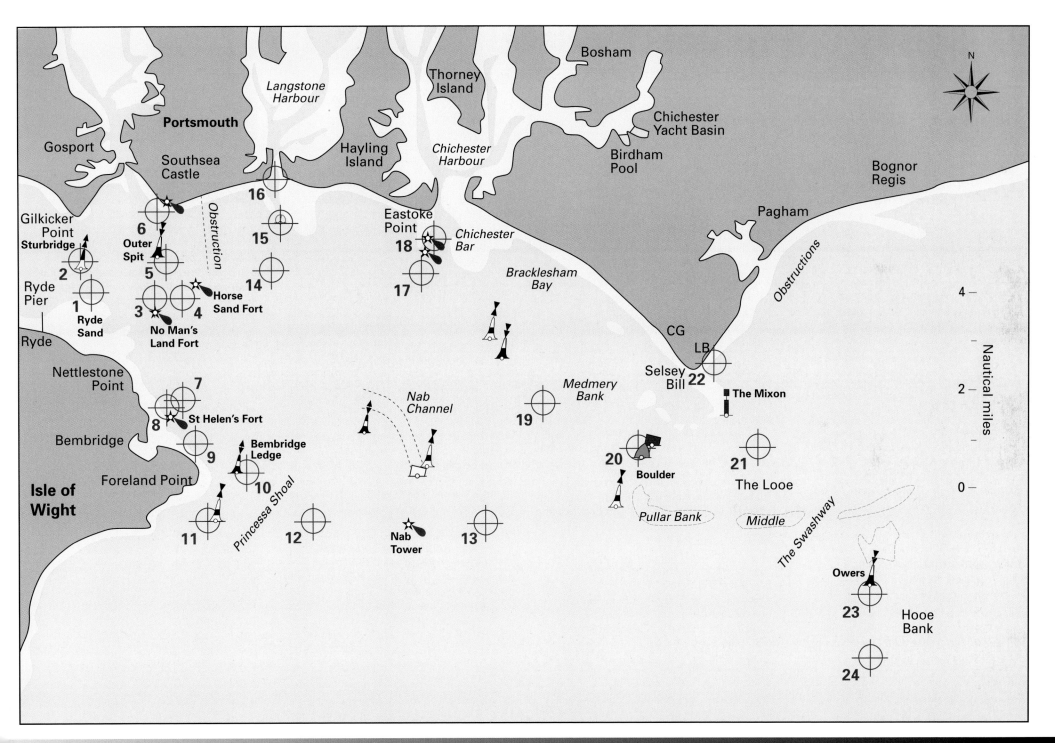

**Selsey Bill to Beachy Head**

| ⊕ | Waypoint name and position | Latitude | Longitude |
|---|---|---|---|
| 23 1 | Medmery Bank clearing, 3M 245°T from Selsey CG Tower | 50°42.580'N | 000°52.490'W |
| 23 2 | Looe Channel west, 1ca NW of Boulder green buoy | 50°41.640'N | 000°49.230'W |
| 23 3 | Looe Channel east 1M SE of The Mixon red beacon | 50°41.676'N | 000°45.217'W |
| 23 4 | Selsey anchorage, 1ca due S of lifeboat house | 50°43.480'N | 000°46.740'W |
| 23 5 | Owers clearing, 1ca due S of Owers S-card buoy | 50°38.497'N | 000°41.088'W |
| 23 6 | Outer Owers, 1½M due S of Owers S-card buoy | 50°37.096'N | 000°41.088'W |
| 23 7 | East Borough Head, ¾M due N of E-card buoy | 50°42.262'N | 000°39.109'W |
| 23 8 | Littlehampton approach, ½M S of outer green beacon | 50°47.370'N | 000°32.380'W |
| 23 9 | Littlehampton entrance, 50m E of tide gauge | 50°47.881'N | 000°32.425'W |
| 23 10 | Shoreham approach, ½M S of east breakwater head | 50°49.044'N | 000°14.800'W |
| 23 11 | Shoreham entrance, 50m E of west breakwater head | 50°49.487'N | 000°14.843'W |
| 23 12 | Brighton entrance, close SE of west breakwater head | 50°48.473'N | 000°06.345'W |
| 23 13 | Newhaven approach, 1M 170°T from west breakwater head | 50°45.562'N | 000°03.778'E |
| 23 14 | Newhaven entrance, 1ca SE of outer breakwater head | 50°46.488'N | 000°03.612'E |
| 23 15 | Beachy Head inner, 1½M due S of lighthouse | 50°42.530'N | 000°14.490'E |
| 23 16 | Beachy Head outer, 5M due S of lighthouse | 50°39.030'N | 000°14.490'E |

### Refer to Charts
Admiralty charts 536, 1652, 2045, 2154
Imray C9

### Beachy Head overfalls
The dramatic chalk face of Beachy Head, over 160m high with the famous red-and-white striped lighthouse at its foot, has a tidal race extending a good one mile offshore. Parts of the coast close inshore near Beachy Head are shallow. Holywell Bank, which extends almost a mile along the shore to the east of Beachy Head, has a depth of 1.3m at chart datum. Closer to the lighthouse, Head Ledge, which almost dries in patches, extends a good ½ mile south of the cliffs.

## COASTAL DANGERS

### Selsey Bill
For anyone approaching the Solent from the east along the Sussex coast, the low promontory of Selsey Bill, with its dangerous off-lying banks and shoals, is always an uneasy obstacle before the clear stretch towards the Spithead forts. If you are making a cross-Channel landfall near the Nab Tower in fresh weather, Selsey is lurking not far to starboard, a nasty lee shore in a southwesterly and barely seven miles from the Nab.

The main danger area stretches south from Selsey Bill for about three miles to the Boulder, Pullar and Middle Ground banks, and southeast for six miles to the southern tip of the Outer Owers. The inshore areas of drying rock and sand lie up to 1½ miles from the Bill, from the Mixon off to the SSE, past the Dries and the Grounds to the southwest and then the Streets to the west.

The narrow Looe channel runs between these inner dangers and the outer banks, a useful short-cut round Selsey in daylight and reasonable weather. But tide is a critical factor around the Bill. The streams run strongly through the narrow west end of the Looe and play funny tricks near the banks. Although the Looe channel is easier these days with GPS, you still have to be careful in a summer haze when the buoys can be difficult to pick up and the coast invisible as you go round.

### Bognor Spit
For any boats coasting close inshore between Littlehampton and Selsey Bill, the long drying ledge known as Bognor Spit should be given a wide berth. Bognor Spit lies just over five miles northeast of the Mixon beacon off Selsey Bill, and it extends about one mile offshore.

### Pagham Harbour obstructions
A few miles southwest of Bognor Spit are the numerous obstructions of Pagham Harbour, most of which are old concrete caissons which came to grief during the period the Mulberry Harbours were waiting to be towed across to Normandy before D-Day.

VisitEastbourne.com

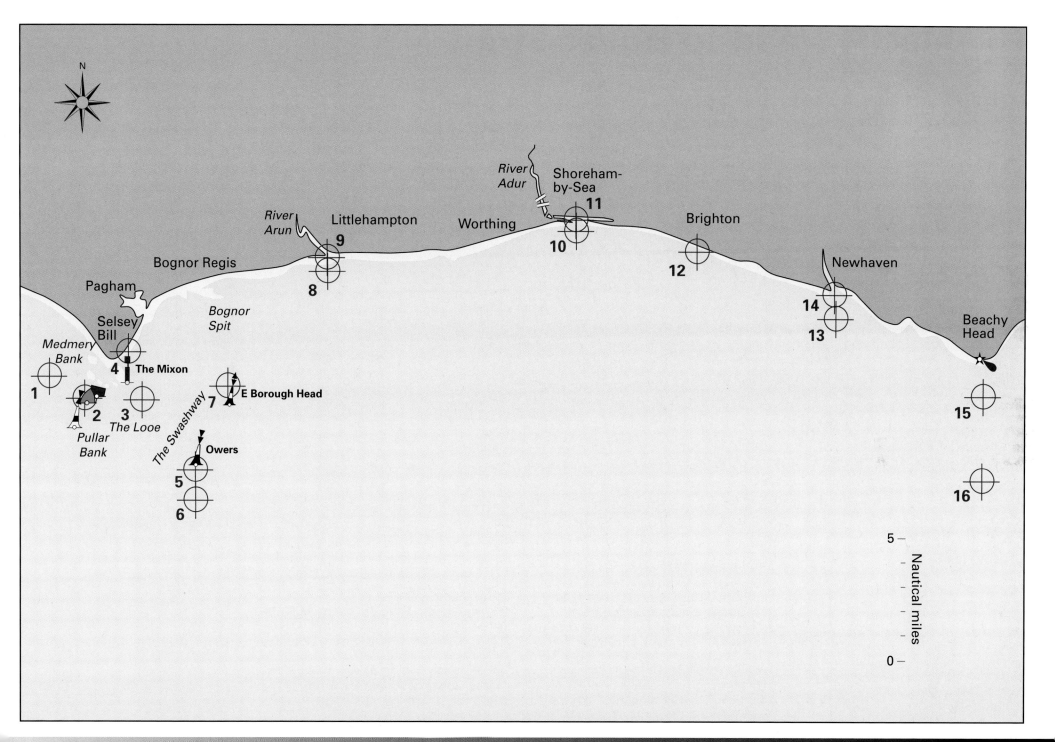

N

River
Adur
Shoreham-
by-Sea

River
Arun

Littlehampton

Worthing

Brighton

Newhaven

Bognor Regis

**11**

Beachy
Head

Pagham

**9**

**10**

**12**

Selsey
Bill

Bognor
Spit

**8**

**14**

Medmery
Bank

**13**

**4**  **The Mixon**

**1**

E Borough Head

**15**

**2**  **3**

**7**

Pullar
Bank

The Looe

Owers

**5**

**16**

**6**

5 —

Nautical miles

0 —

| ⊕ | Waypoint name and position | Latitude | Longitude |
|---|---|---|---|
| 24 1 | Beachy Head inner, 1½M due S of lighthouse | 50°42.530'N | 000°14.490'E |
| 24 2 | Beachy Head outer, 5M due S of lighthouse | 50°39.030'N | 000°14.490'E |
| 24 3 | Eastbourne entrance, near Sovereign Harbour fairway buoy | 50°47.400'N | 000°20.710'E |
| 24 4 | Royal Sovereign north, midway between tower and red buoy | 50°43.845'N | 000°25.951'E |
| 24 5 | Royal Sovereign south, 1M due S of tower | 50°42.470'N | 000°26.090'E |
| 24 6 | Royal Sovereign inner, 2.6M due N of tower | 50°46.070'N | 000°26.090'E |
| 24 7 | Rye fairway, actual position of fairway buoy | 50°54.040'N | 000°48.040'E |
| 24 8 | Dungeness inner, 1M SE of lighthouse | 50°54.115'N | 000°59.666'E |
| 24 9 | Dungeness outer, 2½M SE of lighthouse | 50°53.064'N | 001°01.354'E |
| 24 10 | Folkestone approach, 2ca SE from ferry pierhead | 51°04.422'N | 001°11.913'E |
| 24 11 | Dover west entrance, 1½ca 120°T from Admiralty pierhead | 51°06.613'N | 001°19.863'E |
| 24 12 | Dover east approach, 2ca 100°T from E Arm pierhead | 51°07.274'N | 001°20.900'E |
| 24 13 | Varne LANBY, actual position | 51°01.290'N | 001°23.900'E |
| 24 14 | Colbart SW S-card buoy, actual position | 50°48.870'N | 001°16.320'E |
| 24 15 | Colbart N-card buoy, actual position | 50°57.460'N | 001°23.290'E |
| 24 16 | Calais Approach W-card buoy, 2ca due W of buoy | 50°58.890'N | 001°44.754'E |
| 24 17 | Calais entrance, near Calais west pierhead | 50°58.344'N | 001°50.357'E |
| 24 18 | ZC2 yellow buoy off Cap Gris-Nez, actual position | 50°53.540'N | 001°31.890'E |
| 24 19 | Cap Gris-Nez clearing, 1.2M 300°T from lighthouse | 50°52.678'N | 001°33.339'E |
| 24 20 | Bassure de Baas inner, ½M E of N-card buoy | 50°48.534'N | 001°33.821'E |
| 24 21 | Bassure de Baas outer, 1M W of N-card buoy | 50°48.534'N | 001°31.487'E |
| 24 22 | Boulogne approach, ZC1 yellow buoy, actual position | 50°44.990'N | 001°27.210'E |
| 24 23 | Boulogne entrance, 2ca NW of south breakwater head | 50°44.599'N | 001°33.866'E |
| 24 24 | Le Touquet approach, 1M 340°T from Mérida W-card buoy | 50°33.790'N | 001°32.856'E |

### Refer to Charts
Admiralty charts 536, 1892, 2451
Imray C8

### Le Colbart
This narrow bank lies in mid-Channel, running SSW–NNE some nine miles opposite Cap Gris-Nez. The shallowest depths range from about 1.5m to 4.5m at LAT. In quiet weather most boats can pass over Le Colbart at most tides, but the bank soon becomes dangerous as the wind freshens and the sea builds up.

### Calais – Ridens de la Rade
This narrow bank runs WSW–ENE off Calais, forming a partial natural breakwater up to a mile offshore. The shallowest depths are about 0.8m at LAT ½ mile seaward of Calais breakwaters, with a wider, more shoal area further east over a mile off the old hoverport.

In reasonably quiet weather, with sufficient rise of tide, it is safe for boats to cut across Ridens de la Rade, especially when leaving Calais near high water. However, the bank is dangerous in fresh to strong onshore winds, or in fresh northeasterlies or southwesterlies when the tide is weather-going.

## COASTAL DANGERS

### Beachy Head
The dramatic chalk face of Beachy Head, over 160m high with the famous red-and-white striped lighthouse at its foot, has a tidal race extending a good mile offshore. Parts of the coast close inshore near Beachy Head are very shallow. Holywell Bank, which extends almost a mile along the shore to the east of Beachy Head, has a least depth of 1.3m at chart datum. Closer to the lighthouse, Head Ledge, which almost dries in patches, extends a good ½ mile south of the cliffs.

### Royal Sovereign
The Royal Sovereign shoals, which lie from between five and eight miles east of Beachy Head, represent a very uneven area of seabed and a consequently uneasy stretch of water. Boats on passage between Beachy Head and Dungeness will either pass clear outside the impressive Royal Sovereign light-tower and thus stay in relatively deep and undisturbed water, or they will keep well inshore to the north of the shoals, following the coast past Eastbourne Bay and Pevensey Bay. The Royal Sovereign red buoy lies just under one mile north of the tower on the south edge of the Sovereign shoals.

### Dungeness
The long, low promontory of Dungeness is perhaps the bleakest headland in the English Channel. It is little more than a low shingle bank which is steep-to on its seaward edge. Boats can pass very close, although the ebb tide runs at over two knots at springs, kicking up a nasty steep sea if the stream is weather-going.

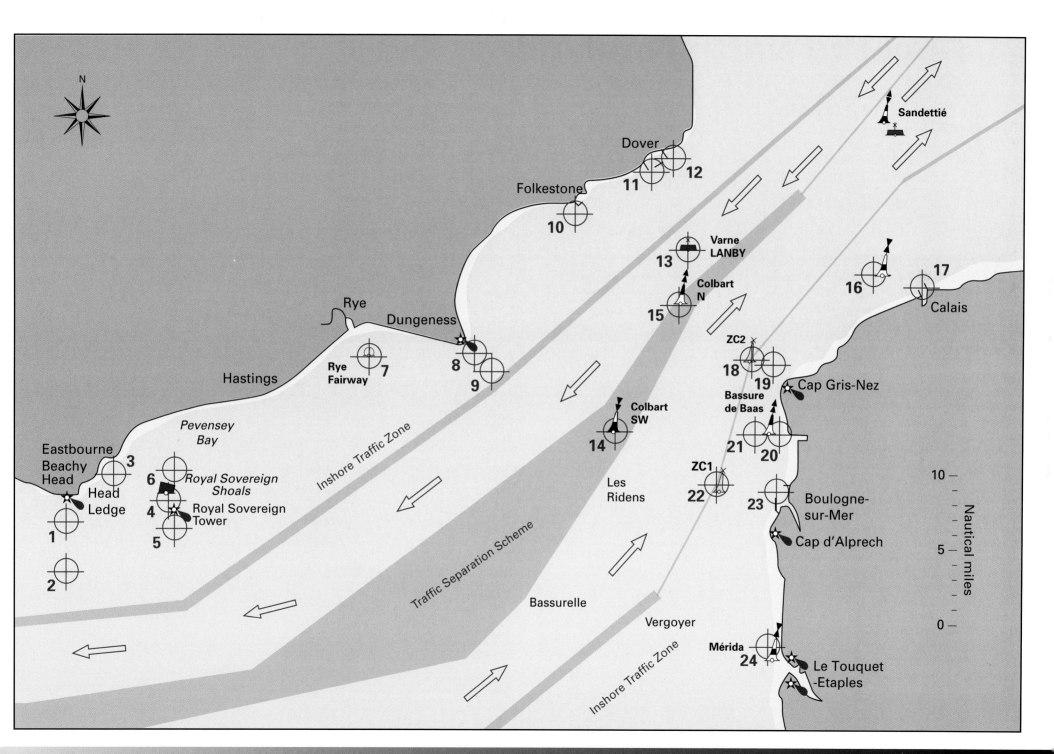

N

Sandettié

Dover
12
Folkestone 11
10

Varne
LANBY
13
Colbart
N
15

16 17
Calais

Rye
Dungeness
Rye
Fairway 7
8
9

ZC2
18
19 Cap Gris-Nez
Bassure
de Baas
21 20

Hastings

Colbart
SW
14

Pevensey
Bay

Eastbourne
Beachy
Head 3
6 Royal Sovereign
Shoals
4 Royal Sovereign
Tower
Head
Ledge

1

5

2

Inshore Traffic Zone

Les
Ridens

ZC1

22

23 Boulogne-
sur-Mer

Cap d'Alprech

Traffic Separation Scheme

Bassurelle

Vergoyer

Inshore Traffic Zone

Mérida
24 Le Touquet
-Etaples

10 —

Nautical miles

5 —

0 —

| ⊕ | | Waypoint name and position | Latitude | Longitude |
|---|---|---|---|---|
| 25 | 1 | Dover west entrance, 1½ca 120°T from Admiralty pierhead | 51°06.613'N | 001°19.863'E |
| 25 | 2 | Dover east approach, 2ca 100°T from E Arm pierhead | 51°07.274'N | 001°20.900'E |
| 25 | 3 | SW Goodwin SW clearing, ½M 250°T from S-card buoy | 51°08.332'N | 001°28.120'E |
| 25 | 4 | SW Goodwin SE clearing, ½M 110°T from S-card buoy | 51°08.332'N | 001°29.605'E |
| 25 | 5 | E Goodwin light-float W clearing, ¼M due W of light-float | 51°13.263'N | 001°35.984'E |
| 25 | 6 | East Goodwin E-card buoy, actual position | 51°15.670'N | 001°35.690'E |
| 25 | 7 | Gull Stream South, between S Brake and W Goodwin buoys | 51°15.698'N | 001°27.088'E |
| 25 | 8 | Gull Stream Mid, between Brake red buoy and NW Goodwin | 51°16.778'N | 001°28.364'E |
| 25 | 9 | Goodwin Knoll green conical buoy, actual position | 51°19.570'N | 001°32.200'E |
| 25 | 10 | Ramsgate Quern, 2ca due E of N-card buoy | 51°19.412'N | 001°26.428'E |
| 25 | 11 | Ramsgate entrance, midway between outer pierheads | 51°19.504'N | 001°25.440'E |
| 25 | 12 | North Foreland, 1M due E of lighthouse | 51°22.493'N | 001°28.274'E |
| 25 | 13 | Elbow N-card buoy, actual position | 51°23.230'N | 001°31.590'E |

### Refer to Charts
Admiralty charts 323, 1828
Imray C8

## COASTAL DANGERS

### Goodwin Sands

The Goodwins are probably the most notorious dangers in the English Channel, extensive drying sands lying up to seven miles offshore between Ramsgate and South Foreland. The Goodwins should be avoided in all circumstances, and are well marked on their east, north and south sides.

The well-used channel between the Goodwins and the Kent coast is partly sheltered by the banks in onshore winds. The wide, southern entrance to this channel lies between South Foreland and the SW Goodwin S-cardinal buoy. Working north, you need to pick up Goodwin Fork S-cardinal buoy and then the narrow gate between South Brake red buoy and West Goodwin green buoy. From this gate, you can make good north true for four miles, passing safely east of Brake Sand, until you join the Ramsgate entrance channel.

Gull Stream is a buoyed channel running SW–NE for just over five miles between the West Goodwin buoy and the north entrance between Gull E-cardinal buoy and Goodwin Knoll green buoy.

### Brake Sand

The Brake is a nasty area of banks stretching from ½ mile to nearly four miles south of Ramsgate entrance. The shallowest, drying area is about 2½ miles south of Ramsgate. Making between Quern N-cardinal buoy and the gateway formed by South Brake red buoy and West Goodwin green, boats should leave the Brake safely to the west. Alternatively, pass inside Brake Sand via the Ramsgate Channel, using B1 and B2 green conical buoys to clear the west edge of the shoals.

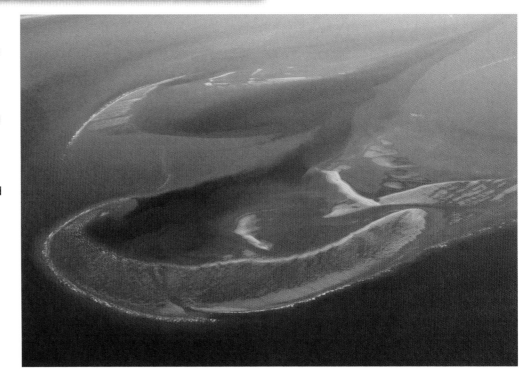

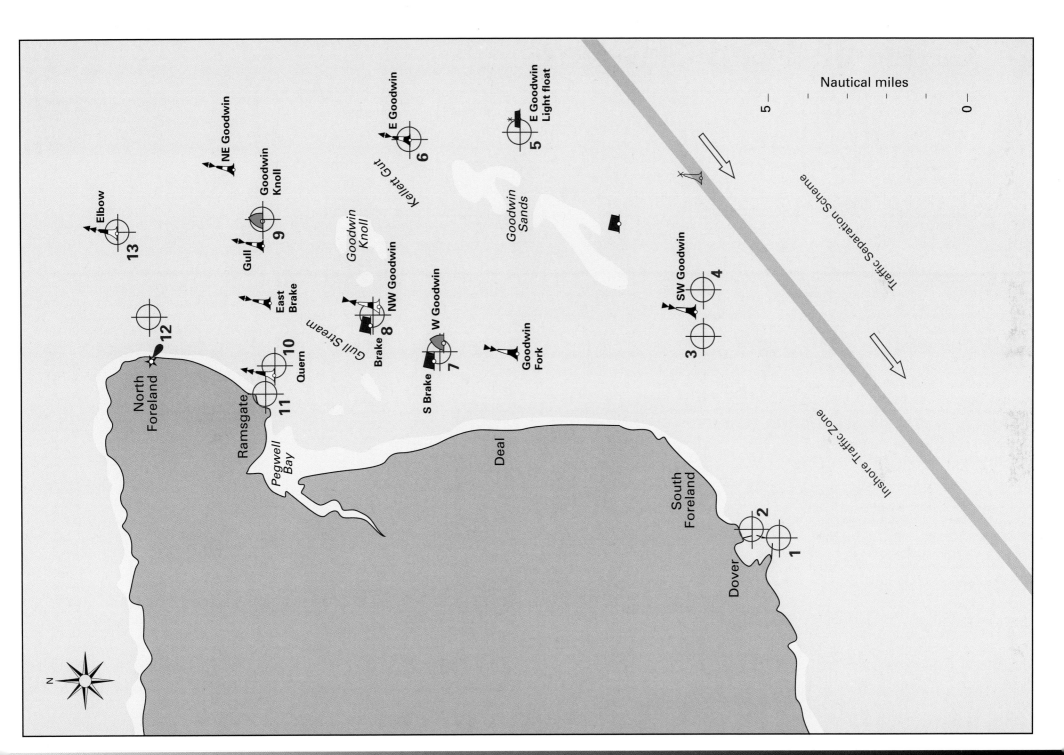

Nautical miles

5

0

Traffic Separation Scheme

Inshore Traffic Zone

NE Goodwin

Goodwin Knoll
9

Gull

East Brake

Elbow
13

Goodwin Knoll

NW Goodwin

Brake
8

Kellett Gut

E Goodwin
6

E Goodwin Light float
5

Goodwin Sands

SW Goodwin
4

3

W Goodwin
7

S Brake

Goodwin Fork

Gull Stream

North Foreland
12

Ramsgate

Pegwell Bay

Quern
10

11

Deal

South Foreland

Dover

2

1

N

| ⊕ | Waypoint name and position | Latitude | Longitude |
|---|---|---|---|
| 26 1 | Ruytingen SW green buoy, actual position | 51°05.000'N | 001°46.840'E |
| 26 2 | Calais entrance, near Calais west pierhead | 50°58.344'N | 001°50.357'E |
| 26 3 | Calais CA6 red buoy, actual position | 50°58.630'N | 001°49.920'E |
| 26 4 | Calais channel inner, 0.33M 265°T from west pierhead | 50°58.214'N | 001°49.885'E |
| 26 5 | Calais channel outer, 8ca 320°T from Sangatte lighthouse | 50°57.809'N | 001°45.711'E |
| 26 6 | Calais Approach W-card buoy, 2ca due W of buoy | 50°58.890'N | 001°44.754'E |
| 26 7 | Les Quénocs clearing, 2ca NW of Les Quénocs N-card buoy | 50°56.984'N | 001°40.899'E |
| 26 8 | La Barrière inner, 8ca SE of Abbeville W-card buoy | 50°55.525'N | 001°38.463'E |
| 26 9 | La Barrière outer, ¼M NW of Abbeville W-card buoy | 50°56.255'N | 001°37.309'E |
| 26 10 | ZC2 yellow buoy off Cap Gris-Nez, actual position | 50°53.540'N | 001°30.890'E |
| 26 11 | Cap Gris-Nez clearing, 1.2M 300°T from lighthouse | 50°52.678'N | 001°33.339'E |

**Refer to Charts**
Admiralty charts 1351, 1892
Imray C8

## COASTAL DANGERS

### Ridens de la Rade

This narrow bank runs WSW–ENE off Calais, forming a partial natural breakwater up to a mile offshore. The shallowest depths are about 0.8m at LAT ½ mile seaward of Calais breakwaters, with a wider, more shoal area further east over a mile off the old hoverport.

In reasonably quiet weather, with sufficient rise of tide, it is safe for boats to cut across Ridens de la Rade, especially when leaving Calais near high water. However, the bank is dangerous in fresh to strong onshore winds, or in fresh northeasterlies or southwesterlies when the tide is weather-going.

### Ferry traffic

More than natural coastal dangers, the greatest threat to yachts in the Dover Strait is posed by the almost continuous and rapid movement of cross-Channel ferries. The Strait is one of the busiest seaways in the world, with shipping movements monitored by the Channel Navigation Information Service run by Dover Coastguard and the French 'Crossma' station at Cap Gris-Nez.

### Cap Blanc-Nez

About six miles WSW of Calais entrance, various shoal patches lie up to 1½ miles seaward of Cap Blanc-Nez, a prominent rise in the cliffs some 130m high. Le Rouge Riden bank has a minimum depth of 1.3m, and a shallow wreck, with only 0.2m over it, lies about ¼ mile inside Les Quénocs N-cardinal buoy. Yachts should stay outside a line between this buoy and Cap Gris-Nez, to avoid La Barrière shoals and Banc à la Ligne.

### Banc à la Ligne

The shallow Banc à la Ligne extends within a couple of miles northeast of Cap Gris-Nez, with depths in parts only just above chart datum. Boats making between Cap Gris-Nez and Calais need to make for ⊕26–8 and stay outside Les Quénocs N-cardinal buoy.

### Shipping lanes

It is a legal requirement that you cross the Dover Strait shipping lanes at right-angles, regardless of what the tide happens to be doing. Low-powered vessels and sailing yachts should not make allowance for the tidal stream while crossing if, by doing so, they will not have a heading nearly at right angles to the traffic flow.

For most craft, therefore, the enforced strategy will be one of dashing across the 10-mile-wide shipping lanes as quickly as possible while keeping careful track of the effect of the tide. Because of the powerful streams in the Dover Strait – up to 3½–4 knots at top of springs – it is best to time your departure so that the overall effect of the tide works in your favour.

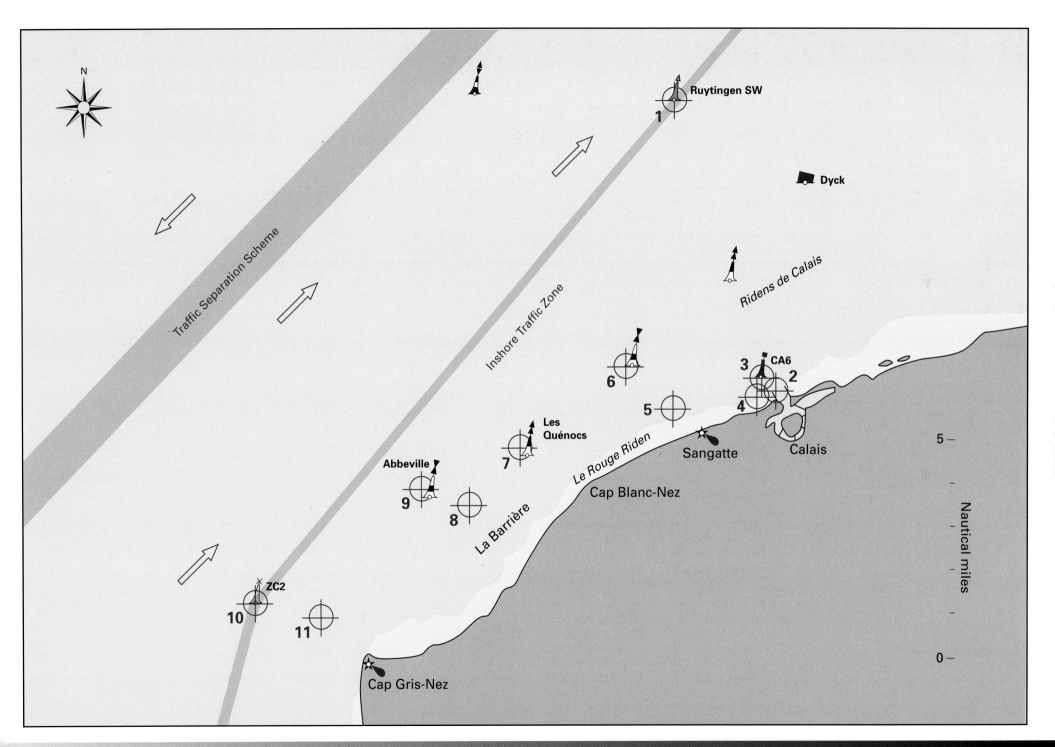

N

Traffic Separation Scheme

Inshore Traffic Zone

Ruytingen SW
1

Dyck

Ridens de Calais

6

3 CA6
2
4

5

Les
Quénocs
7

Sangatte

Calais

Le Rouge Riden

Cap Blanc-Nez

Abbeville
9

8

La Barrière

Nautical miles

5 —

ZC2
10

11

Cap Gris-Nez

0 —

# Boulogne to Dieppe

| ⊕ | Waypoint name and position | Latitude | Longitude |
|---|---|---|---|
| 27 1 | Boulogne approach, actual position of ZC1 yellow buoy | 50°44.990'N | 001°27.210'E |
| 27 2 | Boulogne entrance, 2ca NW of south breakwater head | 50°44.599'N | 001°33.866'E |
| 27 3 | Vergoyer North, actual position of N-card buoy | 50°39.670'N | 001°22.210'E |
| 27 4 | Le Touquet approach, ½M 300°T from Mérida W-card buoy | 50°33.103'N | 001°32.746'E |
| 27 5 | Bassurelle, actual position of red TSS buoy | 50°32.740'N | 000°57.690'E |
| 27 6 | Somme estuary, AT-SO fairway buoy, actual position | 50°14.000'N | 001°28.080'E |
| 27 7 | Somme entrance, midway between S1 and S2 channel buoys | 50°13.197'N | 001°30.360'E |
| 27 8 | Le Tréport approach, ½M NW of west pierhead | 50°04.236'N | 001°21.584'E |
| 27 9 | Le Tréport entrance, midway between pierheads | 50°03.880'N | 001°22.179'E |
| 27 10 | Dieppe approach, 1M 320°T of west breakwater head | 49°57.041'N | 001°03.981'E |
| 27 11 | Dieppe entrance, 1ca NNE of west breakwater head | 49°56.350'N | 001°05.000'E |
| 27 12 | Roches d'Ailly, ½M due N of N-card buoy | 49°56.922'N | 000°56.675'E |

**Refer to Charts**
Admiralty charts 438, 1354, 1355, 2148, 2451
Imray C31

## COASTAL DANGERS

### Le Colbart
This narrow bank lies in mid-Channel, running SSW–NNE some nine miles off the French coast opposite Cap Gris-Nez. The shallowest depths range from about 1.5m to 4.5m at LAT. In quiet weather, most boats can pass over Le Colbert at most tides, but the bank soon becomes dangerous as the wind freshens and the sea builds up.

### Bassure de Baas
This narrow bank, not quite three miles long, lies 2–3 miles off the French coast not far north of Boulogne. The north tip is marked by Bassure de Baas N-cardinal bell buoy. Although there is plenty of water for boats over most of the banks, a shallow wreck, with only 1m over it, lies about six cables south of the buoy.

### Le Touquet approaches
The shallow Baie d'Étaples and the estuary of La Cranche river mostly dry for up to a mile offshore and boats should only approach in quiet weather near high water.

The buoyed channel runs fairly close along the north shore of the estuary and is approached opposite Pointe de Lornel. About 1½ miles southwest of Pointe de Lornel, right in the middle of the estuary, Mérida W-cardinal buoy marks a shallow wreck which just dries at chart datum.

### Baie de Somme approaches
The approaches to the Somme estuary dry for a considerable distance offshore, in fact for just over three miles WNW of Pointe du Hourdel. Yachts should only approach in quiet weather and in the last two hours before high water. The buoyed channel, which is liable to change, winds into the estuary from a position just north of the outer 'AT-SO' N-cardinal buoy, then leading between S1 green and S2 red buoys.

Note that various submerged obstructions, some with barely 1m over them and some almost drying at chart datum, lie up to two miles offshore between four and eight miles south of the outer Somme N-cardinal buoy. These obstructions should be given a wide berth if you are coasting between the Somme and Le Tréport or Dieppe.

### Dieppe approaches
The approaches to Dieppe are largely straightforward, but are rough in heavy weather because of the uneven seabed and relatively shallow depths. The Berneval W-cardinal buoy, just over seven miles north of Dieppe entrance, marks a wreck with 2.5m over it.

### Pointe d'Ailly
This prominent headland, five miles west of Dieppe entrance, is fringed by the drying Roches d'Ailly for nearly ½ mile offshore. There are also several wrecks lurking off the headland, up to 1½ miles offshore. The shallowest wreck has only 1.2m over it and is marked on its seaward side by Roches d'Ailly N-cardinal whistle buoy; boats on passage round Pointe d'Ailly should keep outside this buoy.

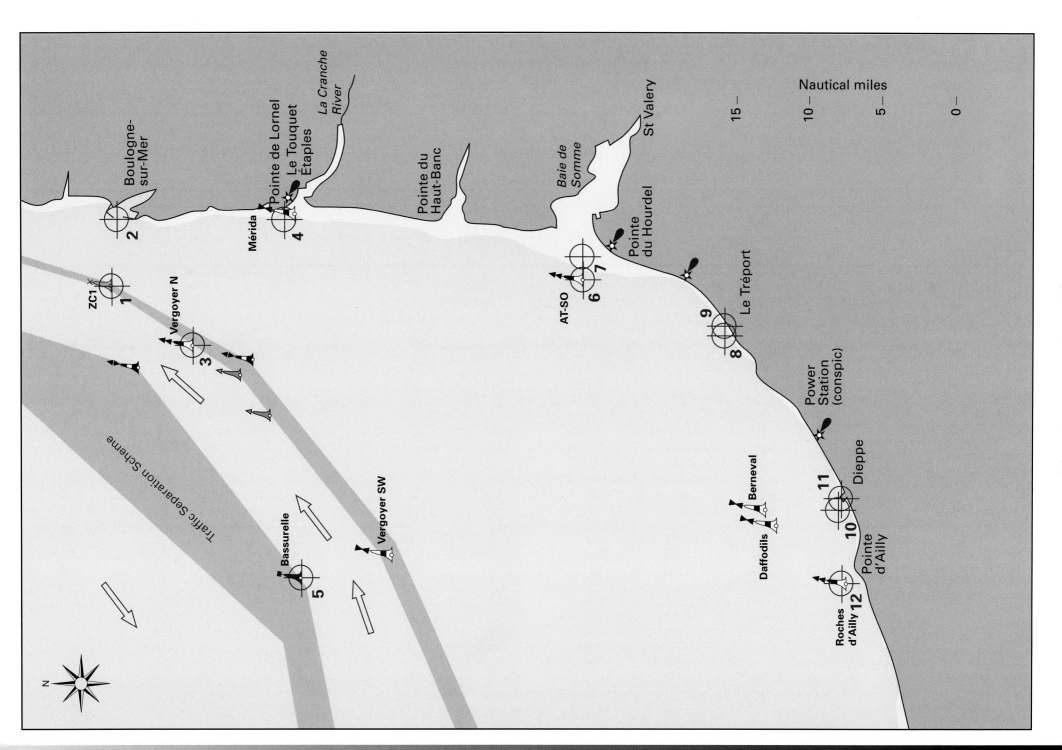

| ⊕ | Waypoint name and position | Latitude | Longitude |
|---|---|---|---|
| 28 1 | Dieppe approach, 1M 320°T of west breakwater head | 49°57.041'N | 001°03.981'E |
| 28 2 | Dieppe entrance, 1ca NNE of west breakwater head | 49°56.350'N | 001°05.000'E |
| 28 3 | Roches d'Ailly, ½M due N of N-card buoy | 49°56.922'N | 000°56.675'E |
| 28 4 | St Valery-en-Caux approach, 1M due N of west pierhead | 49°53.400'N | 000°42.540'E |
| 28 5 | St Valery-en-Caux entrance, 250m N of west pierhead | 49°52.535'N | 000°42.540'E |
| 28 6 | Paluel clearing, ¼M due N of Paluel N-card buoy | 49°52.470'N | 000°38.030'E |
| 28 7 | Pointe Fagnet clearing, ¾M NW of signal station | 49°46.576'N | 000°21.357'E |
| 28 8 | Fécamp approach, 1M due W of north pierhead | 49°46.899'N | 000°20.273'E |
| 28 9 | Fécamp entrance, 2ca due W of outer pierheads | 49°45.920'N | 000°21.500'E |
| 28 10 | Étretat clearing, 1½M NW of Aiguille d'Étretat | 49°43.490'N | 000°09.885'E |
| 28 11 | Cap d'Antifer outer, 2½M NW of lighthouse | 49°42.794'N | 000°07.221'E |
| 28 12 | Cap d'Antifer inner, 1M NW of lighthouse | 49°41.722'N | 000°08.836'E |

**Refer to Charts**
Admiralty charts 1354, 1355, 2146, 2148, 2451
Imray C31

## COASTAL DANGERS

### Dieppe approaches
The approaches to Dieppe are largely straightforward, but are rough in heavy weather because of the uneven seabed and relatively shallow depths. The Berneval W-cardinal buoy, just over seven miles north of Dieppe entrance, marks a wreck with 2.5m over it.

### Pointe d'Ailly
This prominent headland, five miles west of Dieppe entrance, is fringed by the drying Roches d'Ailly for nearly ½ mile offshore. There are also several wrecks lurking off the headland, up to 1½ miles offshore. The shallowest wreck has only 1.2m over it and is marked on its seaward side by Roches d'Ailly N-cardinal whistle buoy; boats on passage round Pointe d'Ailly should keep outside this buoy.

### Approaches to Fécamp
The approaches and entrance to Fécamp are mostly straightforward, but boats coming along the coast from the east should give Pointe Fagnet a wide berth as they come round to line up for Fécamp pierheads. This sheer chalk headland, just northeast of Fécamp entrance, is fringed with rocks for two cables offshore.

### Port du Havre-Antifer
The huge deepwater port of Havre-Antifer lies just over one mile south of Cap d'Antifer. The massive main breakwater extends nearly 1½ miles offshore and the deep buoyed approach channel leads in from the northwest from the A7 and A8 buoys 12 miles offshore.

Boats should avoid the Havre-Antifer approach channel if possible, or else cross it at right-angles as quickly as possible. Vessels coasting between Fécamp and Le Havre should give the Havre-Antifer breakwater a good one mile berth, both on account of shipping and to avoid the possibility of being set down on to the breakwater by the tide.

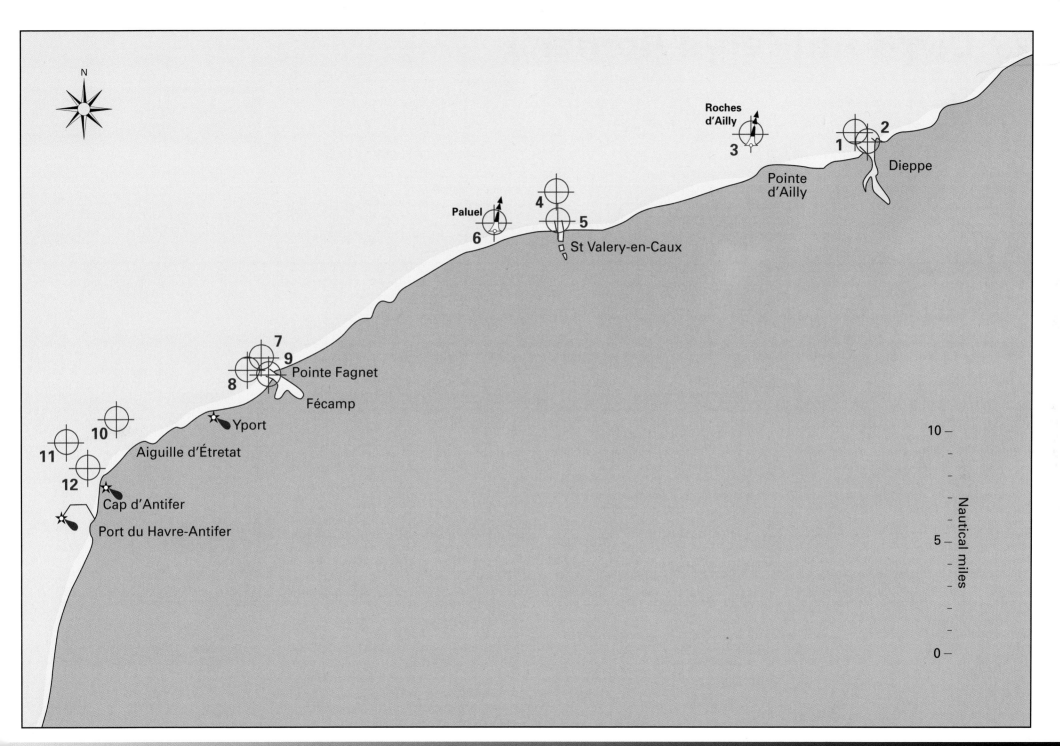

N

Roches
d'Ailly

3

1  2

Dieppe

Pointe
d'Ailly

Paluel

4

5

6

St Valery-en-Caux

7

9

Pointe Fagnet

8

Fécamp

Yport

Aiguille d'Étretat

10

11

12

Cap d'Antifer

Port du Havre-Antifer

10

Nautical miles

5

0

# 29 Cap d'Antifer to Honfleur

| ⊕ | | Waypoint name and position | Latitude | Longitude |
|---|---|---|---|---|
| 29 | 1 | Cap d'Antifer outer, 2½M NW of lighthouse | 49°42.794'N | 000°07.221'E |
| 29 | 2 | Cap d'Antifer inner, 1M NW of lighthouse | 49°41.722'N | 000°08.836'E |
| 29 | 3 | Le Havre outer approach, between LH3 and LH4 buoys | 49°30.970'N | 000°03.930'W |
| 29 | 4 | Le Havre approach channel, close E of LH7 green buoy | 49°30.250'N | 000°00.700'W |
| 29 | 5 | Le Havre inner approach, 2M 245°T of Cap de la Hève lighthouse | 49°29.906'N | 000°01.368'E |
| 29 | 6 | Le Havre entrance, on leading line between pierheads | 49°29.127'N | 000°05.388'E |
| 29 | 7 | Seine outer, close N of Chenal de Rouen No.2 red buoy | 49°27.415'N | 000°01.350'E |
| 29 | 8 | Seine entrance, close N of Chenal de Rouen No.4 red buoy | 49°26.985'N | 000°02.600'E |
| 29 | 9 | Amfard SW, close N of Amfard SW red buoy | 49°26.315'N | 000°04.820'E |
| 29 | 10 | Seine inner, close N of Chenal de Rouen No.10 red buoy | 49°26.115'N | 000°06.390'E |
| 29 | 11 | Honfleur approach, close N of Chenal de Rouen No.20 red buoy | 49°25.865'N | 000°13.710'E |
| 29 | 12 | Ratelets, 2ca due W of W-card buoy | 49°25.290'N | 000°01.580'E |
| 29 | 13 | Deauville outer, on leading line, 1M from outer green beacon | 49°23.207'N | 000°03.413'E |
| 29 | 14 | Deauville inner, 50m 060°T from outer green beacon | 49°22.340'N | 000°04.190'E |

## Refer to Charts
Admiralty charts 2146, 2613
Imray C31,C32

## Approaches to Deauville-Trouville
The approaches to Deauville-Trouville are shallow, especially on the north side where the Banc de Trouville extends well offshore beyond a direct line between Les Ratelets W-cardinal buoy and Deauville-Trouville entrance. Strangers should only approach Deauville-Trouville in quiet weather above half-flood. The approach is dangerous in strong onshore winds.

## COASTAL DANGERS

### Port du Havre-Antifer
The huge deepwater port of Havre-Antifer lies just over one mile south of Cap d'Antifer. The massive main breakwater extends nearly 1½ miles offshore and the deep buoyed approach channel leads in from the northwest from the A7 and A8 buoys 12 miles offshore.

Boats should avoid the Havre-Antifer approach channel if possible, or else cross it at right-angles as quickly as possible. Vessels coasting between Fécamp and Le Havre should give the Havre-Antifer breakwater a good one mile berth, both on account of shipping and to avoid the possibility of being set down on to the breakwater by the tide.

### Cap de la Hève
Just north of Le Havre approaches, the area off Cap de la Hève is littered with various wrecks and their corresponding buoys. Most of these present no danger to yachts, except perhaps the wreck with only 2.8m over it, just over four miles WNW of Cap de la Hève lighthouse, which is marked on its north side by a N-cardinal buoy. Boats approaching Le Havre from the north can therefore keep fairly close in round Cap de la Hève, a mile or so offshore, aiming to join the buoyed entrance channel at the LH11 and LH12 pair of buoys.

### Le Havre approaches
Le Havre is fairly straightforward to approach navigationally, the main danger being posed by shipping coming in and out especially at night. Boats following the main buoyed channel into Le Havre should stay just outside the line of the buoys as far as LH11 and LH12. Thereafter you need to keep inside the buoys to avoid Banc de l'Éclat on the north side and the wide shoals of the outer Seine estuary on the south side.

### Approaches to La Seine
Like all the estuaries of the great French rivers, the Seine is littered with sandbanks and can be uncomfortable to enter or leave in fresh onshore winds. The approaches are well buoyed though, because large ships go right up to Rouen, some 70 miles inland.

Tidal streams in the Seine estuary can be strong and boats need to time their entrance or exit carefully. If you are bound for Honfleur, about half-flood is a good time to enter the Chenal de Rouen at No.2 red buoy. This long buoyed channel into the Seine carries plenty of heavy shipping, so yachts should keep just north (i.e. the wrong side) of the trail of red buoys. If bound for Honfleur, turn south across the fairway just after No.20 red, allowing for cross-tide when aiming for the entrance. The streams can run strongly here with some nasty swirls and back-eddies. If you round up into the stream to take the sails down, do this well before reaching the narrow gap or you could be swept past.

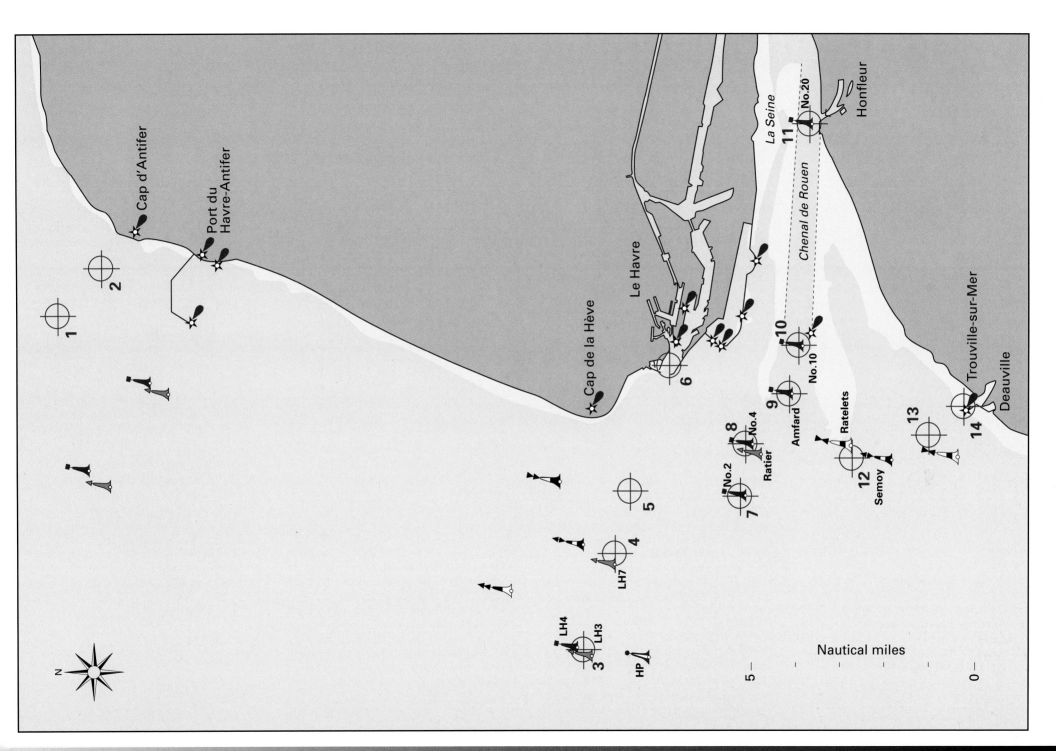

Cap d'Antifer

Port du
Havre-Antifer

Cap de la Hève

Le Havre

La Seine

Chenal de Rouen

No.20

Honfleur

No.10

11

10

9

Amfard

Ratelets

Trouville-sur-Mer

Deauville

No.2

No.4

8

Ratier

Semoy

12

13

14

7

5

4

LH7

LH4

LH3

3

HP

N

Nautical miles

5

0

# 30 La Seine to Ouistreham

**Refer to Charts**
Admiralty charts 1349, 2146, 2613
Imray C32

| ⊕ | Waypoint name and position | Latitude | Longitude |
|---|---|---|---|
| 30 1 | LHA, ½M due N of Le Havre light-float | 49°31.880'N | 000°09.860'W |
| 30 2 | Le Havre outer approach, between LH3 and LH4 buoys | 49°30.970'N | 000°03.930'W |
| 30 3 | Le Havre approach channel, close E of LH7 green buoy | 49°30.250'N | 000°00.700'W |
| 30 4 | Le Havre inner approach, 2M 245°T from Cap de la Hève LH | 49°29.906'N | 000°01.368'E |
| 30 5 | Le Havre entrance, on leading line between pierheads | 49°29.127'N | 000°05.388'E |
| 30 6 | RNA fairway buoy, actual position | 49°28.630'N | 000°05.510'W |
| 30 7 | Seine outer, close N of Chenal de Rouen No.2 red buoy | 49°27.415'N | 000°01.350'E |
| 30 8 | Seine entrance, close N of Chenal de Rouen No.4 red buoy | 49°26.985'N | 000°02.600'E |
| 30 9 | Amfard SW, close N of Amfard SW red buoy | 49°26.315'N | 000°04.820'E |
| 30 10 | Seine inner, close N of Chenal de Rouen No.10 red buoy | 49°26.115'N | 000°06.390'E |
| 30 11 | Honfleur approach, close N of Chenal de Rouen No.20 red buoy | 49°25.865'N | 000°13.710'E |
| 30 12 | Ratelets, 2ca due W of W-card buoy | 49°25.290'N | 000°01.580'E |
| 30 13 | Deauville outer, on leading line, 1M from outer green beacon | 49°23.207'N | 000°03.413'E |
| 30 14 | Deauville inner, 50m 060°T from outer green beacon | 49°22.340'N | 000°04.190'E |
| 30 15 | Dives approach, 1½M 338°T from leading lighthouse | 49°19.199'N | 000°06.088'W |
| 30 16 | Dives entrance, on leading line, close E of No.7 green buoy | 49°17.929'N | 000°05.280'W |
| 30 17 | Ouistreham outer, 2ca E of E-cardinal buoy on leading line | 49°20.420'N | 000°14.510'W |
| 30 18 | Ouistreham entrance, between outer light beacons | 49°18.020'N | 000°14.690'W |

## COASTAL DANGERS

### Cap de la Hève

Just north of Le Havre approaches, the area off Cap de la Hève is littered with various wrecks and their corresponding buoys. Most of these present no danger to yachts, except perhaps the wreck with only 2.8m over it, just over four miles WNW of Cap de la Hève lighthouse, which is marked on its north side by a N-cardinal buoy. Boats approaching Le Havre from the north can therefore keep fairly close in round Cap de la Hève, a mile or so offshore, aiming to join the buoyed entrance channel at the LH11 and LH12 pair of buoys.

### Le Havre approaches

Le Havre is fairly straightforward to approach navigationally, the main danger being posed by shipping coming in and out, especially at night. Boats following the main buoyed channel into Le Havre should stay just outside the line of the buoys as far as LH11 and LH12. Thereafter you need to keep inside the buoys to avoid Banc de l'Éclat on the north side and the wide shoals of the outer Seine estuary on the south side.

### Approaches to La Seine

Like all the estuaries of the great French rivers, the Seine is littered with sandbanks and can be uncomfortable to enter or leave in fresh onshore winds. The approaches are well buoyed though, because large ships go right up to Rouen, some 70 miles inland.

Tidal streams in the Seine estuary can be strong and boats need to time their entrance or exit carefully. If you are bound for Honfleur, about half-flood is a good time to enter the Chenal de Rouen at No.2 red buoy. This long buoyed channel into the Seine carries plenty of heavy shipping, so yachts should keep just north (i.e. the wrong side) of the trail of red buoys. If bound for Honfleur, turn south across the fairway just after No.20 red, allowing for cross-tide when aiming for the entrance. The streams can run strongly here with some nasty swirls and back-eddies. If you round up into the stream to take the sails down, do this well before reaching the narrow gap or you could be swept past.

## Approaches to Deauville-Trouville

The approaches to Deauville-Trouville are shallow, especially on the north side where the Banc de Trouville extends well offshore beyond a direct line between Les Ratelets W-cardinal buoy and Deauville-Trouville entrance. Strangers should only approach Deauville-Trouville in quiet weather above half-flood. The approach is dangerous in strong onshore winds.

## Approaches to Dives-sur-Mer

The approaches to Dives are shallow, with banks drying for a good ¾ mile offshore. Strangers should only approach in the last two hours before high water. The lock gate into Port Guillaume is normally open for about three hours each side of local high water.

## Approaches to Ouistreham

The outer approaches to Ouistreham are shallow, although the buoyed channel is dredged for the ferries and can be entered at any state of tide from a position just east of Ouistreham E-cardinal buoy. The approaches to Ouistreham are rough-going in strong onshore winds, when you need to be sure of your position if closing the coast.

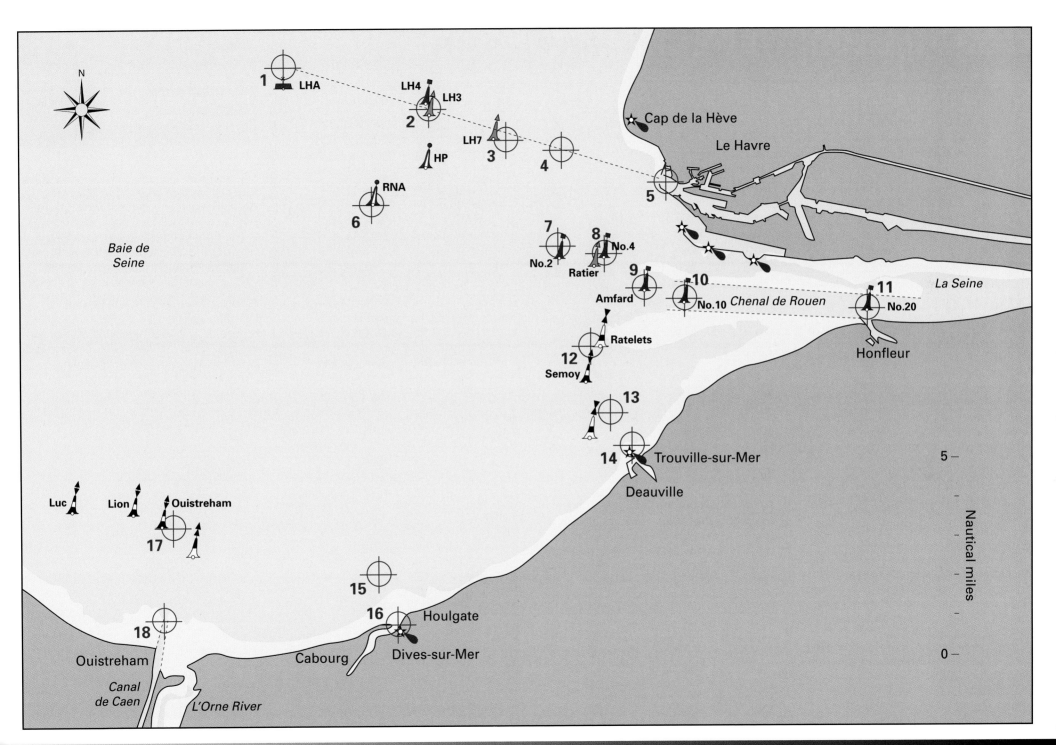

N

1 LHA

LH4 LH3

2

LH7

3

4

HP

RNA

6

Cap de la Hève

Le Havre

5

7

8 No.4

No.2

Ratier

9

Amfard

10

11 La Seine

No.10 Chenal de Rouen

No.20

Honfleur

Ratelets

12

Semoy

13

14 Trouville-sur-Mer

Deauville

Baie de
Seine

Luc

Lion Ouistreham

17

5 —

Nautical miles

15

16 Houlgate

Cabourg

Dives-sur-Mer

18

Ouistreham

0 —

Canal
de Caen

L'Orne River

# Ouistreham to Port-en-Bessin

| ⊕ | Waypoint name and position | Latitude | Longitude |
|---|---|---|---|
| 31  1 | Ouistreham outer, 2ca E of E-card buoy on leading line | 49°20.420'N | 000°14.510'W |
| 31  2 | Ouistreham entrance, between outer light beacons | 49°18.020'N | 000°14.690'W |
| 31  3 | Essarts de Langrune, 1ca due N of N-card buoy | 49°22.670'N | 000°21.300'W |
| 31  4 | Courseulles offing, 3M N of Courseulles E pierhead | 49°23.260'N | 000°27.680'W |
| 31  5 | Courseulles fairway buoy, actual position | 49°21.280'N | 000°27.680'W |
| 31  6 | Courseulles approach, 7ca 018°T from E pierhead | 49°20.929'N | 000°27.065'W |
| 31  7 | Courseulles entrance, close E of outer green beacon | 49°20.418'N | 000°27.325'W |
| 31  8 | Arromanches clearing, ½M N of Roseberry E-card buoy | 49°23.652'N | 000°36.329'W |
| 31  9 | Port-en-Bessin outer, 2M 024°T from W pierhead | 49°22.998'N | 000°44.167'W |

**Refer to Charts**
Admiralty charts 1349, 2136, 2613
Imray C32

caissons just under one mile SSE of Harpagas E-cardinal buoy. Care must be taken once inside the Mulberry harbour, where there are also drying obstructions and wrecks. Unless the weather is very calm, stay well clear of this whole area when coasting past, keeping outside the Roseberry E-cardinal buoy.

## COASTAL DANGERS

### Approaches to Ouistreham
The outer approaches to Ouistreham are shallow, although the buoyed channel is dredged for the ferries and can be entered at any state of tide from a position just east of Ouistreham E-cardinal buoy. The approaches to Ouistreham are rough-going in strong onshore winds, when you need to be sure of your position if closing the coast.

### Les Essarts de Langrune
A broad rocky plateau, Les Essarts de Langrune, stretches along the Normandy coast for four miles east of Courseulles-sur-Mer and the shoals extend up to two miles offshore. Drying rocks lurk to 1½ miles offshore and the plateau is marked on its northeast side by Essarts de Langrune N-cardinal bell buoy. Boats coasting between Ouistreham and Courseulles should pass outside, or at least close to this buoy. About midway between Ouistreham E-cardinal buoy and Essarts de Langrune N-cardinal, the Luc E-cardinal buoy guards the east side of a wreck, parts of which dry 2.9m at LAT. Yachts should pass well outside the Luc buoy.

### Plateau du Calvados
Opposite and to the west of Courseulles-sur-Mer, the Plateau du Calvados is an even broader area of drying rocks and shoals, extending about seven miles along the coast and up to two miles offshore. This shoal area, which is well-littered with wrecks, is not marked directly by buoys. Boats coasting past Courseulles in either direction should stay 2½–3 miles offshore, preferably outside a direct line between Essarts de Langrune N-cardinal and Roseberry E-cardinal buoys.

### Arromanches and the Mulberry harbour
Some six miles west of Courseulles-sur-Mer, the still substantial remains of the famous wartime 'Mulberry harbour' conceived by Winston Churchill provide a dramatic reminder of the Normandy landings which helped turn the tide of the war. The area is littered with wrecks, the outer of which, the Roseberry, lies nearly 2¾ miles offshore with 2.2m over it, marked on its east side by Roseberry E-cardinal buoy. Further inshore, just opposite Arromanches, the Harpagas wreck has only 0.3m over it and is also marked on its east side by an E-cardinal buoy.

The numerous caissons of the Mulberry harbour lie off Arromanches just inside the Rochers du Calvados, still forming a partially enclosing breakwater three miles long. Yachts can enter the Mulberry harbour in quiet weather, passing between a red and a green buoy which mark a gap in the

### Approaches to Port-en-Bessin
The approaches to the fishing harbour of Port-en-Bessin are straightforward, but the shore dries out on either side of the harbour as far out as the two outer breakwater heads. Boats should keep a good ½ mile offshore until opposite the entrance.

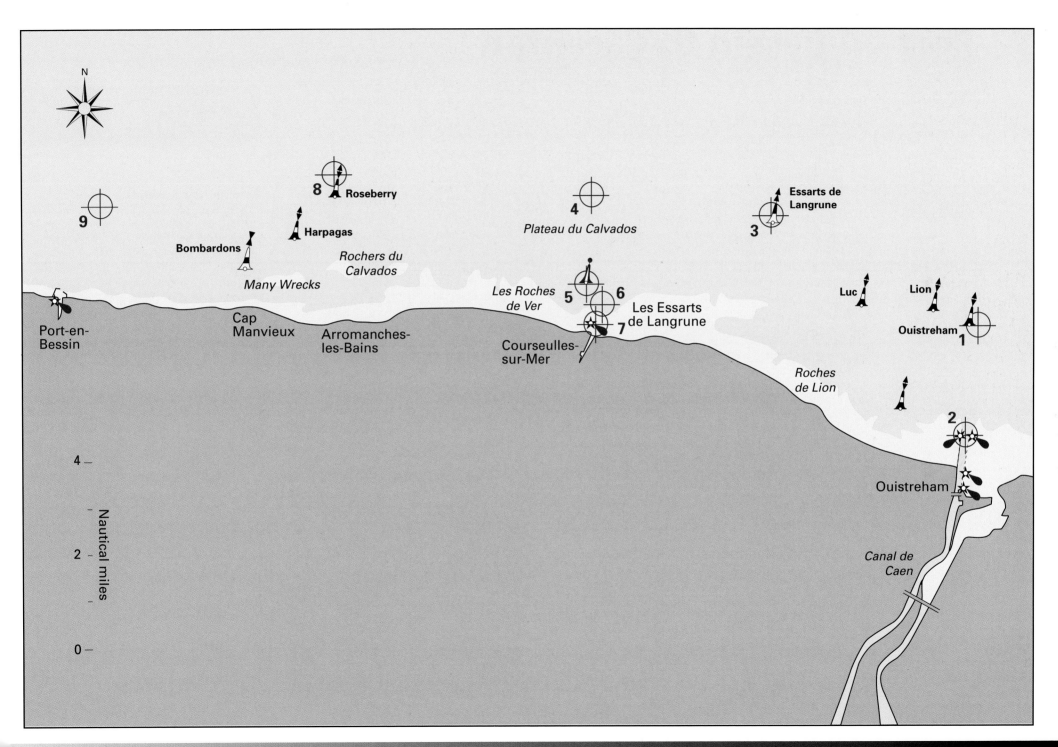

N

Roseberry 8

9

Harpagas

Bombardons

Rochers du
Calvados

Many Wrecks

Plateau du Calvados 4

Essarts de
Langrune

3

Port-en-
Bessin

Cap
Manvieux

Arromanches-
les-Bains

Les Roches
de Ver

5

6

Les Essarts
de Langrune

Luc

Lion

Ouistreham

1

Courseulles-
sur-Mer

7

Roches
de Lion

2

4 —

Ouistreham

Nautical miles

2 —

Canal de
Caen

0 —

| ⊕ | Waypoint name and position | Latitude | Longitude |
|---|---|---|---|
| 32 **1** | Port-en-Bessin outer, 2M 024°T from W pierhead | 49°22.998′N | 000°44.167′W |
| 32 **2** | Omaha clearing, 6ca 020°T from middle N-card buoy | 49°23.780′N | 000°51.580′W |
| 32 **3** | Broadsword clearing, ¾M N of Broadsword E-card buoy | 49°26.090′N | 000°52.960′W |
| 32 **4** | St Pierre du Mont, 1¼M due N of 39 m spot height | 49°24.730′N | 000°57.310′W |
| 32 **5** | Cardonnet E-card buoy, actual position | 49°26.830′N | 001°01.100′W |
| 32 **6** | Grandcamp No.3, ¼M due N of No.3 N-card buoy | 49°25.170′N | 001°03.690′W |
| 32 **7** | Grandcamp outer, on leading line 2¾M 326°T from pierheads | 49°25.710′N | 001°05.280′W |
| 32 **8** | Grandcamp entrance, between outer pierheads | 49°23.451′N | 001°02.967′W |
| 32 **9** | Isigny outer, ¼M NE of Isigny N-card buoy | 49°24.510′N | 001°06.080′W |
| 32 **10** | Isigny approach, 2¼M 352°T from Pte du Grouin beacons | 49°23.650′N | 001°07.650′W |
| 32 **11** | Isigny entrance, between Pte du Grouin beacons | 49°21.417′N | 001°07.173′W |
| 32 **12** | Carentan C1 fairway buoy, actual position | 49°25.440′N | 001°07.080′W |
| 32 **13** | Carentan outer, between No.1 and No.2 entrance buoys | 49°23.914′N | 001°08.453′W |
| 32 **14** | Carentan entrance, between outer training wall beacons | 49°21.935′N | 001°09.907′W |

### Refer to Charts
Admiralty charts 1349, 2135, 2136, 2613
Imray C32

### Banc du Cardonnet
This long narrow bank lies about four miles offshore opposite the Baie du Grand Vey, and extends for about six miles parallel to the coast between Iles St-Marcouf and the Est du Cardonnet E-cardinal buoy. It is safe to cross the Banc du Cardonnet for up to 1½ miles southeast of Iles St-Marcouf but further southeast the Cardonnet bank is littered with wrecks with uncertain depths over them.

## COASTAL DANGERS

### Approaches to Port-en-Bessin
The approaches to the fishing harbour of Port-en-Bessin are straightforward, but the shore dries out on either side of the harbour as far out as the two outer breakwater heads. Yachts should keep a good ½ mile offshore until opposite the entrance.

### Omaha Beach
Between three and six miles west of Port-en-Bessin, the famous Omaha Beach is still encumbered with numerous wrecks and obstructions for a good ¾ mile offshore. Three N-cardinal buoys guard these dangers, and yachts should stay outside these buoys when coasting between Port-en-Bessin and Grandcamp-Maisy.

### Broadsword wreck
This wreck, with 2.4m over it, lies 2½ miles offshore opposite the west end of Omaha Beach, marked on its east side by the Broadsword E-cardinal buoy.

### Les Roches de Grandcamp
This wide drying plateau fringes the coast for nearly five miles opposite Grandcamp-Maisy, from near Pointe du Hoc in the east to the Isigny entrance channel in the west. Les Roches de Grandcamp extend up to 1½ miles offshore and are guarded by three N-cardinal buoys. Grandcamp-Maisy harbour can be approached for two hours each side of local high water, from a fairway position between No.3 and No.5 N-cardinal buoys.

### Approaches to Carentan
The Baie du Grand Vey, which forms the outer approaches to Carentan and Isigny, is a broad expanse of mostly drying sand. Two buoyed channels – the Passe de Carentan and Passe d'Isigny – lead across these shoals and can be negotiated for about two hours each side of high water, although strangers bound for Carentan should aim to arrive off the C1 fairway buoy an hour before local high water or just before.

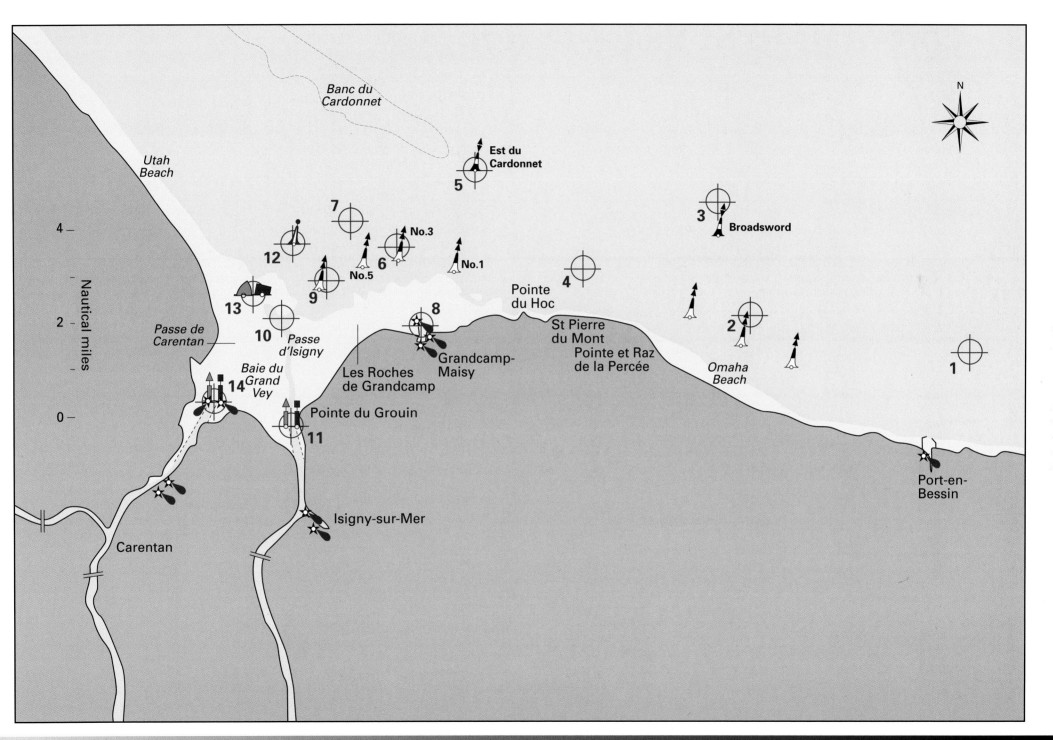

Banc du
Cardonnet

Utah
Beach

N

Est du
Cardonnet

**5**

**7**

**3**    Broadsword

4 —

Nautical miles

**12**

No.3

No.5    **6**

No.1

**9**

**4**

2 —

Pointe
du Hoc

**13**

**8**

St Pierre
du Mont

Passe de
Carentan

**10**

Passe
d'Isigny

Grandcamp-
Maisy

Pointe et Raz
de la Percée

**2**

0 —

Baie du
Grand
Vey

Les Roches
de Grandcamp

Omaha
Beach

**14**

**1**

Pointe du Grouin

**11**

Port-en-
Bessin

Carentan

Isigny-sur-Mer

# 33 Carentan to St Vaast-la-Hougue

| ⊕ | Waypoint name and position | Latitude | Longitude |
|---|---|---|---|
| 33 1 | Cardonnet E-card buoy, actual position | 49°26.830'N | 001°01.100'W |
| 33 2 | Grandcamp No.3, ¼M due N of No.3 N-card buoy | 49°25.170'N | 001°03.690'W |
| 33 3 | Grandcamp outer, on leading line 2¾M 326°T from pierheads | 49°25.710'N | 001°05.280'W |
| 33 4 | Grandcamp entrance, between outer pierheads | 49°23.451'N | 001°02.967'W |
| 33 5 | Isigny outer, ¼M NE of Isigny N-card buoy | 49°24.510'N | 001°06.080'W |
| 33 6 | Carentan C1 fairway buoy, actual position | 49°25.440'N | 001°07.080'W |
| 33 7 | Carentan outer, between No.1 and No.2 entrance buoys | 49°23.914'N | 001°08.453'W |
| 33 8 | Cardonnet west clearing, 3¼M due W of E-card buoy | 49°26.830'N | 001°06.120'W |
| 33 9 | Cardonnet north, ¾M N of Norfalk E-card buoy | 49°29.520'N | 001°03.480'W |
| 33 10 | St Marcouf west, 2ca W of St Marcouf W-card buoy | 49°29.730'N | 001°12.280'W |
| 33 11 | St Marcouf NE, ½M NE of Ile du Large lighthouse | 49°30.238'N | 001°08.221'W |
| 33 12 | St Floxel E-card buoy, actual position | 49°30.640'N | 001°13.940'W |
| 33 13 | St Vaast E approach, 2¼M 150°T from Pte de Saire lighthouse | 49°34.390'N | 001°12.050'W |
| 33 14 | Le Gavendest clearing, 1ca SE of Le Gavendest S-card buoy | 49°34.300'N | 001°13.780'W |
| 33 15 | St Vaast Passe du Nord, on leading line ¾M S of Fort L'Ilet | 49°34.300'N | 001°14.510'W |
| 33 16 | St Vaast entrance, 1½ca due E of outer pierhead | 49°35.170'N | 001°15.180'W |
| 33 17 | Pointe de Saire clearing, 1¾M E of Pointe de Saire lighthouse | 49°36.366'N | 001°11.083'W |

**Refer to Charts**
Admiralty charts 1349, 2135
Imray C32

### Roches St Floxel
Five miles south of St Vaast, some rocky ledges known as Roches St Floxel jut out from the coast for almost one mile. The extremity of these dangers is marked by St Floxel E-cardinal buoy.

### Approaches to St Vaast-la-Hougue
The approaches to St Vaast, although rather rocky, are well marked and quite straightforward by day or night. Coming from the north round Pointe de Saire, you have to stay well out to the east to clear the rocky dangers east and south of Ile de Tatihou before turning west to follow the Passe du Nord south of two S-cardinal buoys and into the Petite Rade.

Coming from the southeast outside Iles St-Marcouf and the banks, you would normally keep a good mile northeast of Iles St-Marcouf and join the Passe du Nord once clear to the north of Banc de la Rade. Coming from the south inside Iles St-Marcouf and the banks, you would normally approach St Vaast from a position close east of St Floxel E-cardinal buoy.

## COASTAL DANGERS

### Approaches to Carentan
The Baie du Grand Vey, which forms the outer approaches to Carentan and Isigny, is a broad expanse of mostly drying sand. Two buoyed channels – the Passe de Carentan and Passe d'Isigny – lead across these shoals and can be negotiated for about two hours each side of high water, although strangers bound for Carentan should aim to arrive off the C1 fairway buoy an hour before local high water or just before.

### Utah Beach
The Utah Bench stretches northwest from the west side of Baie du Grand Vey, marked at its southeast end by the prominent American monument. Various wrecks, some awash at chart datum, still lie over one mile offshore. Boats following the Normandy coast between Carentan and St Vaast-la-Hougue should therefore keep just outside a direct line between Carentan 'C1' red-and-white fairway buoy and St Floxel E-cardinal buoy.

### Banc du Cardonnet
This long narrow bank lies about four miles offshore opposite the Baie du Grand Vey, and extends for about six miles parallel to the coast between Iles St-Marcouf and the Est du Cardonnet E-cardinal buoy. It is safe to cross the Banc du Cardonnet for up to 1½ miles southeast of Iles St-Marcouf but further southeast the Cardonnet bank is littered with wrecks with uncertain depths over them.

### Iles St-Marcouf
These two small islands lie about four miles north of Utah Beach, more or less in the middle of the long line of banks which curves parallel to the shore between St Vaast and the Est du Cardonnet E-cardinal buoy.

Iles St-Marcouf are fairly steep-to and in quiet weather you can anchor off the southwest side of the north island, Ile du Large, for lunch. The south island, Ile de Terre, is a bird sanctuary and landing is prohibited.

The banks northwest of Iles St-Marcouf are shoal with numerous wrecks and should be avoided.

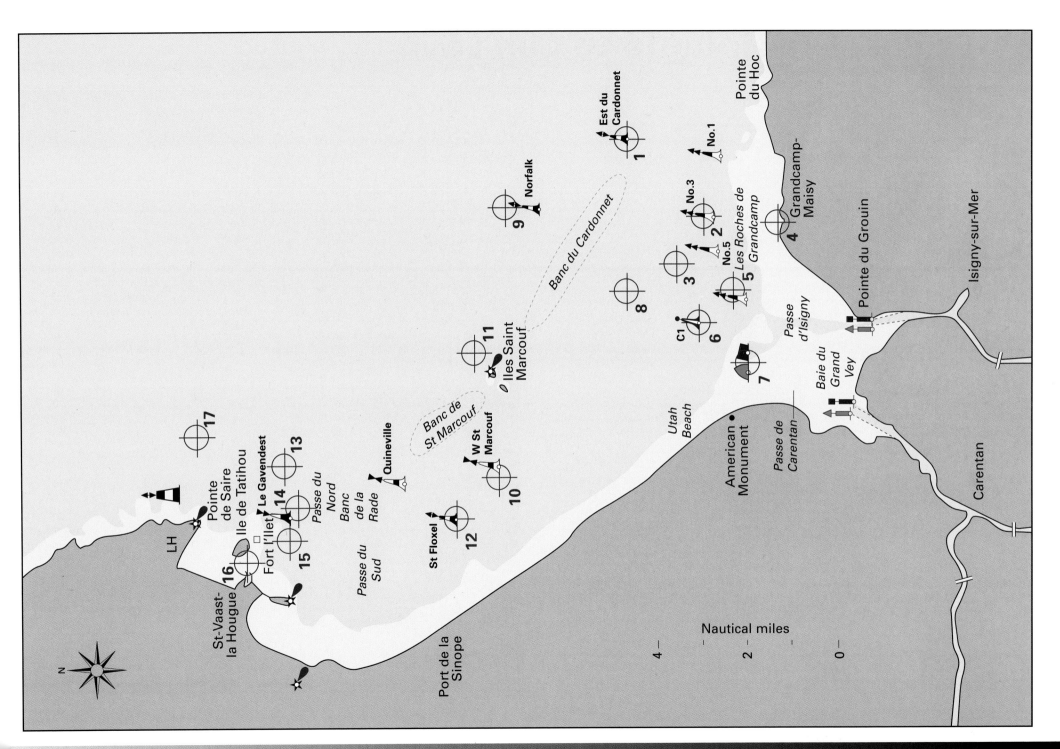

Pointe du Hoc

Est du Cardonnet

No.1

No.3

No.5 *Les Roches de Grandcamp*

Grandcamp-Maisy

Norfalk

Pointe du Grouin

Isigny-sur-Mer

Banc du Cardonnet

Passe d'Isigny

c1

Baie du Grand Vey

Iles Saint Marcouf

*Utah Beach*

Passe de Carentan

Carentan

Banc de St Marcouf

Quineville

W St Marcouf

American Monument

17

13

St Floxel

*Banc de la Rade*

*Passe du Nord*

Pointe de Saire

Ile de Tatihou

Le Gavendest

Fort l'Ilet

LH

St-Vaast-la-Hougue

*Passe du Sud*

Port de la Sinope

N

Nautical miles

4    2    0

| ⊕ | Waypoint name and position | Latitude | Longitude |
|---|---|---|---|
| 34 1 | Pointe de Saire clearing, 1¾M E of Pointe de Saire lighthouse | 49°36.366'N | 001°11.083'W |
| 34 2 | St Vaast E approach 2¼M 150°T from Pointe de Saire lighthouse | 49°34.390'N | 001°12.050'W |
| 34 3 | Le Gavendest clearing, 1ca SE of Le Gavendest S-card buoy | 49°34.300'N | 001°13.780'W |
| 34 4 | St Vaast Passe du Nord, on leading line ¾M S of Fort L'Ilet | 49°34.300'N | 001°14.510'W |
| 34 5 | St Vaast entrance, 1½ca due E of outer pierhead | 49°35.170'N | 001°15.180'W |
| 34 6 | Barfleur north clearing, 4M due N of lighthouse | 49°45.780'N | 001°15.960'W |
| 34 7 | Barfleur east clearing, 4M due E of lighthouse | 49°41.780'N | 001°09.791'W |
| 34 8 | Barfleur NE clearing, 3M 063°T from lighthouse | 49°43.120'N | 001°11.820'W |
| 34 9 | Barfleur approach, 1¼M 040°T from breakwater head on leading line | 49°41.270'N | 001°14.230'W |
| 34 10 | Barfleur entrance, breakwater head actual position | 49°40.310'N | 001°15.470'W |
| 34 11 | Basse du Rénier, ½M due N of N-card buoy | 49°45.340'N | 001°22.090'W |
| 34 12 | La Pierre Noire, 1ca due N of W-card buoy | 49°43.640'N | 001°29.070'W |
| 34 13 | Port Lévi approach, ¾M due W of Fort Lévi | 49°41.420'N | 001°29.780'W |
| 34 14 | Port Lévi anchorage, 1½ca due W of S pierhead | 49°41.220'N | 001°28.720'W |

### Refer to Charts
Admiralty charts 1114, 1349, 2135
Imray C32

### Basse du Rénier
Between Pointe de Barfleur and Cap Lévi, numerous rocky dangers extend up to two miles offshore. Les Équets N-cardinal buoy marks the northwest extremity of Banc de St Pierre and the Plateau des Équets; the Basse du Rénier N-cardinal buoy marks the furthest offlying dangers. La Pierre Noire W-cardinal buoy, not quite two miles north of Cap Lévi, serves as a corner mark for the westernmost of the dangers along this stretch of coast.

## COASTAL DANGERS

### Approaches to St Vaast-la-Hougue
The approaches to St Vaast, although rather rocky, are well marked and quite straightforward by day or night. Coming from the north round Pointe de Saire, you have to stay well out to the east to clear the rocky dangers east and south of Ile de Tatihou before turning west to follow the Passe du Nord south of two S-cardinal buoys and into the Petite Rade.

Coming from the south-east outside Iles St-Marcouf and the banks, you would normally keep a good mile north-east of Iles St-Marcouf and join the Passe du Nord once clear to the north of Banc de la Rade. Coming from the south inside Iles St-Marcouf and the banks, you would normally approach St Vaast from a position close east of St Floxel E-cardinal buoy.

### Pointe de Barfleur
A significant tidal race extends 3–4 miles east and north-east from Pointe de Barfleur, with heavy breaking seas when the stream is weather-going, especially at springs. Give the Barfleur Race a wide berth or, better still, round Pointe de Barfleur at slack water. Pointe de Barfleur is a low rocky promontory on both its north and east sides and, even at slack water, should be given a generous offing as you go round. On the north side, the Banc de St Pierre and the Plateau des Équets extend for more than 1½ miles offshore and are marked on their north-west corner by Les Équets N-cardinal buoy.

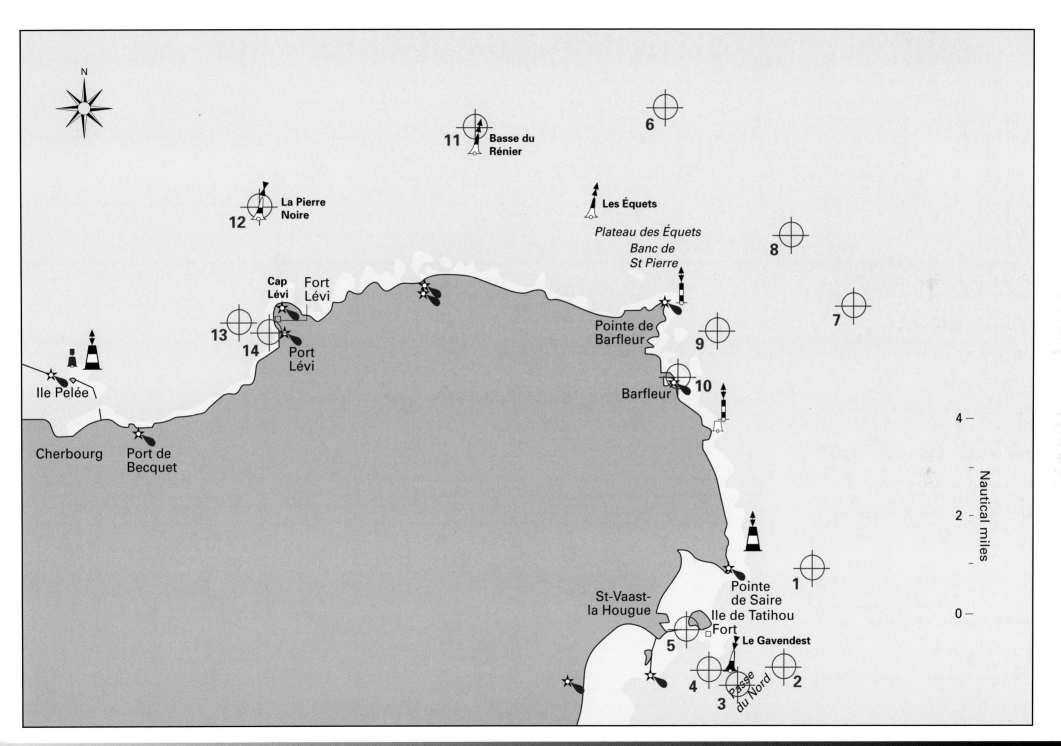

N

11 Basse du Rénier

Les Équets

6

La Pierre Noire

12

8

Plateau des Équets
Banc de St Pierre

Cap Lévi

Fort Lévi

7

13

Pointe de Barfleur

9

14

Port Lévi

Ile Pelée

Barfleur 10

Cherbourg

Port de Becquet

4

St-Vaast-la Hougue

2

Pointe de Saire

1

Nautical miles

St-Vaast-la Hougue

Ile de Tatihou

Fort

5

Le Gavendest

4

Passe du Nord

3

2

0

# 35 Approaches to Cherbourg and Omonville

| ⊕ | Waypoint name and position | Latitude | Longitude |
|---|---|---|---|
| 35 1 | La Pierre Noire, 1ca due N of W-card buoy | 49°43.640'N | 001°29.070'W |
| 35 2 | Port Lévi approach, ¾M due W of Fort Lévi | 49°41.420'N | 001°29.780'W |
| 35 3 | Port Lévi anchorage, 1½ca due W of S pierhead | 49°41.220'N | 001°28.720'W |
| 35 4 | Cherbourg east entrance, 6ca 025°T from Fort de L'Est | 49°40.824'N | 001°35.544'W |
| 35 5 | Cherbourg west entrance, 1½ca W of Fort de l'Ouest | 49°40.450'N | 001°39.090'W |
| 35 6 | CH1 fairway buoy, actual position | 49°43.240'N | 001°42.090'W |
| 35 7 | Raz de Bannes, 6ca N of N-card beacon tower | 49°41.920'N | 001°44.530'W |
| 35 8 | Omonville east approach, 1M 077°T from leading light | 49°42.462'N | 001°48.607'W |
| 35 9 | Omonville entrance, 1½ca E of L'Étonnard green beacon tower | 49°42.330'N | 001°49.633'W |
| 35 10 | Basse Bréfort, 2ca N of N-card buoy | 49°44.100'N | 001°51.150'W |

**Refer to Charts**
Admiralty charts 1112, 1114
Imray C32, C33A

## COASTAL DANGERS

### Cap Lévi

Rocks and rocky banks extend for nearly 1¾ miles north of Cap Lévi. The most seaward danger of significance to boats is La Pierre Noire Rock, with 2.2m over it, which lies about 1¼ miles north of Cap Lévi. La Pierre Noire is guarded by a W-cardinal buoy, which acts as a corner mark for the westernmost of the extensive area of offshore dangers between Pointe de Barfleur and Cap Lévi.

### Ile Pelée

On the east side of Cherbourg east entrance, an area of drying reefs extends seawards from the east fort for three cables. This plateau is guarded on its north edge by Ile Pelée red beacon tower and an E-cardinal beacon tower, but it is important not to confuse these two towers if approaching Cherbourg east entrance in poor visibility.

### Ferry traffic

Cherbourg is a busy cross-Channel ferry port and care must be taken to keep clear of shipping when entering or leaving either the east or west entrance.

### Raz de Bannes

Just over three miles west of Cherbourg west entrance, an area of drying rocky ledges juts six cables offshore opposite the village and beach of Urville. These dangers are marked on their north edge by the Raz de Bannes N-cardinal beacon tower. Just under ½ mile WNW of this tower is an isolated rock with only 1m over it at chart datum.

### Pointe de Jardeheu

About eight miles WNW of Cherbourg west entrance, just beyond the pleasant harbour of Omonville-la-Rouge, the promontory of Pointe de Jardeheu is fringed by drying rocks on both sides and just over ½ mile seaward. The extremity of these dangers is marked by the Basse Bréfort N-cardinal whistle buoy, which most boats leave fairly close to the south on their way between Cherbourg and Cap de la Hague.

If leaving Omonville for Cap de la Hague, you need to make a positive circle around Les Tataquets, Basse de Moitié and La Coque rocks before steering to pass outside the Basse Bréfort buoy, making due allowance for the west-going tide on the way.

### Inshore Eddy

A west-going eddy runs close inshore between Cherbourg and Cap de la Hague, starting about three hours before HW Dover off Cherbourg and much earlier further west. By taking advantage of this eddy, it is possible to carry a fair stream from Cherbourg either to St Peter Port, or direct to St Helier via Corbière Point.

Cap de la Hague is just over 14 miles from Cherbourg west entrance, so most yachts bound for Guernsey or Jersey would be aiming to pass Cherbourg Fort de l'Ouest 2½–3 hours before slack water in the Race ie at around 3½ hours before HW Dover.

Yachts making for Alderney from Cherbourg should leave up to an hour earlier and then hold well up to the north when crossing between Cap de la Hague and the northeast corner of Alderney. You need to be skirting the north end of the Race during the last of the north-going run and then the brief period of slack, to avoid being sucked south of Alderney by the new southwest-going stream in the Race.

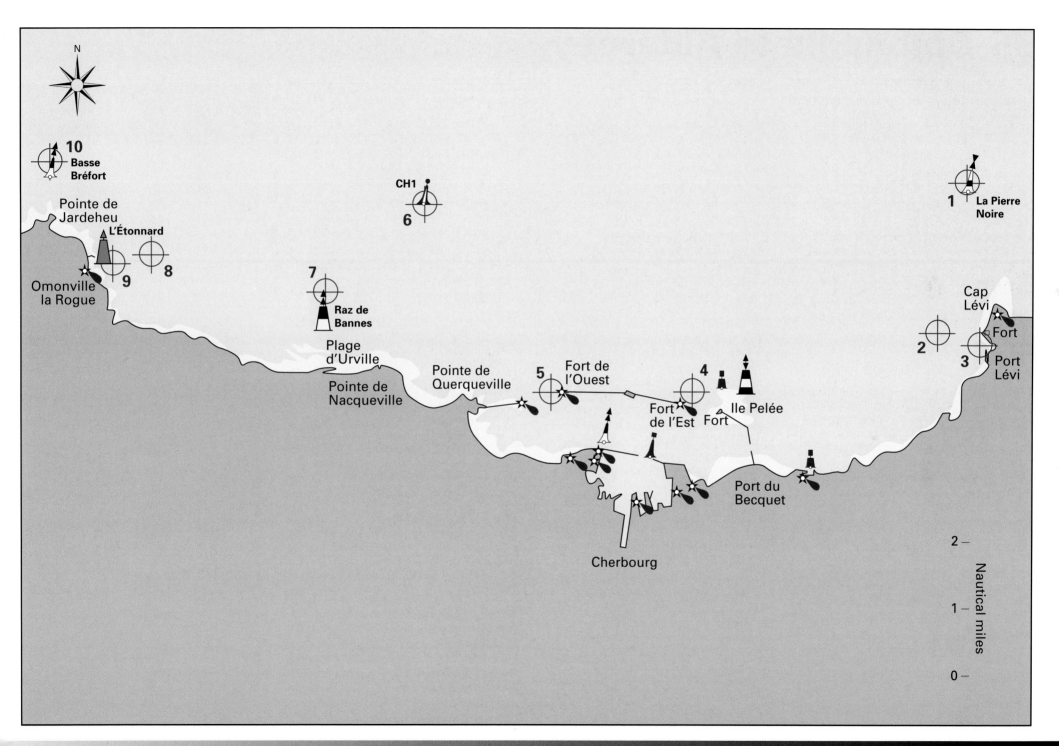

N

**10** Basse Bréfort

Pointe de Jardeheu

L'Étonnard

**8**

**9**

Omonville la Rogue

CH1

**6**

**1** La Pierre Noire

**7** Raz de Bannes

Plage d'Urville

Pointe de Nacqueville

Pointe de Querqueville

**5** Fort de l'Ouest

Fort de l'Est

Fort

Ile Pelée

**4**

Cap Lévi

Fort

**2**

**3** Port Lévi

Port du Becquet

Cherbourg

2 —

1 —

0 —

Nautical miles

# 36 Omonville to Alderney

| ⊕ | | Waypoint name and position | Latitude | Longitude |
|---|---|---|---|---|
| 36 | 1 | Omonville east approach, 1M 077°T from leading light | 49°42.462'N | 001°48.607'W |
| 36 | 2 | Omonville entrance, 1½ca E of L'Étonnard green beacon tower | 49°42.330'N | 001°49.633'W |
| 36 | 3 | Basse Bréfort, 2ca N of N-card buoy | 49°44.100'N | 001°51.150'W |
| 36 | 4 | Cap de la Hague, 8ca due N of La Plate tower | 49°44.770'N | 001°55.740'W |
| 36 | 5 | Alderney Race north inner, 4M due E of Alderney lighthouse | 49°43.785'N | 002°03.724'W |
| 36 | 6 | Alderney outer approach, 6½ca N of Château à L'Étoc lighthouse | 49°44.585'N | 002°10.631'W |
| 36 | 7 | The Swinge, ¾M due W of Fort Clonque | 49°42.800'N | 002°15.120'W |
| 36 | 8 | Swinge South approach, 1½M 214°T from Les Étacs west edge | 49°41.035'N | 002°15.768'W |
| 36 | 9 | Alderney Race South, 3½M S of old Telegraph Tower | 49°38.779'N | 002°13.268'W |
| 36 | 10 | Jobourg clearing, 3½M SW of Nez de Jobourg | 49°37.868'N | 002°00.251'W |
| 36 | 11 | Diélette NW offing, 3.2M 326°T from N power station tower | 49°34.859'N | 001°55.632'W |
| 36 | 12 | Diélette entrance, 2ca 320°T from Jetée Ouest light | 49°33.329'N | 001°52.008'W |

### Refer to Charts
Admiralty charts 60, 1114, 3653
Imray C33A, 2500.1, 2500.6

### The Swinge
The Swinge channel, between Alderney and Burhou, can kick up savage overfalls with even a light wind over the tide. Spring rates can exceed 6–7 knots and the Swinge should be taken as near to slack water as possible – that is, at around half-tide (up or down) at Braye Harbour.

## COASTAL DANGERS

### Pointe de Jardeheu
About eight miles WNW of Cherbourg west entrance, just beyond the pleasant harbour of Omonville-la-Rouge, the promontory of Pointe de Jardeheu is fringed by drying rocks on both sides and just over ½ mile seaward. The extremity of these dangers is marked by the Basse Bréfort N-cardinal whistle buoy, which most boats leave fairly close to the south on their way between Cherbourg and Cap de la Hague.

If leaving Omonville for Cap de la Hague, you need to make a positive circle around Les Tatquets, Basse de Moitié and La Coque rocks before steering to pass outside the Basse Bréfort buoy, making due allowance for the west-going tide on the way.

### Cap de la Hague
This rather bleak promontory, right at the northwest tip of the Cherbourg peninsula, is an important psychological gateway between the Normandy coast and the more rugged cruising grounds of Brittany and the Channel Islands. Cap de la Hague, together with Quénard Point at the east tip of Alderney, forms the famous tidal gateway of the Alderney Race.

Cap de la Hague is fringed with drying rocks on its north and west sides. On the Channel side, the dangers extend nearly ¾ mile northwest of the blockhouse on Cap de la Hague. La Plate N-cardinal beacon tower, standing not quite ½ mile offshore, should itself be cleared by a good ½ mile to be sure of avoiding Petite Grune (dries 0.6m) and La Grande Grune (with only 1.3m over it) as you round Cap de la Hague.

On the west side of Cap de la Hague, La Foraine drying reefs extend a good six cables beyond Gros du Raz lighthouse, and are marked on their west side by La Foraine W-cardinal beacon tower. Boats bound for Diélette, Carteret marina or direct for Jersey, should aim to pass a couple of miles west of Cap de la Hague – that is, something over half a mile west of La Foraine buoy.

### Nez de Jobourg
Three miles south of Cap de la Hague, the promontory of Nez de Jobourg has dangerous rocks lurking almost one mile to the WNW, ½ mile to the west and (Les Calenfriers and Les Huquets de Jobourg) 1½ miles to the south. This far northwest tip of Normandy needs a wide berth if you are heading south from the Alderney Race towards Diélette, Carteret marina or direct for Jersey.

### The Alderney Race
Streams are powerful in the Alderney Race, with areas of heavy overfalls, especially with a weather-going tide. Spring rates reach 5–6 knots through most of the Race, but 8–9 knots locally.

### Alderney, Braye Harbour approach
East of Braye harbour entrance, the Grois Rocks and Boués Briées extend up to ¼ mile north and NNE of Château à L'Étoc Point. On the west side of Braye harbour entrance, avoid the old submerged breakwater which extends about three cables northeast of the existing breakwater.

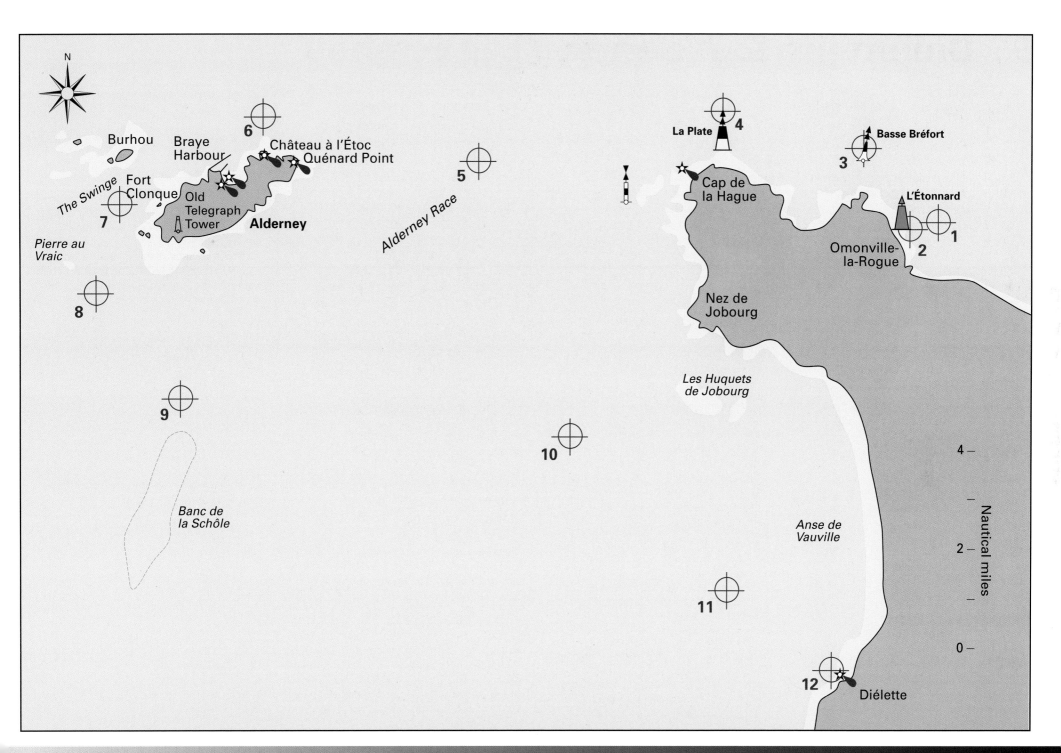

N

Burhou

Braye
Harbour

Château à l'Étoc
Quénard Point

**6**

Fort
Clonque

The Swinge

Old
Telegraph
Tower

**Alderney**

**7**

Pierre au
Vraic

**8**

**5**

Alderney Race

La Plate **4**

**3**

Basse Bréfort

L'Étonnard

Cap de
la Hague

**1**

**2**

Omonville-
la-Rogue

Nez de
Jobourg

**9**

Les Huquets
de Jobourg

**10**

Banc de
la Schôle

Anse de
Vauville

4 —

2 —

0 —

Nautical miles

**11**

**12**

Diélette

# Diélette to Carteret and Les Écrehou

| ⊕ | Waypoint name and position | Latitude | Longitude |
|---|---|---|---|
| 37 1 | Jobourg clearing, 3½M SW of Nez de Jobourg | 49°37.868'N | 002°00.251'W |
| 37 2 | Diélette NW offing, 3.2M 326°T from N power station | 49°34.859'N | 001°55.632'W |
| 37 3 | Diélette entrance, 2ca 320°T from Jetée Ouest light | 49°33.329'N | 001°52.008'W |
| 37 4 | Flamanville clearing, 2½M W of power station towers | 49°32.207'N | 001°56.707'W |
| 37 5 | Les Trois Grunes west, ¼M due W of W-card buoy | 49°21.840'N | 001°55.577'W |
| 37 6 | Les Trois Grunes north clearing, 6ca due N of buoy | 49°22.440'N | 001°55.210'W |
| 37 7 | Les Trois Grunes south clearing, 6ca due S of buoy | 49°21.240'N | 001°55.210'W |
| 37 8 | Cap de Carteret, ¾M SW of lighthouse | 49°21.880'N | 001°49.230'W |
| 37 9 | Carteret approach, 1M 190°T from west pierhead | 49°21.102'N | 001°47.592'W |
| 37 10 | Carteret entrance, 2ca due S of east pierhead beacon | 49°21.970'N | 001°47.300'W |
| 37 11 | Portbail approach, 2ca SE of RW fairway buoy | 49°18.237'N | 001°44.549'W |
| 37 12 | Déroute N outer, 5M 230°T from Cap de Carteret lighthouse | 49°19.231'N | 001°54.267'W |
| 37 13 | Déroute N inner, 8ca E of Écrevière S-card buoy | 49°15.270'N | 001°50.930'W |
| 37 14 | Écrevière, ¼M due S of Écrevière S-card buoy | 49°15.020'N | 001°52.130'W |
| 37 15 | Les Écrehou approach, 1½M 202°T from Bigorne Rock | 49°15.740'N | 001°55.770'W |
| 37 16 | Les Dirouilles West, 2¼M NE of Sorel Point N tip | 49°17.280'N | 002°07.180'W |
| 37 17 | Les Écrehou SW, 1½M NE of La Coupe Point, Jersey | 49°15.042'N | 001°59.907'W |

### Refer to Charts
Admiralty charts 3653, 3655
Imray C33A, 2500.5, 2500.6

## COASTAL DANGERS

### Diélette approach
This stretch of coast is a lee shore in westerlies or northwesterlies, so it is not prudent to run for Diélette in fresh to strong winds from this quarter. There are drying dangers just off the coast within ¾ mile either side of Diélette harbour, so choose your spot with care if anchoring outside the harbour. Diélette has an attractive marina with a half-tide sill.

### Flamanville to Carteret
Parts of the coast between Cap de Flamanville and Cap de Carteret are shallow to within a mile of the shore. The Chausée des Cagnes juts out seawards for three cables not far southeast of Cap de Flamanville. Pointe du Rozel, about three miles SSE of Cap de Flamanville, has drying

ledges and shoal patches extending offshore for a radius of almost a mile. Further south, towards Cap de Carteret, the drying plateau known as Roches du Rit extends for nearly ¾ mile offshore opposite Les Dunes d'Hatainville, with shoal water reaching out another ½ mile.

Between Pointe du Rozel and Roches du Rit, the Banc de Surtainville has shoal patches extending from 1½–2½ miles offshore. The shallowest patch, Basse Bihard with 2m over it, lies about 2½ miles southwest of Pointe du Rozel.

### Approaches to Carteret
The approaches to Carteret are shallow and therefore rough-going in fresh onshore winds. Strangers should not, in any event, close the coast near Carteret except within a couple of hours of high water.

### Plateau des Trois-Grunes
This small rocky plateau, parts of which dry up to 1.6m, lies about 3½ miles west of Cap de Carteret and is marked on its west side by Les Trois Grunes W-cardinal buoy.

### Banks between Les Écrehou and the mainland
There are various banks and shoals strung out between the French mainland and the rocky plateau of rocks and islets known as Les Écrehou. Close southeast of Les Écrehou, the Écrevière Bank dries up to 2.3m and stretches SSE from L'Écrevière Rock for nearly 1½ miles. The tip of the bank is marked by a S-cardinal buoy. There is then a deep channel, about 1½ miles wide, between the east side of Les Écrehou and the Basses de Taillepied shoals, parts of which have less than a metre over them,

with a rocky patch drying 0.7m near the northwest tip of the shoal area.

Basses de Taillepied are about five miles offshore, and there are more shoals between Taillepied and the mainland, parts of which dry or almost dry at chart datum. These banks merge into the coastal shoals off Portbail, a small drying harbour which should only be approached near high water.

### Les Écrehou
This fascinating plateau of reefs and islets can be visited in quiet weather, but pilotage around Les Écrehou needs great care, especially as the tides are very strong in this area. Strangers should approach from the SSW, using the waypoints given in this directory and following the advice of a reliable pilot book. A good time to arrive is around half-ebb, when there is plenty of water in the approach channel but enough of the key rocks exposed to make them clearly visible.

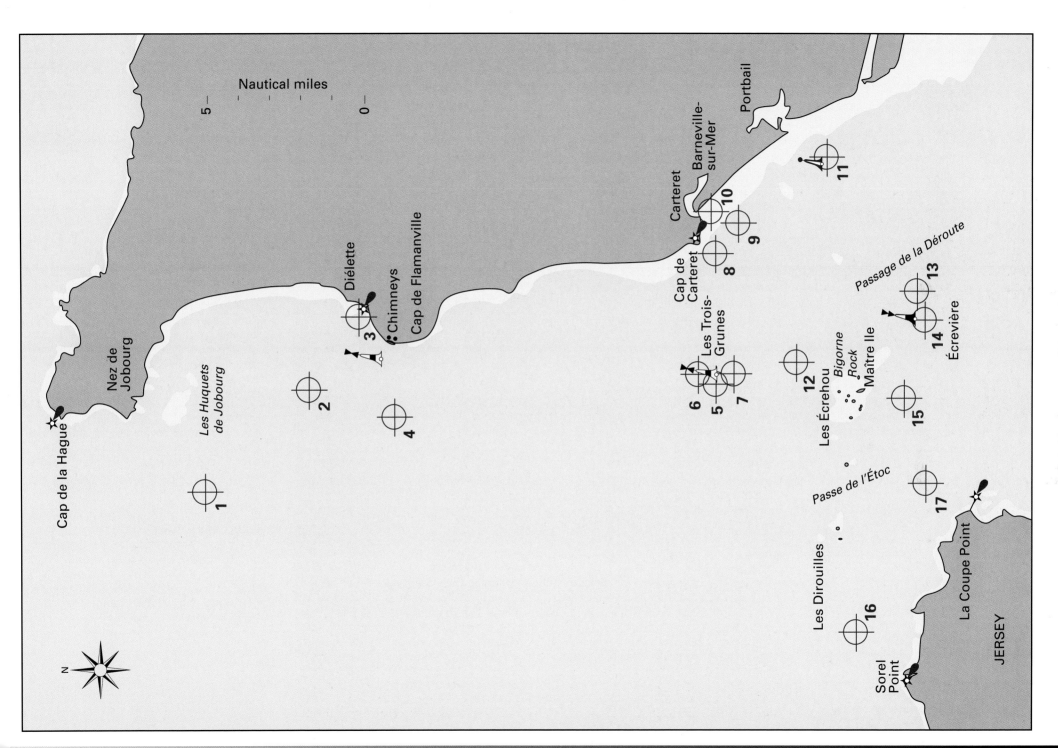

Nautical miles

5                    0

N

Cap de la Hague

Nez de Jobourg

Les Huquets de Jobourg

Diélette

Chimneys

Cap de Flamanville

Carteret

Barneville-sur-Mer

Portbail

Cap de Carteret

Les Trois-Grunes

Les Écrehou

Bigorne Rock

Maître Ile

Passage de la Déroute

Écrevière

Passe de l'Étoc

Les Dirouilles

Sorel Point

La Coupe Point

JERSEY

1
2
3
4
5
6
7
8
9
10
11
12
13
14
15
16
17

# 38 Alderney Race to Guernsey

| ⊕ | | Waypoint name and position | Latitude | Longitude |
|---|---|---|---|---|
| 38 | 1 | Cap de la Hague, 8ca due N of La Plate tower | 49°44.770′N | 001°55.740′W |
| 38 | 2 | Alderney Race north inner, 4M due E of Alderney lighthouse | 49°43.785′N | 002°03.724′W |
| 38 | 3 | Alderney outer approach, 6½ca N of Château à L'Étoc lighthouse | 49°44.585′N | 002°10.631′W |
| 38 | 4 | The Swinge, ¾M due W of Fort Clonque | 49°42.800′N | 002°15.120′W |
| 38 | 5 | Swinge South approach, 1½M 214°T from Les Étacs west edge | 49°41.035′N | 002°15.768′W |
| 38 | 6 | Casquets west clearing, 2M due W of Casquets lighthouse | 49°43.320′N | 002°25.698′W |
| 38 | 7 | Alderney Race South, 3½M S of old Telegraph Tower | 49°38.779′N | 002°13.268′W |
| 38 | 8 | Jobourg clearing, 3½M SW of Nez de Jobourg | 49°37.868′N | 002°00.251′W |
| 38 | 9 | Diélette NW offing, 3.2M 326°T from N power station tower | 49°34.859′N | 001°55.632′W |
| 38 | 10 | Diélette entrance, 2ca 320°T from Jetée Ouest light | 49°33.329′N | 001°52.008′W |
| 38 | 11 | Schôle Bank East, 10M due S of Quénard Point lighthouse | 49°33.750′N | 002°09.860′W |
| 38 | 12 | East Sark, ½M due E of Blanchard E-card buoy | 49°25.360′N | 002°16.660′W |
| 38 | 13 | Little Russel north, 9ca 067°T from Platte Fougère lighthouse | 49°31.183′N | 002°27.866′W |
| 38 | 14 | Roustel, 1ca due W of BW tower | 49°29.230′N | 002°28.970′W |
| 38 | 15 | St Peter Port, 1ca ENE of Castle pierhead | 49°27.347′N | 002°31.309′W |
| 38 | 16 | Little Russel south, 6ca ESE of St Martin's lighthouse | 49°25.100′N | 002°30.840′W |
| 38 | 17 | Big Russel north, 2M E of Grande Amfroque beacons | 49°30.578′N | 002°21.569′W |
| 38 | 18 | Big Russel south, 1M E of Lower Heads S-card buoy | 49°25.850′N | 002°27.020′W |
| 38 | 19 | Sark, Havre Gosselin, 1½ca due S of Les Dents Rocks | 49°25.420′N | 002°23.710′W |
| 38 | 20 | Guernsey south coast, 1½M S of Corbière tower | 49°23.745′N | 002°37.154′W |
| 38 | 21 | Les Hanois W clearing, 2M due W of lighthouse | 49°26.100′N | 002°45.205′W |
| 38 | 22 | Lower Heads south clearing, 1ca due S of S-card buoy | 49°25.750′N | 002°28.550′W |
| 38 | 23 | Sark north clearing, ½M due N of Bec du Nez light | 49°27.590′N | 002°22.170′W |
| 38 | 24 | Little Sark west clearing, 8½ca 222°T from Les Dents | 49°24.940′N | 002°24.580′W |
| 38 | 25 | Sark south clearing, 9ca 230°T from S tip of L'Étac | 49°23.480′N | 002°23.090′W |

## Refer to Charts

Admiralty charts 60, 807, 808, 3653, 3654
Imray C33A, 2500.2, 2500.6

## Herm Island

Herm is surrounded by wide expanses of drying rocks. Approaching the Little Russel from Alderney, be sure you are well north of Platte Boue and Boufresse, the most northeasterly (and unmarked) out-lying dangers.

## Guernsey North Coast

Along the northwest coast of Guernsey, between Les Hanois and Platte Fougère, dangers extend up to two miles offshore. In poor visibility, be sure you are approaching either safely west of Les Hanois or east of Platte Fougère.

## Les Hanois

The rocks off the southwest tip of Guernsey extend 1¾ miles WNW of Pleinmont Point, over ½ mile seaward of the lighthouse. Give this corner a safe berth, particularly when rounding from the N and especially if the tide is NE going as you approach Les Hanois.

## Guernsey South Coast

Guernsey's south coast is relatively steep-to, but the west end has several patches – notably Les Kaines (drying 1.2m) and Les Lieuses (drying 4–5m) – which lie nearly ½ mile offshore. Give these dangers a wide berth at half-tide or below.

## COASTAL DANGERS

### Alderney Race

Streams are powerful in the Alderney Race, with areas of heavy overfalls especially on a weather-going tide. Spring rates reach 5–6 knots through most of the Race, but 8–9 knots locally.

### The Swinge

The Swinge channel, between Alderney and Burhou, can kick up savage overfalls with even a light wind over the tide. Spring rates can reach 6–7 knots and the Swinge should be taken as near slack water as possible, at around half-tide (up or down) at Braye Harbour.

### The Casquets

Although the main island of the Casquets is comparatively steep-to and can be passed within ½ mile on its west side, the whole area around these reefs is notorious for strong tides, patches of overfalls and an uneasy swell. Strangers on passage are advised to leave Casquets lighthouse a good 1½–2 miles to the east.

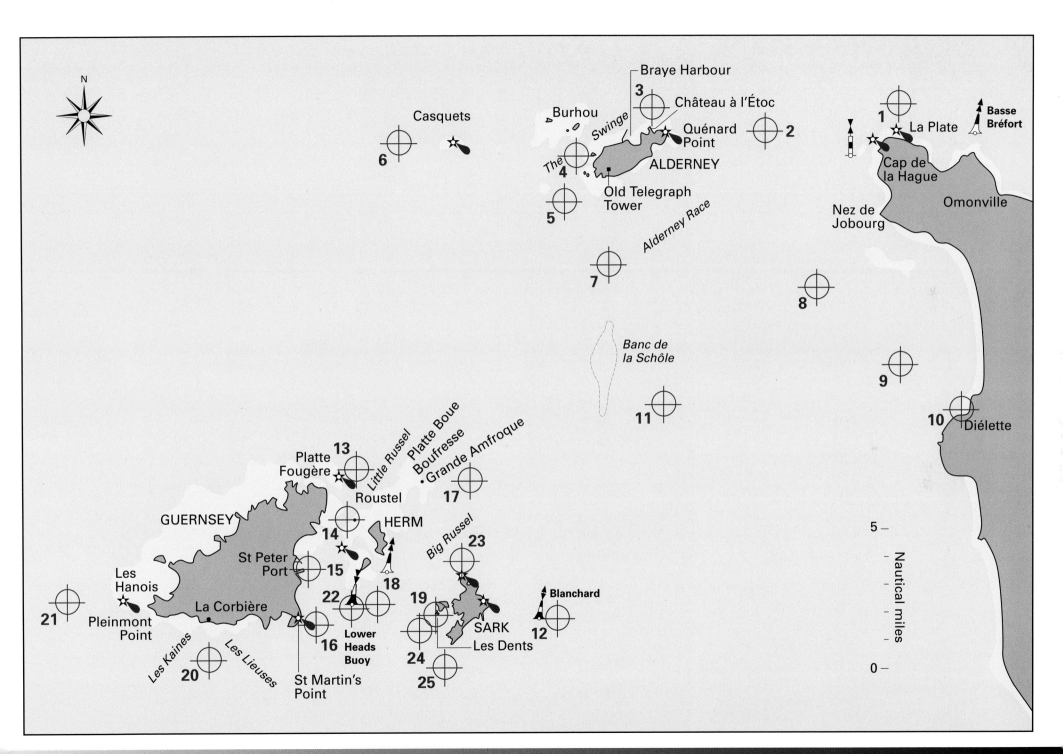

N

Casquets
6

Burhou
Braye Harbour
3
Château à l'Étoc
Quénard
Point
The Swinge
4
ALDERNEY
2
Old Telegraph
Tower
5
Alderney Race
7
Banc de
la Schôle
11

1
La Plate
Basse
Bréfort
Cap de
la Hague
Omonville
Nez de
Jobourg
8
9
10
Diélette

Platte Boue
Boufresse
13
Platte
Fougère
Little Russel
Grande Amfroque
Roustel
17
GUERNSEY
HERM
14
Big Russel
23
St Peter
Port
15
18
19
Blanchard
Les
Hanois
22
24
SARK
12
21
La Corbière
Lower
Heads
Buoy
16
Les Dents
25
Pleinmont
Point
Les Kaines
Les Lieuses
20
St Martin's
Point

5 —

Nautical miles

0 —

# 39 Guernsey, Jersey and Roches Douvres

| ⊕ | Waypoint name and position | Latitude | Longitude |
|---|---|---|---|
| 39 1 | Little Russel north, 9ca 067°T from Platte Fougère lighthouse | 49°31.183′N | 002°27.866′W |
| 39 2 | Roustel, 1ca due W of BW tower | 49°29.230′N | 002°28.970′W |
| 39 3 | St Peter Port, 1ca ENE of Castle pierhead | 49°27.347′N | 002°31.309′W |
| 39 4 | Little Russel south, 6ca ESE of St Martin's lighthouse | 49°25.100′N | 002°30.840′W |
| 39 5 | Big Russel north, 2M E of Grande Amfroque beacons | 49°30.578′N | 002°21.569′W |
| 39 6 | Big Russel south, 1M E of Lower Heads buoy | 49°25.850′N | 002°27.020′W |
| 39 7 | Guernsey south coast, 1½M S of Corbière tower | 49°23.745′N | 002°37.154′W |
| 39 8 | Les Hanois, 2M due W of lighthouse | 49°26.100′N | 002°45.205′W |
| 39 9 | East Sark, ½M due E of Blanchard E-card buoy | 49°25.360′N | 002°16.660′W |
| 39 10 | Les Dirouilles West, 2¼M NE of Sorel Point N tip | 49°17.280′N | 002°07.180′W |
| 39 11 | Les Écrehou SW, 1½M NE of La Coupe Point, Jersey | 49°15.042′N | 001°59.907′W |
| 39 12 | Desormes West, 1ca W of Desormes W-card buoy | 49°18.940′N | 002°18.138′W |
| 39 13 | La Corbière West, 1.2M due W of lighthouse | 49°10.790′N | 002°16.837′W |
| 39 14 | Noirmont Point, 2ca due S of lighthouse | 49°09.710′N | 002°10.080′W |
| 39 15 | St Helier entrance, 2¼ca 200°T from Platte beacon | 49°09.944′N | 002°07.466′W |
| 39 16 | Roches Douvres west clearing, 3M WNW of lighthouse | 49°07.431′N | 002°53.071′W |
| 39 17 | Roches Douvres east, 3½M due E of lighthouse | 49°06.300′N | 002°43.584′W |
| 39 18 | Lower Heads south clearing, 1ca due S of S-card buoy | 49°25.750′N | 002°28.550′W |
| 39 19 | Sark south clearing, 9ca 230°T from S tip of L'Étac | 49°23.480′N | 002°23.090′W |
| 39 20 | Les Trois Grunes north clearing, 6ca due N of buoy | 49°22.440′N | 001°55.210′W |
| 39 21 | Les Trois Grunes west, ¼M due west of W-card buoy | 49°21.840′N | 001°55.577′W |
| 39 22 | Les Trois Grunes south clearing, 6ca due S of buoy | 49°21.240′N | 001°55.210′W |

## Refer to Charts
Admiralty charts 2669, 3654, 3655
Imray C33A, 2500.1

## Jersey North Coast
Approaching Jersey from northward, especially direct from the Alderney Race, avoid the Paternosters which lie 2–3 miles offshore between Grosnez Point and Sorel Point. Further east, from 3–5 miles off the NE corner of Jersey, are Les Dirouilles plateau and the numerous reefs around Les Écrehou islands.

## La Corbière Point
Drying rocks lurk up to ½ mile west and WNW of La Corbière. Rounding the point from the north to line up for the Western Passage to St Helier, stay at least ¾ mile west of the lighthouse until you have passed nicely south of it and cleared these dangers.

## Roches Douvres
The Roches Douvres plateau is about two miles across from west to east and 1½ miles from north to south. The tides set strongly in this area, especially between Roches Douvres and Plateau de Barnouic. It is important to pass both these areas of rocks a distance off, preferably keeping 'down-tide' of the dangers. The clearing waypoints in this directory have been set with this in mind.

## COASTAL DANGERS

### Guernsey North Coast
Along the northwest coast of Guernsey, between Les Hanois and Platte Fougère, dangers extend up to two miles offshore. In poor visibility, be sure you are approaching either safely west of Les Hanois or east of Platte Fougère.

### Les Hanois
The rocks off the southwest tip of Guernsey extend 1¾ miles WNW of Pleinmont Point, more than ½ mile seaward of the lighthouse. Give this corner a safe berth, particularly when rounding from the north and if the tide is northeast-going as you approach Les Hanois.

### Guernsey South Coast
Guernsey's south coast is relatively steep-to, but the west end has several patches – notably Les Kaines (drying 1.2m) and Les Lieuses (drying 4–5m) – which lie nearly ½ mile offshore. Give these dangers a wide berth at half-tide or below.

### Herm
The island of Herm is surrounded by large expanses of drying rocks. Approaching the north end of the Little Russel channel from the direction of Alderney, be sure you are well north of Platte Boue and Boufresse.

### Sark
There are many off-lying rocks around Sark, especially on the northeast side between Bec du Nez and Creux Harbour, and off the south and west coasts of Little Sark. The streams round Sark can be strong, up to four or five knots at springs off the east and west coasts, up to six knots in the Goulet between Creux Harbour and Les Burons Rocks, and up to seven knots in the Gouliot Passage between Brecqhou and the west coast. Night navigation around Sark is not advisable.

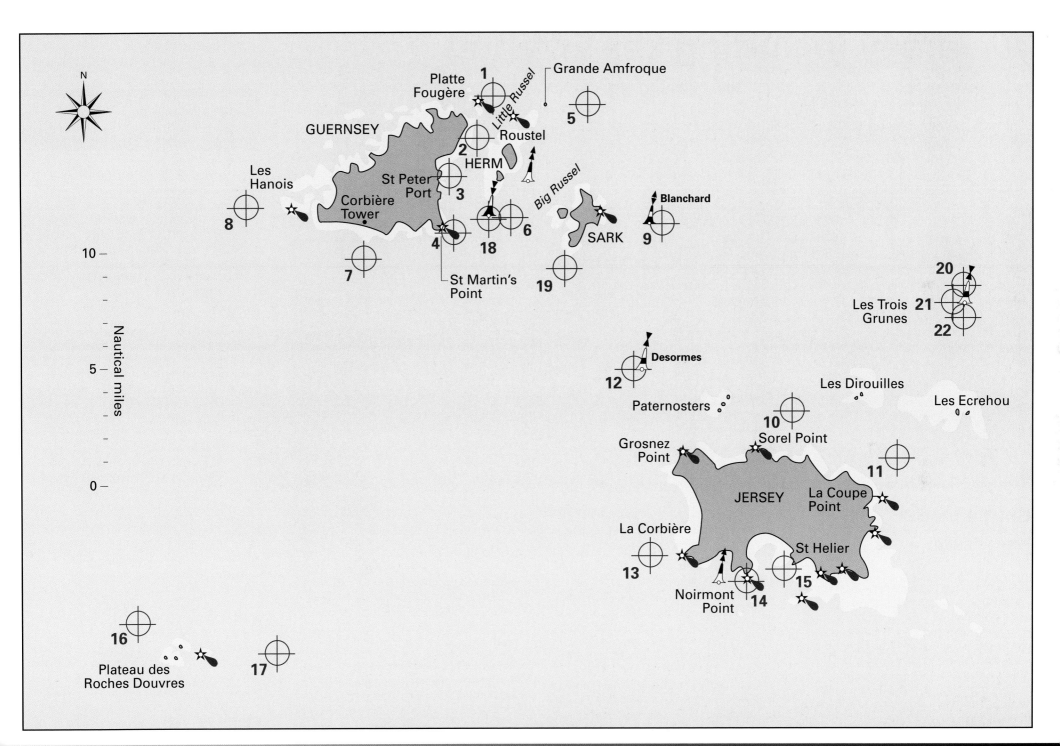

N

GUERNSEY

Platte
Fougère

1

Grande Amfroque

5

Little Russel

Roustel

2

HERM

Les
Hanois

St Peter
Port

3

Big Russel

Blanchard

8

Corbière
Tower

4

18

6

SARK

9

7

St Martin's
Point

19

20

Les Trois
Grunes

21

22

Desormes

12

Paternosters

Les Dirouilles

Les Ecrehou

10

Sorel Point

Grosnez
Point

11

La Corbière

JERSEY

La Coupe
Point

13

St Helier

16

Noirmont
Point

14

15

17

Plateau des
Roches Douvres

10

Nautical miles

5

0

# 40 Jersey including Les Écrehou

| ⊕ | | Waypoint name and position | Latitude | Longitude |
|---|---|---|---|---|
| 40 | 1 | Déroute N outer, 5M 230°T from Cap de Carteret lighthouse | 49°19.231′N | 001°54.267′W |
| 40 | 2 | Déroute N inner, 8ca E of Écrevière S-card buoy | 49°15.270′N | 001°50.930′W |
| 40 | 3 | Écrevière, ¼M due S of Écrevière S-card buoy | 49°15.020′N | 001°52.130′W |
| 40 | 4 | Les Écrehou approach, 1½M 202°T from Bigorne rock | 49°15.740′N | 001°55.770′W |
| 40 | 5 | Les Dirouilles West, 2¼M NE of Sorel Point N tip | 49°17.280′N | 002°07.180′W |
| 40 | 6 | Les Écrehou SW, 1½M NE of La Coupe Point, Jersey | 49°15.042′N | 001°59.907′W |
| 40 | 7 | Desormes West, 1ca W of Desormes W-card buoy | 49°18.940′N | 002°18.138′W |
| 40 | 8 | Plemont Point, ¾M NE of headland NE tip | 49°16.160′N | 002°12.780′W |
| 40 | 9 | Grosnez West, 3½M due W of Grosnez Point lighthouse | 49°15.500′N | 002°20.190′W |
| 40 | 10 | La Corbière West, 1.2M due W of lighthouse | 49°10.790′N | 002°16.837′W |
| 40 | 11 | La Corbière SW, 2½M SW of lighthouse on leading line | 49°09.050′N | 002°17.704′W |
| 40 | 12 | La Corbière South, 1M due S of lighthouse | 49°09.790′N | 002°15.010′W |
| 40 | 13 | Noirmont Point, 2ca due S of lighthouse | 49°09.710′N | 002°10.080′W |
| 40 | 14 | St Helier entrance, 2¼ca 200°T from Platte beacon | 49°09.944′N | 002°07.466′W |
| 40 | 15 | East Passage outer, 2ca S of Demie de Pas beacon | 49°08.810′N | 002°06.150′W |
| 40 | 16 | Canger Rock West, ½M NW of W-card buoy | 49°07.705′N | 002°00.921′W |
| 40 | 17 | Frouquier Aubert, ¾M due S of S-card buoy | 49°05.330′N | 001°58.840′W |
| 40 | 18 | Violet SW, 6ca WSW of Violet fairway buoy | 49°07.581′N | 001°57.973′W |
| 40 | 19 | Violet North, 8½ca 353°T from Violet fairway buoy | 49°08.660′N | 001°57.270′W |
| 40 | 20 | Gorey SE, 1.6M 118°T from Gorey pierhead | 49°11.047′N | 001°59.212′W |
| 40 | 21 | Gorey NE outer, 1¾M 050°T from Mont Orgueil | 49°13.080′N | 001°59.090′W |
| 40 | 22 | Gorey NE inner, 7ca 050°T from Mont Orgueil | 49°12.393′N | 002°00.344′W |

### Refer to Charts
Admiralty charts 1136, 1137, 1138, 3655
Imray C33A, 2500.4, 2500.5, 2500.6

St Helier. The Western Passage is the main 'big-ship' channel to St Helier, leading close along Jersey's southwest coast inside the off-lying dangers. Arriving from the east and south, most boats use the Eastern Passage which leads between the Hinguette Rocks and the coastal dangers north of the Demie de Pas beacon tower.

## Violet Bank
This vast area of drying rocks lies off the southeast corner of Jersey, extending southeast from La Rocque Point for over three miles. Although the Violet Bank looks pretty horrific on a chart, the dangers are reasonably compact on the south side, and the passage between St Helier and Gorey via the Violet Channel is fairly straightforward in reasonable visibility. Perhaps the greatest care is needed when on passage between St Helier and Granville, when the various drying dangers extending southeastwards beyond the Violet Bank need to be left well clear to the north.

## Jersey East Coast
The east side of the Violet Bank extends eastwards for up to two miles off La Rocque Point, with drying dangers extending north to Grouville Bay and the southeast approaches to Gorey. The seaward side of these dangers is marked by various spar beacons, but care must be taken that these are not confused. Outlying reefs also extend east and southeast of the Violet fairway buoy and their beacons must be identified with care as you come through the Violet Channel.

## COASTAL DANGERS

### Pierres de Lecq
This plateau of drying and above-water rocks, also known as the Paternosters, lies between 1½ and three miles off the west end of Jersey's north coast, between Grosnez Point and Sorel Point. The plateau is about 1¼ miles across and represents a particular danger for boats arriving off the northwest corner of Jersey direct from the Alderney Race, or for vessels coasting inshore around Jersey. The Desormes W-cardinal buoy lies just over three miles WNW of Pierres de Lecq.

Further east, from 3–5 miles off the northeast corner of Jersey, are Les Dirouilles plateau and the numerous reefs around Les Écrehou islands.

### Jersey West Coast
Rocky shoals extend up to a mile seaward of Jersey's west coast and boats should keep well off St Ouen Bay when approaching Corbière Point from the north, or when bound northwards having rounded Corbière. The Rigdon Bank, a couple of miles southeast of Grosnez Point, should be avoided except in quiet weather. The Rigdon has only 3m over it at chart datum

and any swell can break heavily over these shoals in even a moderate onshore wind.

### La Corbière
Drying rocks lurk up to ½ mile W and WNW of La Corbière. Rounding the point from the north to line up for the Western Passage to St Helier, stay at least ¾ mile W of the lighthouse until you have passed nicely south of it and cleared these dangers.

### Approaches to St Helier
There are numerous drying rocks off the south coast of Jersey, through or inside which lead the various approach passages to

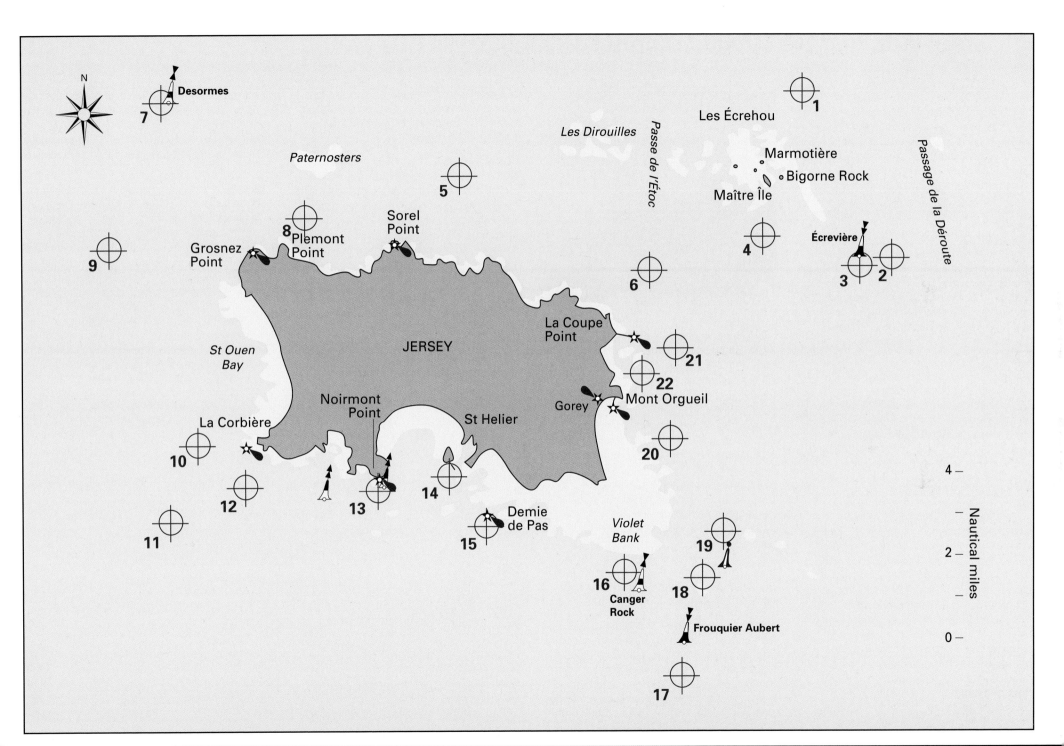

N

Desormes

7

Paternosters

Les Dirouilles

Passe de l'Étoc

Les Écrehou

Marmotière

Bigorne Rock

Maître Île

1

Passage de la Déroute

5

8 Plemont
Point

Sorel
Point

Grosnez
Point

9

6

4

Écrevière

3    2

La Coupe
Point

JERSEY

21

St Ouen
Bay

22

Gorey    Mont Orgueil

La Corbière

Noirmont
Point

St Helier

20

10

14

12    13

Demie
de Pas

Violet
Bank

19

11

15

16

18

Canger
Rock

Frouquier Aubert

17

4 —

— 3

Nautical miles

2 —

— 1

0 —

Various drying rocks, some marked by beacons, litter the east approaches to Gorey. Just over one mile seaward of Gorey harbour, parts of the Banc du Château have less than 1m over them, and the shallowest part of the Middle Bank has only 0.4m at chart datum. There are numerous rocks off and in St Catherine Bay, just north of Gorey, which become significant below half-tide.

## Les Écrehou

This fascinating plateau of reefs and islets can be visited in quiet weather, but pilotage around Les Écrehou needs great care, especially as the tides are very strong in this area. Strangers should approach from the SSW using the waypoints given in this directory and following the advice of a reliable pilot book.

A good time to arrive is around half-ebb, when there is plenty of water in the approach channel but enough of the key rocks exposed to make them clearly visible. The visitors' buoys off Gorey offer a convenient point of departure for a day trip to Les Écrehou. GPS has made it much simpler and safer to visit intriguing rocky corners such as the anchorage south of Marmotière island.

## Crab-pot buoys

Watch out for crab-pot floats all around Jersey and Les Écrehou, especially during strong spring tides when even the largest buoys can be pulled under until they are almost invisible. Catching one of these lines round a rudder or skeg can be serious if a boat is then held stern-to the powerful streams, which can reach five knots in places. This is one of the most significant hazards of night navigation around the Channel Islands.

## Drifting net

The waters around Jersey have become renowned for discarded pieces of net drifting just below the surface – a menace to yachts and motor boats alike. The area between Jersey and Plateau des Minquiers seems particularly prone, and also the popular route to St Malo between Les Minquiers and Iles Chausey. Some of these abandoned nets can be extremely large, but even quite a small section round a prop can put a yacht in danger. So when motoring in calm weather around the Channel Islands, Les Minquiers or Chausey, be sure to pass down-tide of dangers where possible. With no wind you need time to think if a tough piece of net jumps onto the prop – time to try shifting ahead and astern, call a nearby boat or put out a Pan-Pan if things look dicey; maybe anchor if depth allows.

## Beware half-tide

Half-tide around Jersey is when the streams are most powerful, but is also the time when many rocky shoals are at their most dangerous – neither safely covered, nor easily visible. At high water you can sail over many of the nasty green areas marked on the chart and at low water it's usually patently obvious that you can't, but half-tide can catch even professional mariners and fishermen unawares.

## Fast Ferries

Fast ferries operate between Guernsey, Jersey and St Malo, with service speeds up to 37 knots in any reasonable weather. Yachts and motor boats must keep from under the feet of these monsters and you can take simple precautions by staying slightly off the regular tram-lines that fast ferries follow.

On passage between St Malo and Jersey, fast ferries usually leave the St Malo estuary east of Ile de Cézembre by the Grande Conchée passage and then head just east of north for the SE Minquiers buoy. With a reasonable rise of tide they then strike due north along the 2°W line of longitude, passing east of the main body of Les Minquiers as far as the North Minquiers buoy, and thence direct to the Demie de Pas beacon off St Helier. Nearer low water, however, they go round the NE Minquiers buoy to give the Caux des Minquiers reefs a wide berth.

Fast ferries on passage from Jersey to Guernsey come out of St Helier by the Western Passage, usually keep a mile west of La Corbière lighthouse and then head directly for a position about half a mile east of St Peter Port pierheads. You can easily draw these routes on your Channel Islands passage chart and aim to stay clear of them if only by a quarter mile or so. You'll be pleased you did this if poor visibility clamps in, especially if you ever hear the snarl of one of these ferries approaching, or see a huge bold echo moving at astonishing speed across your radar screen.

| ⊕ | | Waypoint name and position | Latitude | Longitude |
|---|---|---|---|---|
| 41 | 1 | La Corbière West, 1.2M due W of lighthouse | 49°10.790'N | 002°16.837'W |
| 41 | 2 | La Corbière SW, 2½M SW of lighthouse on leading line | 49°09.050'N | 002°17.704'W |
| 41 | 3 | La Corbière South, 1M due S of lighthouse | 49°09.790'N | 002°15.010'W |
| 41 | 4 | Noirmont Point, 2ca due S of lighthouse | 49°09.710'N | 002°10.080'W |
| 41 | 5 | St Helier entrance, 2¼ca 200°T from Platte beacon | 49°09.944'N | 002°07.466'W |
| 41 | 6 | East Passage outer, 2ca S of Demie de Pas beacon | 49°08.810'N | 002°06.150'W |
| 41 | 7 | Canger Rock West, ½M NW of W-card buoy | 49°07.705'N | 002°00.921'W |
| 41 | 8 | Frouquier Aubert, ¾M due S of S-card buoy | 49°05.330'N | 001°58.840'W |
| 41 | 9 | Violet SW, 6ca WSW of Violet fairway buoy | 49°07.581'N | 001°57.973'W |
| 41 | 10 | Violet North, 8½ca 353°T from Violet fairway buoy | 49°08.660'N | 001°57.270'W |
| 41 | 11 | Gorey SE, 1.6M 118°T from Gorey pierhead | 49°11.047'N | 001°59.212'W |
| 41 | 12 | Gorey NE outer, 1¾M 050°T from Mont Orgueil | 49°13.080'N | 001°59.090'W |
| 41 | 13 | Gorey NE inner, 7ca 050°T from Mont Orgueil | 49°12.393'N | 002°00.344'W |
| 41 | 14 | Les Minquiers Demie de Vascelin buoy, actual position | 49°00.810'N | 002°05.170'W |
| 41 | 15 | N Minquiers N-card buoy, actual position | 49°01.640'N | 002°00.580'W |
| 41 | 16 | NE Minquiers, 1ca 060°T from E-card buoy | 49°00.894'N | 001°55.146'W |
| 41 | 17 | Les Ardentes NE, 4.66M 356°T from L'Enseigne beacon | 48°58.310'N | 001°50.810'W |
| 41 | 18 | Les Ardentes W, 3.2M 192°T from NE Minquiers E-card buoy | 48°57.738'N | 001°56.249'W |
| 41 | 19 | Chausey N approach, 2M 336°T from L'Enseigne beacon | 48°55.490'N | 001°51.580'W |
| 41 | 20 | Chausey N entrance, 1M 336°T from L'Enseigne beacon | 48°54.580'N | 001°50.970'W |
| 41 | 21 | L'État clearing, 7ca NE of L'État BW beacon | 48°55.170'N | 001°45.460'W |
| 41 | 22 | Chausey NE clearing, 6ca NE of Canuettes E-card beacon tower | 48°54.470'N | 001°43.600'W |
| 41 | 23 | Chausey East, midway between Anvers and Le Founet buoys | 48°53.560'N | 001°41.630'W |
| 41 | 24 | Pointe du Roc NW, 1¼M 297°T from lighthouse | 48°50.640'N | 001°38.460'W |
| 41 | 25 | St Germain-sur-Ay offing, 4M 247°T from conspic. house at St Germain-sur-Ay Plage | 49°12.048'N | 001°44.199'W |
| 41 | 26 | Basse Jourdan E, 1ca E of Basse Jourdan E-card buoy | 49°06.850'N | 001°43.800'W |
| 41 | 27 | Le Sénéquet clearing, 2½M W of Le Sénéquet lighthouse | 49°05.480'N | 001°43.535'W |
| 41 | 28 | Les Nattes clearing, ¾M W of Les Nattes buoy | 49°03.460'N | 001°43.000'W |
| 41 | 29 | La Catheue East, 8ca E of La Catheue buoy | 48°57.670'N | 001°42.740'W |
| 41 | 30 | Anvers east, 6ca E of Anvers E-card buoy | 48°53.906'N | 001°40.166'W |
| 41 | 31 | Chausey S approach, 1M 152°T from La Crabière-Est beacon | 48°51.594'N | 001°48.699'W |
| 41 | 32 | Chausey S entrance, ½M 152°T from La Crabière-Est beacon | 48°52.042'N | 001°49.060'W |
| 41 | 33 | Chausey SW, ¾M SW of La Cancalaise S-card beacon | 48°51.376'N | 001°51.919'W |
| 41 | 34 | Chausey W, 2.8M 260°T from L'Enseigne BW beacon | 48°53.213'N | 001°54.554'W |
| 41 | 35 | SE Minquiers, 2ca 130°T of SE Minquiers E-card buoy | 48°53.297'N | 001°59.857'W |
| 41 | 36 | S Minquiers, 2ca S of S Minquiers S-card buoy | 48°53.090'N | 002°10.100'W |
| 41 | 37 | SW Minquiers W-card buoy, actual position | 48°54.350'N | 002°19.410'W |
| 41 | 38 | NW Minquiers N-card buoy, actual position | 48°59.630'N | 002°20.590'W |

## Refer to Charts

Admiralty charts 1137, 3655, 3656
Imray C33B, 2500.7

## COASTAL DANGERS

### Plateau des Minquiers

This notorious plateau of reefs, islets and banks lies about 10 miles south of Jersey. The total extent of the Minquiers is almost as large as Jersey itself, with the main drying areas of sand and rock comprising some 25 square miles. The edges of the plateau are guarded by cardinal buoys, and the only outcrop large enough to count as a real island is Maitresse Ile, near the eastern edge of the reefs. Strangers passing around Plateau des Minquiers, either west or east-about, should stay outside the area bounded by the six main cardinal buoys.

### Iles Chausey

This compact plateau of reefs and islets lies about 20 miles southeast of Jersey. The Chausey plateau is just over six miles wide from east to west and three miles from north to south.

The limit of dangers is mostly fairly obvious and steep-to, but you should be careful to keep a safe offing when skirting the west side of Chausey, perhaps en route between St Helier and the south entrance to Chausey Sound.

### Les Ardentes

This rather nasty reef lies just over three miles southeast of the NE Minquiers E-cardinal buoy and a similar distance north of the Chausey plateau. Les Ardentes is covered most of the time, drying 2.1m at chart datum but needs watching below half-tide. The reef is marked on its east side by an E-cardinal buoy.

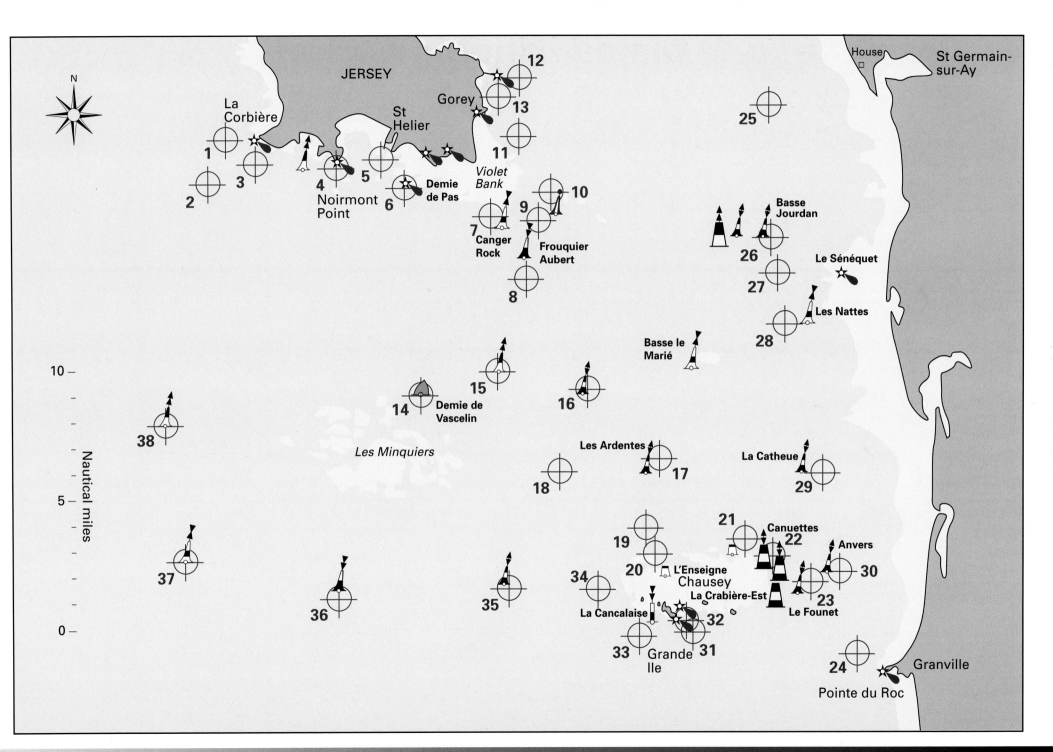

JERSEY

La Corbière

1

2

3

4 Noirmont Point

5

6 Demie de Pas

St Helier

Gorey

12

13

11 Violet Bank

7 Canger Rock

8

9

10

Frouquier Aubert

House

St Germain-sur-Ay

25

Basse Jourdan

26

27 Le Sénéquet

28 Les Nattes

Basse le Marié

14 Demie de Vascelin

15

16

Les Minquiers

Les Ardentes

17

18

La Catheue

29

19

20

21

22 Canuettes

Anvers

30

34 L'Enseigne Chausey

La Crabière-Est

23 Le Founet

38

37

36

35

La Cancalaise

32

33 Grande Ile

31

24 Pointe du Roc

Granville

10

Nautical miles

5

0

N

# *42* Granville to St Malo including Cancale

| ⊕ | | Waypoint name and position | Latitude | Longitude |
|---|----|---------------------------------------------------------|------------|-------------|
| 42 | 1 | Pointe du Roc NW, 1¼M 297°T from lighthouse | 48°50.640'N | 001°38.460'W |
| 42 | 2 | Granville approach, 7ca 210°T from Pointe du Roc lighthouse | 48°49.460'N | 001°37.310'W |
| 42 | 3 | Granville marina approach, 100m S of Jetée Ouest pierhead | 48°49.810'N | 001°36.230'W |
| 42 | 4 | Le Videcoq clearing, 2ca S of Videcoq W-card buoy | 48°49.460'N | 001°42.060'W |
| 42 | 5 | Pierre d'Herpin E, 1.3M E of Pierre d'Herpin lighthouse | 48°43.772'N | 001°46.956'W |
| 42 | 6 | La Fille clearing, 2ca N of La Fille N-cardinal buoy | 48°44.360'N | 001°48.460'W |
| 42 | 7 | Le Grand Ruet, ¼M NE of Herpin islet | 48°43.455'N | 001°49.592'W |
| 42 | 8 | Vieille Rivière N, between Ruet and Grande Bunouze buoys | 48°43.250'N | 001°50.550'W |
| 42 | 9 | Pointe Chatry, ¼M E of headland | 48°41.802'N | 001°50.357'W |
| 42 | 10 | Cancale N approach, 2ca NW of Ile des Rimains N tip | 48°41.150'N | 001°49.830'W |
| 42 | 11 | Chenal de la Bigne outer, 1.3M N of Pointe du Meinga | 48°43.460'N | 001°56.230'W |
| 42 | 12 | Rochefort clearing, ½M N of W-card beacon tower | 48°43.392'N | 001°58.295'W |
| 42 | 13 | Petits Pointus outer, 1M 035°T from St Servantine buoy | 48°42.760'N | 002°00.100'W |
| 42 | 14 | Grande Conchée outer, 1½M 015°T from La Conchée fort | 48°42.504'N | 002°02.051'W |
| 42 | 15 | La Petite Porte outer, 150m NE of fairway buoy | 48°41.436'N | 002°07.204'W |
| 42 | 16 | La Petite Porte inner, 3ca 310°T from Le Grand Jardin | 48°40.390'N | 002°05.320'W |
| 42 | 17 | La Grande Porte outer, 75m SW of No.2 red buoy | 48°40.332'N | 002°07.401'W |
| 42 | 18 | Le Grand Jardin West, 250m W of Le Grand Jardin | 48°40.210'N | 002°05.180'W |
| 42 | 19 | Le Buron, 100m NE of Le Buron green tower | 48°39.360'N | 002°03.610'W |
| 42 | 20 | St Malo entrance, 125m SW of main north pierhead | 48°38.453'N | 002°02.030'W |

## Refer to Charts

Admiralty charts 2700, 3659
Imray C33B, 2500.7, 2500.8

## COASTAL DANGERS

### Approaches to Granville

The approaches to Granville are shallow and rough in strong westerlies or southwesterlies although the area is sheltered from any long fetch by Iles Chausey and Plateau des Minquiers to the WNW and by the mainland coast to the southwest.

Coastal shoals extend several miles seaward of Granville, both north and south of Pointe du Roc. The shallowest areas lie up to three miles SSW of Granville, with drying patches on the Banc de Tombelaine and further seaward. Strangers should only approach Granville within two hours of local high water.

## Baie du Mont St Michel

This wide shallow bay starts to open up half-a-dozen miles south of Granville, a hostile area of powerful tides and drying sands. The prominent Mont St Michel, down in the southeast corner of the bay, is a rather eerie landmark as you cruise southwest from Granville. The Baie du Mont St Michel is best given a wide berth by boats, except for the northwest corner where the attractive drying harbour at Cancale or the anchorages a mile or two north of the harbour are straightforward enough to visit.

## Approaches to Cancale

There are various dangers as you approach Cancale from the north or northeast, but most are safely covered above half tide. In Le Grand Ruet channel, between Pierre d'Herpin lighthouse and Herpin islet, the Basse du Milieu rock only has 1.1m over it at chart datum. There are also overfalls and whirlpools in this channel during the strongest hours of the tide. About three cables NNW of Pointe du Grouin, the Grande Bunouze Rock (dries 1.6m) is marked on its seaward side by a N-cardinal buoy.

In the Grande Rade de Cancale, between Ile des Landes and Ile des Rimains, the Banc de Chatry has only 0.4m over it at chart datum. There is also a drying rock off the small headland ½ mile SSE of Pointe Chatry.

## Les Tintiaux

West of Pointe du Grouin, between Cancale and St Malo, various drying reefs lie up to one mile north of the coast. The most extensive are Les Tintiaux Rocks, up to ½ mile north and a mile northeast of Pointe du Meinga. About 1½ miles west of Les Tintiaux, the Rochefort rocks are marked by a W-cardinal beacon tower.

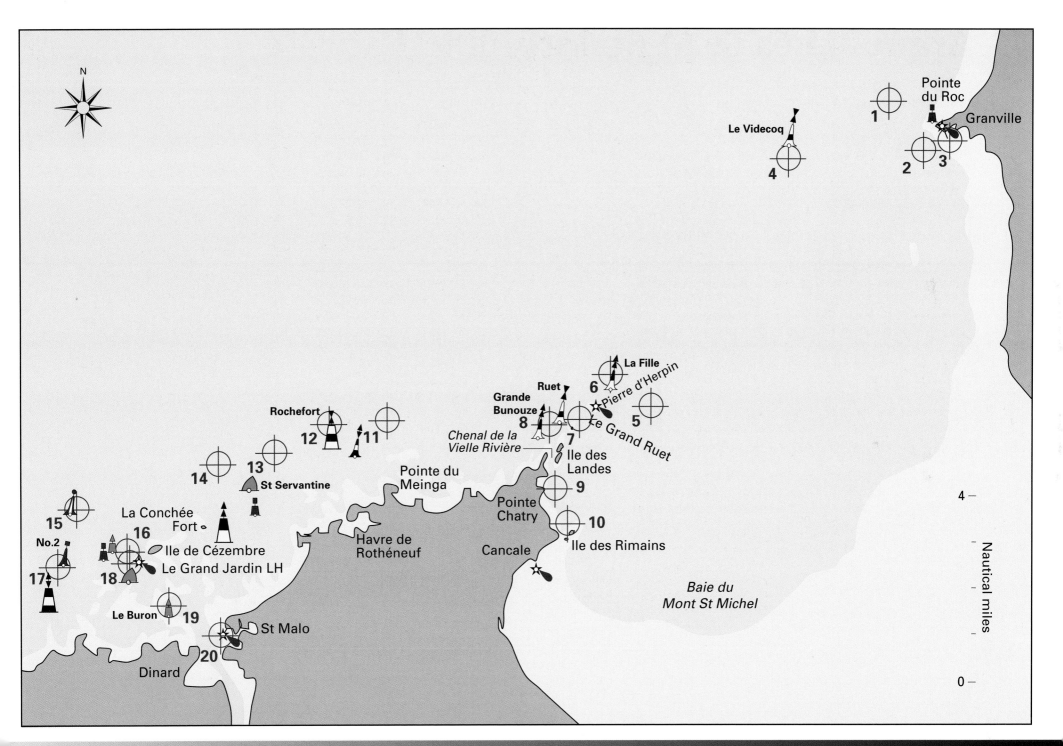

N

Pointe
du Roc

1

Granville

2  3

Le Videcoq

4

La Fille

Ruet

6  Pierre d'Herpin

Grande
Bunouze

8  7  Le Grand Ruet

5

Rochefort

Chenal de la
Vielle Rivière

9

Ile des
Landes

12  11

14  13

St Servantine

Pointe du
Meinga

Pointe
Chatry

10

Ile des Rimains

15

La Conchée
Fort

Ile de Cézembre

Havre de
Rothéneuf

Cancale

No.2

16

17  18

Le Grand Jardin LH

Baie du
Mont St Michel

Le Buron  19

St Malo

20

Dinard

4 —

0 —

Nautical miles

# *43* Approaches to St Malo

| ⊕ | | Waypoint name and position | Latitude | Longitude |
|---|---|---|---|---|
| 43 | 1 | Chenal de la Bigne outer, 1.3M N of Pointe du Meinga | 48°43.460'N | 001°56.230'W |
| 43 | 2 | Basse Rochefort, 110m SE of E-card buoy | 48°42.654'N | 001°57.253'W |
| 43 | 3 | Chenal de la Bigne inner, 100m E of La Bigne green beacon | 48°41.660'N | 001°58.640'W |
| 43 | 4 | Les Létruns, 75m SE of Les Létruns green buoy | 48°40.689'N | 002°00.582'W |
| 43 | 5 | Le Grand Bey, 7ca 007°T from Le Grand Bey fort | 48°39.850'N | 002°01.900'W |
| 43 | 6 | Le Petit Bey, 4ca 003°T from Le Petit Bey fort | 48°39.554'N | 002°02.256'W |
| 43 | 7 | Rochefort clearing, ½M N of W-card beacon tower | 48°43.392'N | 001°58.295'W |
| 43 | 8 | Petits Pointus outer, 1M 035°T from St Servantine buoy | 48°42.760'N | 002°00.100'W |
| 43 | 9 | St Servantine, ¼M E of St Servantine green buoy | 48°41.934'N | 002°00.567'W |
| 43 | 10 | Grande Conchée outer, 1½M 015°T from La Conchée fort | 48°42.504'N | 002°02.051'W |
| 43 | 11 | Grande Conchée inner, 3ca E of La Conchée fort | 48°41.053'N | 002°02.196'W |
| 43 | 12 | Rade de St Malo, ½M 123°T from Le Buron green tower | 48°39.051'N | 002°03.027'W |
| 43 | 13 | La Petite Porte outer, 150m NE of fairway buoy | 48°41.436'N | 002°07.204'W |
| 43 | 14 | La Petite Porte inner, 3ca 310°T from Le Grand Jardin | 48°40.390'N | 002°05.320'W |
| 43 | 15 | Le Grand Jardin West, 250m W of Le Grand Jardin | 48°40.210'N | 002°05.180'W |
| 43 | 16 | Le Buron, 100m NE of Le Buron green tower | 48°39.360'N | 002°03.610'W |
| 43 | 17 | St Malo entrance, 125m SW of main north pierhead | 48°38.453'N | 002°02.030'W |
| 43 | 18 | Banchenou, ¼M N of Banchenou green buoy | 48°40.690'N | 002°11.480'W |
| 43 | 19 | Vieux Banc NE, 300m NE of Vieux Banc N-card buoy | 48°42.492'N | 002°08.963'W |
| 43 | 20 | Vieux Banc SW, 2ca SW of Vieux Banc W-card buoy | 48°41.704'N | 002°10.419'W |
| 43 | 21 | La Grande Porte outer, 75m SW of No.2 red buoy | 48°40.332'N | 002°07.401'W |
| 43 | 22 | La Grande Porte inner, 1.4ca N of Boujaron green beacon | 48°40.310'N | 002°05.967'W |
| 43 | 23 | Le Décollé outer, 600m SW of No.2 red buoy | 48°39.972'N | 002°07.880'W |
| 43 | 24 | Le Décollé inner, ½M 314°T from Grand Genillet W beacon | 48°39.020'N | 002°06.410'W |

## Refer to Charts

Admiralty charts 2700, 3659
Imray C33B, 2500.8

## COASTAL DANGERS

### Strong tides

There are strong tides in the outer approaches to St Malo, especially at springs during the middle hours of the flood. Even navigators of fast motor boats need to allow for this when arriving off St Malo, especially as the mainland and Ile de Cézembre may be visible from some distance offshore in clear visibility. It is important not to become complacent about your arrival as soon as the outer marks have been spotted, because the view from offshore can change drastically with a strong cross-tide.

### East approaches to St Malo

The eastern approach channels to St Malo cut between numerous drying dangers within the area bounded by Pointe du Meinga, Rochefort beacon tower, Ile de Cézembre and Le Grand Bey and Petit Bey forts. The two channels – Chenal de la Grande Conchée and Chenal des Petits Pointus – are straightforward in reasonable visibility and at least two hours above low water.

The important outer marks when approaching St Malo from the east are Ile de Cézembre itself, La Grande Conchée fort and its outer above-water rocks, the St Servantine green buoy and Rochefort W-cardinal beacon tower.

The shallowest parts of the east approach channels are at their inner ends, where they converge to the north and northwest of Le Grand Bey and Le Petit Bey forts. Patches of this area almost dry at chart datum, although at ordinary low springs you can reckon on about 1.2m least depth in calm conditions.

There is plenty of rise of tide over these inner shallows within 3½–4 hours of local high water.

### West approaches to St Malo

There are numerous reefs and islets to the west and southwest of Ile de Cézembre, although the outer dangers are well marked by beacon towers and buoys. The two main west approach channels – Chenal de la Grande Porte and Chenal de la Petite Porte – converge and meet just west of Le Grand Jardin lighthouse, which stands not quite ½ mile southwest of Ile de Cézembre. From here, the wide buoyed fairway leads southeast for just over 2½ miles towards St Malo harbour entrance.

The outer mark for Chenal de la Petite Porte is the St Malo fairway buoy, about two miles northwest of Le Grand Jardin lighthouse. The outer mark for Chenal de la Grande Porte is the No.2 red whistle buoy, about 1¾ miles west of Le Grand Jardin.

Le Vieux Banc shoals and drying rock lie about 1¾ miles WNW of the St Malo fairway buoy, marked by a N-cardinal and a W-cardinal buoy. Be careful not to confuse these buoys in poor visibility, especially near low water.

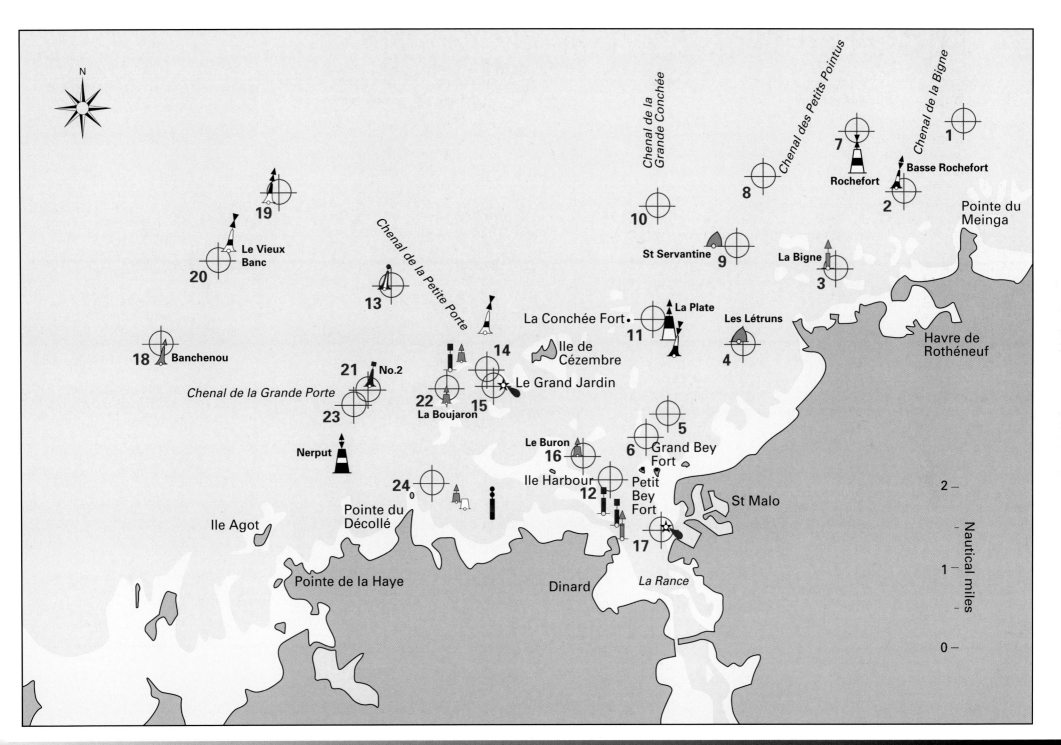

N

Chenal de la Bigne

Chenal des Petits Pointus

Chenal de la Grande Conchée

1

7
Rochefort

Basse Rochefort

2

Pointe du Meinga

8

10

St Servantine
9

La Bigne
3

Havre de Rothéneuf

19

Le Vieux Banc

20

Chenal de la Petite Porte

13

La Plate

La Conchée Fort

11

Les Létruns

4

Ile de Cézembre

14

18 Banchenou

Chenal de la Grande Porte

21 No.2

23

22
La Boujaron

15

Le Grand Jardin

5

Le Buron

16

Grand Bey Fort

6

Nerput

24

Ile Harbour

12

Petit Bey Fort

St Malo

Ile Agot

Pointe du Décollé

17

Pointe de la Haye

Dinard

La Rance

2 —

Nautical miles

1 —

0 —

# 44 St Cast to Erquy

| ⊕ | Waypoint name and position | Latitude | Longitude |
|---|---|---|---|
| 44 1 | Vieux Banc NE, 300m NE of Vieux Banc N-card buoy | 48°42.492'N | 002°08.963'W |
| 44 2 | Vieux Banc SW, 2ca SW of Vieux Banc W-card buoy | 48°41.704'N | 002°10.419'W |
| 44 3 | Banchenou, ¼M N of Banchenou green buoy | 48°40.690'N | 002°11.480'W |
| 44 4 | Les Bourdinots W, 3½ca W of Bourdinots E-card buoy | 48°39.010'N | 002°14.000'W |
| 44 5 | Les Bourdinots E, ¼M E of Bourdinots E-card buoy | 48°39.010'N | 002°13.108'W |
| 44 6 | St Cast entrance, just off marina breakwater | 48°38.381'N | 002°14.564'W |
| 44 7 | Pointe de la Garde, 2ca E of Pointe de la Garde N tip | 48°37.543'N | 002°14.075'W |
| 44 8 | Pointe de la Latte clearing, 6ca NE of La Latte fort | 48°40.540'N | 002°16.400'W |
| 44 9 | Cap Fréhel N clearing, ¾M N of Cap Fréhel lighthouse | 48°41.800'N | 002°19.130'W |
| 44 10 | Cap Fréhel W, 1M W of Cap Fréhel N tip | 48°41.275'N | 002°20.621'W |
| 44 11 | Roches d'Erquy N clearing, 4M N of Cap d'Erquy N tip | 48°42.740'N | 002°29.270'W |
| 44 12 | Les Justières, 4ca 170°T from S-card buoy | 48°40.170'N | 002°26.370'W |
| 44 13 | Chenal d'Erquy SW, 3ca NW of Cap d'Erquy | 48°38.952'N | 002°29.600'W |
| 44 14 | Roches d'Erquy W clearing, 1¼M 260°T from Landas buoy | 48°41.225'N | 002°33.149'W |
| 44 15 | Erquy NW approach outer, 1M 317°T from L'Evette beacon | 48°39.247'N | 002°32.480'W |
| 44 16 | Erquy NW approach inner, 9ca 295°T from outer mole head | 48°38.440'N | 002°29.910'W |
| 44 17 | Erquy W approach outer, 7ca 219°T from L'Evette beacon | 48°37.972'N | 002°32.118'W |
| 44 18 | Erquy W approach inner 1M 268°T from outer mole head | 48°38.030'N | 002°30.190'W |

## Refer to Charts

Admiralty charts 2029, 3659, 3672
Imray C33B

## Roches d'Erquy

An extensive area of drying and above-water rocks lies up to 2½ miles offshore to the north and northeast of Cap d'Erquy. Rohinet, 6m high, is the most obvious above-water rock near high water, but the reefs around Le Grand Pourier become prominent as the tide falls away.

There is a navigable channel, known as Chenal d'Erquy, between these rocks and the shore, passing south of Les Justières and Basses du Courant S-cardinal buoys. The northwest corner of Roches d'Erquy is marked by Les Landas N-cardinal buoy. The northeast corner is unmarked, except by reference to Les Justières S-cardinal buoy.

## COASTAL DANGERS

### Les Bourdinots

This small drying reef lies seven cables northeast of Pointe de St Cast, marked on its northeast edge by an E-cardinal buoy. Pointe de St Cast itself is fringed by drying ledges for about ¼ mile on its north and northeast sides.

### Pointe de la Latte

Basse de la Latte Rock, with only 0.7m over it, lies three cables north of the fort on Pointe de la Latte. Basse Raymonde, which dries 2.7m lies about four cables WNW of the fort. These rocks are only a practical danger if you are coast-hopping near low water.

### Cap Fréhel

A long narrow bank, known as Banc de l'Etendrée, extends for nearly one mile just east of Cap Fréhel. Depths over the bank change from time to time, but the shallowest part has about 1.5m over it at chart datum. At the far west end of this bank, just four cables east of Cap Fréhel lighthouse, Roche de l'Etendrée dries 3.9m and should be given a clear berth when rounding Fréhel.

### Plateau des Portes d'Erquy

This fairly compact plateau of drying and underwater rocks, not quite ¾ mile wide from west to east, lies about 1¼ miles west of Cap d'Erquy and is marked on its northeast edge by L'Evette N-cardinal beacon tower.

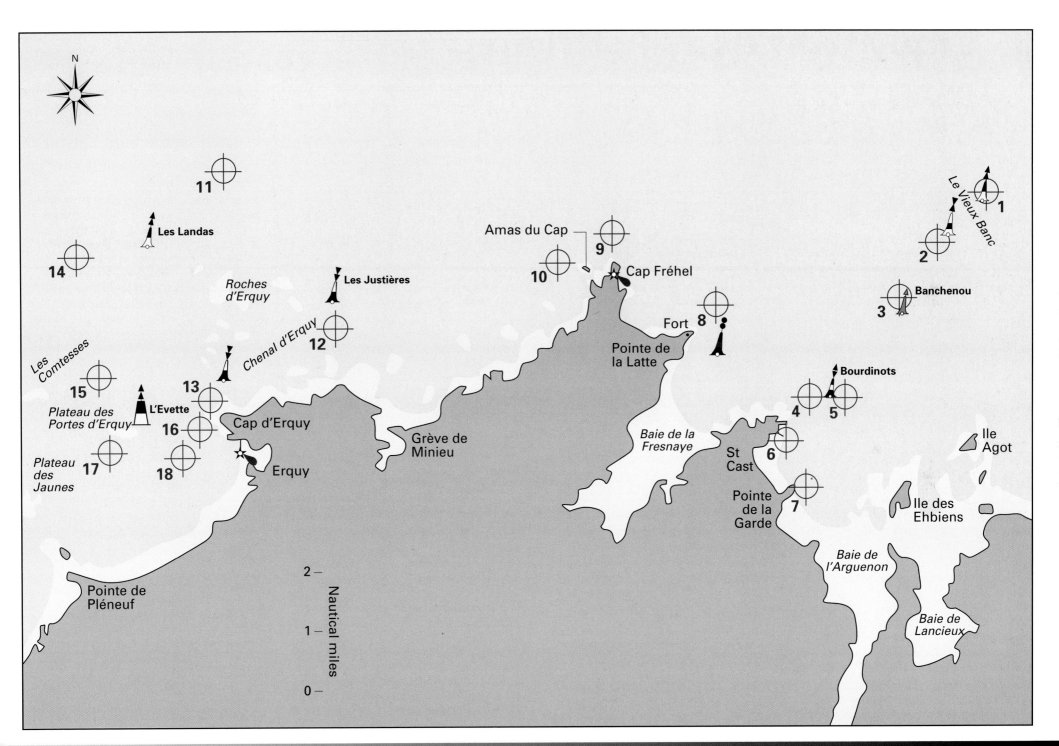

N

Le Vieux Banc

11

Les Landas

Amas du Cap

9

Cap Fréhel

10

Banchenou

3

Roches
d'Erquy

Les Justières

Fort

8

12

Pointe de
la Latte

Chenal d'Erquy

Bourdinots

Les Comtesses

13

Baie de la
Fresnaye

4    5

15

Plateau des
Portes d'Erquy

L'Evette

St
Cast

16

6

Cap d'Erquy

Grève de
Minieu

Plateau
des
Jaunes

17

18

Erquy

Pointe
de la
Garde

7

Ile
Agot

Ile des
Ehbiens

Baie de
l'Arguenon

Pointe de
Pléneuf

2 —

1 —

Nautical miles

0 —

Baie de
Lancieux

# Erquy to St Quay-Portrieux

| ⊕ | Waypoint name and position | Latitude | Longitude |
|---|---|---|---|
| 45 1 | Roches d'Erquy N clearing, 4M N of Cap d'Erquy N tip | 48°42.740'N | 002°29.270'W |
| 45 2 | Petit Léjon N, 1.4M N of W-card buoy | 48°43.200'N | 002°37.554'W |
| 45 3 | Petit Léjon S, 1M S of W-card buoy | 48°40.800'N | 002°37.554'W |
| 45 4 | Roches d'Erquy W clearing, 1¼M 260° from Landas buoy | 48°41.225'N | 002°33.149'W |
| 45 5 | Rohein W clearing, 1M W of Rohein W-card tower | 48°38.800'N | 002°39.280'W |
| 45 6 | Rohein S clearing, 9ca S of Rohein W-card tower | 48°37.900'N | 002°37.770'W |
| 45 7 | Chenal d'Erquy SW, 3ca NW of Cap d'Erquy N tip | 48°38.952'N | 002°29.600'W |
| 45 8 | Erquy NW approach outer, 1M 317° from L'Evette beacon | 48°39.247'N | 002°32.480'W |
| 45 9 | Erquy NW approach inner, 9ca 295°T from outer mole head | 48°38.440'N | 002°29.910'W |
| 45 10 | Erquy W approach outer, 7ca 219°T from L'Evette beacon | 48°37.972'N | 002°32.118'W |
| 45 11 | Erquy W approach inner 1M 268° from outer mole head | 48°38.030'N | 002°30.190'W |
| 45 12 | Les Jaunes north, 1M S of Les Comtesses main rock | 48°37.923'N | 002°34.499'W |
| 45 13 | Petit Bignon west, 1M W of W-card beacon | 48°36.824'N | 002°36.571'W |
| 45 14 | Dahouet approach, 1ca NE of Dahouet N-card buoy | 48°35.231'N | 002°35.327'W |
| 45 15 | Dahouet entrance, 200m NW of La Petite Muette tower | 48°34.890'N | 002°34.390'W |
| 45 16 | Le Légué fairway buoy actual position | 48°34.320'N | 002°41.150'W |
| 45 17 | Le Légué approach, ½M E of Pointe de Chatel Renault | 48°32.380'N | 002°42.330'W |
| 45 18 | Binic E approach, 1½M 096°T from E breakwater head | 48°35.915'N | 002°46.687'W |
| 45 19 | Binic entrance, ½ca SE of E breakwater head | 48°36.035'N | 002°48.929'W |
| 45 20 | St Quay SE approach, 2ca S of Roselière W-card buoy | 48°37.120'N | 002°46.187'W |
| 45 21 | St Quay entrance, 200m 138°T from E breakwater head | 48°38.768'N | 002°48.791'W |
| 45 22 | St Quay N approach, 6ca WNW of Madeux beacon tower | 48°40.620'N | 002°49.661'W |
| 45 23 | Grandes Moulières, 6ca 259°T from Ile Harbour lighthouse | 48°39.881'N | 002°49.386'W |
| 45 24 | Rade de St Quay, 2ca S of Les Noirs W-card buoy | 48°38.895'N | 002°48.462'W |

## Refer to Charts
Admiralty charts 2029, 3672
Imray C33B, C34

at least a quarter of a mile off to enter Erquy harbour from the NW.

**From the west:** You'd approach Erquy from this direction i.e. coming south of Rohein islet, if arriving from St Quay-Portrieux, Binic, Le Légué, or from Dahouet just round the corner on the other side of Pointe de Pléneuf. Simply leave Rohein W-cardinal beacon tower at least three quarters of a mile to the north and Petit Bignon W-cardinal beacon tower at least three quarters of a mile to the south while heading due east true towards Erquy. A couple of miles from Erquy, leave Plateau des Portes rocks (drying 9.4m and usually showing) 3–4 cables to port and L'Evette N-cardinal beacon tower half a mile to port and then make for the end of Erquy's outer mole.

### Plateau des Portes d'Erquy
This fairly compact plateau of drying and underwater rocks, not quite ¾ mile wide from west to east, lies about 1¼ miles west of Cap d'Erquy and is marked on its northeast edge by L'Evette N-cardinal beacon. Les Portes d'Erquy should be left clear to the north if you are coasting inshore between Erquy and Dahouet, Binic or St Quay-Portrieux.

### Plateau des Jaunes
This plateau of drying and above-water rocks extends up to 1¾ miles northwest of Pointe de Pléneuf and must be rounded with care when coasting between Erquy and Dahouet. Le Petit Bignon W-cardinal beacon guards the west edge of the plateau, but the highest rock of the plateau should be skirted by a good ¾ mile as you come round.

## COASTAL DANGERS

### Roches d'Erquy
An extensive area of drying and above-water rocks lies up to 2½ miles offshore to the north and northeast of Cap d'Erquy. Rohinet, 6m high, is the most obvious above-water rock near high water, but the reefs around Le Grand Pourier become prominent as the tide falls away.

There is a navigable channel, known as Chenal d'Erquy, between these rocks and the shore, passing south of Les Justières and

Basses du Courant S-cardinal buoys. The northwest corner of Roches d'Erquy is marked by Les Landas N-cardinal buoy. The northeast corner is unmarked, except by reference to Les Justières S-cardinal buoy.

### Approaching Erquy
**From the east:** Coming from Cap Fréhel by day in reasonable weather and visibility, the best approach is by Chenal d'Erquy, which is much simpler in practice than it looks on the chart. Having rounded Cap Fréhel by half a mile or so and skirted Amas du Cap islet, bring Amas du Cap into transit astern just

touching the north edge of Fréhel at 077°T. Follow this line for four miles until Les Justières S-cardinal buoy is four cables abeam to starboard and then continue for another half mile until Le Verdelet islet (42m high, 3.5 miles SW of Cap d'Erquy) is just open to the north of the large above-water rocks immediately off Cap d'Erquy, bearing 228°T. Come round to the SW on this new transit, but edge seaward of the line as you get near Cap d'Erquy, to leave Basses du Courant S-cardinal buoy fairly close to starboard. Skirt round Cap d'Erquy

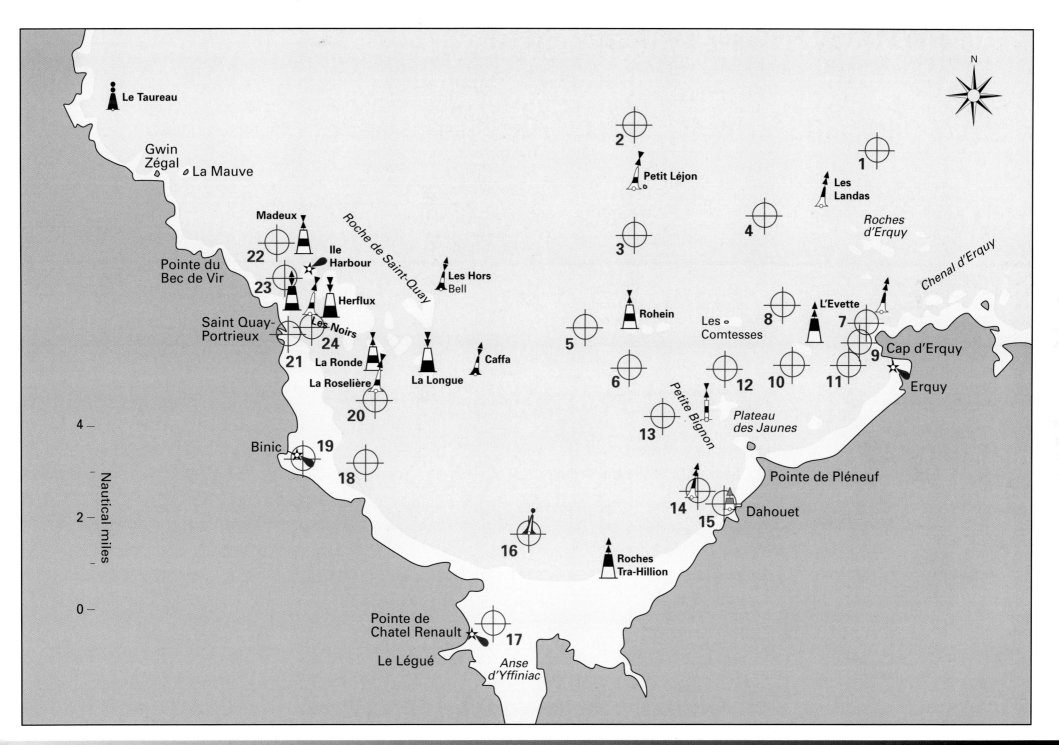

Le Taureau

Gwin
Zégal

La Mauve

Madeux

Roche de Saint-Quay

Ile
Harbour

Les Hors
Bell

2

Petit Léjon

1

Les
Landas

Roches
d'Erquy

Pointe du
Bec de Vir

22

23

Herflux

Les Noirs

24

4

3

Chenal d'Erquy

L'Evette

8

7

Saint Quay-
Portrieux

21

La Ronde

La Roselière

Caffa

La Longue

Rohein

Les
Comtesses

Cap d'Erquy

9

Erquy

5

6

12

10

11

20

13

Petite Bignon

Plateau
des Jaunes

4 —

Nautical miles

Binic

19

18

16

14

15

Dahouet

Pointe de Pléneuf

2 —

Roches
Tra-Hillion

0 —

Pointe de
Chatel Renault

17

Le Légué

Anse
d'Yffiniac

### Rohein

Towards the middle of Baie de St Brieuc, the Rohein W-cardinal tower marks the southwest corner of quite a wide but well-spaced, almost rectangular area of shoals and drying rocks. At the southeast corner are Les Comtesses reefs and at the northwest corner the long Banc des Dahouetins, parts of which have less than 1m depth at chart datum.

Yachts coasting between Erquy and Binic or St Quay-Portrieux would normally pass south of these dangers, leaving Rohein tower a mile or so to the north. Yachts making for Dahouet from Paimpol or Ile de Bréhat would come in through the wide gap between Rohein and the Roches de St Quay, leaving Rohein tower about one mile to the east.

### Petit Léjon

This small outlying reef, which dries 3.1m, lies a couple of miles north of the Rohein plateau and is marked on its west side by Petit Léjon W-cardinal buoy. Yachts on passage between Cap Fréhel and Paimpol would normally pass between Petit Léjon and Le Grand Léjon lighthouse, but the Petit Léjon buoy, being a W-cardinal, should be left well clear to the south in this case.

### Scallop boats

In and around the Bay of St Brieuc, you'll often see quite small fishing boats dredging scallops – those delicious Coquilles St Jacques for which Erquy and its restaurants are so famous. These boats are apt to change course quite dramatically and suddenly, so keep an eye on them if your paths are likely to cross. Be patient with them too, because they do an excellent job!

### Approaching Dahouet

Dahouet entrance lies just over a mile southwest of Pointe de Pléneuf and its prominent off-lying islet of Le Verdelet (42m high). The final approach to this fascinating inlet is made from the northwest, to avoid Plateau des Jaunes rocks that straggle a good mile seawards from Le Verdelet, and to clear various drying dangers scattered up to a mile offshore west of the mouth.

When approaching Dahouet from outside Baie de St Brieuc, it's usually best to make for the outer waypoint 45–5, a mile due west of Rohein W-cardinal beacon tower, and then track 143°T for 4.5 miles towards the inner waypoint 45–14 that leaves Le Dahouet N-cardinal buoy close to starboard. Dahouet entrance gap lies three quarters of a mile southeast of this buoy and a rather drab white and green beacon tower stands more or less in the middle of the mouth. The Rohein approach waypoint is a shade over six miles south of Grand Léjon lighthouse, the outer mark for Baie de St Brieuc.

### Approaching Le Légué and St Brieuc

The head of Baie de St Brieuc is shoal and should only be approached towards high water and in quiet conditions. Le Légué, in any case, is not the most attractive of harbours, although the locked basin is snug once you are safely inside. It may appeal to those with a taste for off-beat ports of call.

### Approaching Binic

The approaches to Binic dry out for about ¾ mile from the outer pierheads. This corner of the Baie de St Brieuc is well sheltered from between northwest through west to south, but is rather exposed to easterlies and northeasterlies. It's best to approach Binic about two hours before high water.

The lock gate into the wet basin is open from up to 2¼ hours before high water to just after high, depending on the tidal height or French 'coefficient'. At dead neaps, with high water less than 8.5m, the gate probably won't open at all.

### Roches de St Quay

To the north of Binic, an extensive area of drying reefs and islets fringes the coast opposite St Quay-Portrieux. The eastern edge of these dangers, some four miles offshore, is marked by the Caffa and Les Hors E-cardinal buoys. At the northwest corner are Madeux W-cardinal tower and the distinctive lighthouse on Ile Harbour. The southern extremity of the plateau is marked by La Roselière W-cardinal buoy and La Longue S-cardinal beacon tower.

Boats approaching St Quay from the south or southeast would normally make for La Roselière buoy before heading northwest towards St Quay harbour entrance, leaving an E-cardinal wreck buoy fairly close to port. Yachts arriving from the north, perhaps from Paimpol, Bréhat or direct from the Channel Islands, would make for a position clear to the northwest of Madeux beacon tower before continuing SSE into the Rade de St Quay-Portrieux.

# 46 Cap Fréhel to Ile de Bréhat

| ⊕ | Waypoint name and position | Latitude | Longitude |
|---|---|---|---|
| 46 1 | Cap Fréhel N clearing, ¾M N of Cap Fréhel lighthouse | 48°41.800'N | 002°19.130'W |
| 46 2 | Cap Fréhel W, 1M W of Cap Fréhel N tip | 48°41.275'N | 002°20.621'W |
| 46 3 | Roches d'Erquy N clearing, 4M N of Cap d'Erquy N tip | 48°42.740'N | 002°29.270'W |
| 46 4 | Grand Léjon S, 1½M 170°T from Grand Léjon lighthouse | 48°43.434'N | 002°39.482'W |
| 46 5 | Grand Léjon N, 2M N of Grand Léjon lighthouse | 48°46.913'N | 002°39.872'W |
| 46 6 | Roches d'Erquy W clearing, 1¼M 260°T from Landas buoy | 48°41.225'N | 002°33.149'W |
| 46 7 | Petit Léjon N, 1.4M N of W-card buoy | 48°43.200'N | 002°37.554'W |
| 46 8 | Petit Léjon S, 1M S of W-card buoy | 48°40.800'N | 002°37.554'W |
| 46 9 | Rohein W clearing, 1M W of Rohein W-card tower | 48°38.800'N | 002°39.280'W |
| 46 10 | Rohein S clearing, 9ca S of Rohein W-card tower | 48°37.900'N | 002°37.770'W |
| 46 11 | Binic E approach, 1½M 096°T from E breakwater head | 48°35.915'N | 002°46.687'W |
| 46 12 | St Quay SE approach, 2ca S of Roselière W-card buoy | 48°37.120'N | 002°46.187'W |
| 46 13 | St Quay N approach, 6ca WNW of Madeux beacon tower | 48°40.620'N | 002°49.661'W |
| 46 14 | Paimpol outer approach, 6.6M 090½°T from Porz-Don lighthouse | 48°47.428'N | 002°51.557'W |
| 46 15 | Basse St Brieuc, 2ca 060°T from E-card buoy | 48°46.373'N | 002°53.379'W |
| 46 16 | Les Calemarguiers, 2ca 060°T from E-card buoy | 48°47.083'N | 002°54.581'W |
| 46 17 | Ferlas SE outer, 3.9M 100°T from Men Joliguet tower | 48°49.420'N | 002°54.394'W |
| 46 18 | Ferlas SE inner, ½ca S of Lel ar Serive S-card buoy | 48°49.930'N | 002°58.760'W |
| 46 19 | Cain ar Monse, ¼M 307°T from N-card buoy | 48°50.324'N | 002°57.005'W |
| 46 20 | Men-Marc'h E approach, 2M 121°T from Men-Marc'h buoy | 48°52.174'N | 002°49.202'W |

## Refer to Charts
Admiralty charts 2027, 2029, 3673
Imray C33B, C34

## COASTAL DANGERS

### Cap Fréhel
A long narrow bank, known as Banc de l'Etendrée, extends for nearly one mile just east of Cap Fréhel. Depths over the bank change from time to time, but the shallowest part has about 1.5m over it at chart datum. At the far west end of this bank, just four cables east of Cap Fréhel lighthouse, Roche de l'Etendrée dries 3.9m and should be given a clear berth when rounding Fréhel.

### Roches d'Erquy
An extensive area of drying and above-water rocks lies up to 2½ miles offshore to the north and northeast of Cap d'Erquy. Rohinet, 6m high, is the most obvious above-water rock near high water, but the reefs around Le Grand Pourier become prominent as the tide falls away.

There is a navigable channel, known as Chenal d'Erquy, between these rocks and the shore, passing south of Les Justières and Basses du Courant S-cardinal buoys. The northwest corner of Roches d'Erquy is marked by Les Landas N-cardinal buoy. The northeast corner is unmarked, except by reference to Les Justières S-cardinal buoy.

### Approaching Erquy from Cap Fréhel
Coming from Cap Fréhel by day in reasonable weather and visibility, the best approach is by Chenal d'Erquy, which is much simpler in practice than it looks on the chart. Having rounded Cap Fréhel by half a mile or so and skirted Amas du Cap islet, bring Amas du Cap into transit astern just touching the north edge of Fréhel at 077°T. Follow this line for four miles until Les Justières S-cardinal buoy is four cables abeam to starboard and then continue for another half mile until Le Verdelet islet (42m high, 3.5 miles SW of Cap d'Erquy) is just open to the north of the large above-water rocks immediately off Cap d'Erquy, bearing 228°T. Come round to the SW on

this new transit, but edge seaward of the line as you get near Cap d'Erquy, to leave Basses du Courant S-cardinal buoy fairly close to starboard. Skirt round Cap d'Erquy at least a quarter of a mile off to enter Erquy harbour from the NW.

### Scallop boats
In and around the Bay of St Brieuc, you'll often see quite small fishing boats dredging scallops. These boats can change course quite dramatically and suddenly, so keep an eye on their movements if your paths are likely to cross.

### Rohein
Towards the middle of Baie de St Brieuc, the Rohein W-cardinal tower marks the southwest corner of quite a wide but well-spaced, almost rectangular area of shoals and drying rocks. At the southeast corner are Les Comtesses reefs and at the northwest corner the long Banc des Dahouetins, parts of which have less than a metre depth at chart datum.

Boats coasting between Erquy and Binic or St Quay-Portrieux would normally pass south of these dangers, leaving Rohein tower a mile or so to the north. Yachts making for Dahouet from Paimpol or Ile de Bréhat would come in through the wide gap between Rohein and the Roches de St Quay, leaving Rohein tower about a mile to the east.

### Petit Léjon
This small outlying reef, which dries 3.1m, lies a couple of miles north of the Rohein plateau and is marked on its west side by

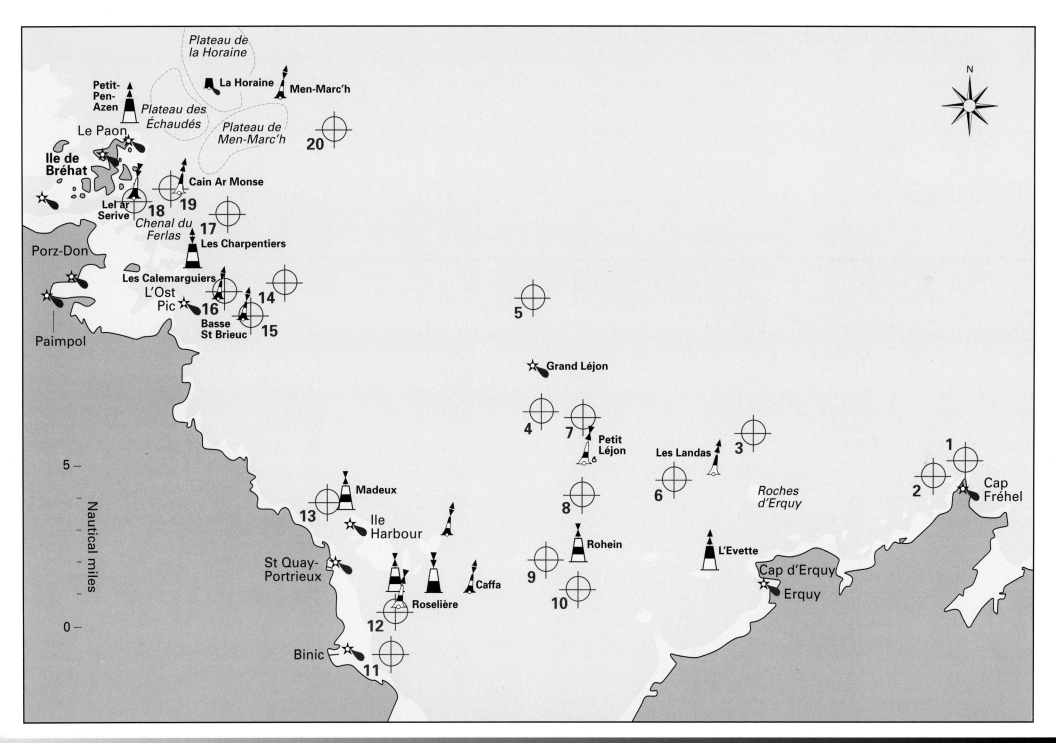

Plateau de
la Horaine

La Horaine

Men-Marc'h

Petit-
Pen-
Azen

Plateau des
Échaudés

Plateau de
Men-Marc'h

20

Le Paon

Ile de
Bréhat

Cain Ar Monse

Lel ar
Serive

18    19

Chenal du
Ferlas

17

Les Charpentiers

Porz-Don

Les Calemarguiers

L'Ost
Pic    16    14

Paimpol

Basse
St Brieuc    15

Grand Léjon

N

Cap
Fréhel

1

2

3

Les Landas

Roches
d'Erquy

6

Petit
Léjon

4    7

8

Madeux

13

Ile
Harbour

Caffa

Rohein

L'Evette

St Quay-
Portrieux

9    10

Cap d'Erquy

Erquy

Roselière

12

Binic

11

5 —

Nautical miles

0 —

5

Petit Léjon W-cardinal buoy. Boats on passage between Cap Fréhel and Paimpol would normally pass between Petit Léjon and Le Grand Léjon lighthouse, but the Petit Léjon buoy, being a W-cardinal, should be left well clear to the south in this case.

## Grand Léjon

The Grand Léjon reef, marked by a lighthouse, lies right in the north approaches to Baie de St Brieuc, more or less on a direct line between Cap Fréhel and Paimpol. The reef is steep-to on its south side but patchy on its north side. Les Bouillons, an outlying head with 1m over it at chart datum, lies three cables northeast of the lighthouse.

## Roches de St Quay

To the north of Binic, an extensive area of drying reefs and islets fringes the coast opposite St Quay-Portrieux, The eastern edge of these dangers, some four miles offshore, is marked by the Caffa and Les Hors E-cardinal buoys. At the northwest corner are Madeux W-cardinal tower and the distinctive lighthouse on Ile Harbour. The southern extremity of the plateau is marked by La Roselière W-cardinal buoy and La Longue S-cardinal beacon tower.

Boats approaching St Quay from the south or southeast would normally make for La Roselière buoy before heading northwest towards St Quay harbour entrance, leaving an E-cardinal wreck buoy fairly close to port. Yachts arriving from the north, perhaps from Paimpol, Bréhat or direct from the Channel Islands, would make for a position clear to the northwest of Madeux beacon tower before continuing SSE into the Rade de St Quay-Portrieux.

## L'Ost-Pic

The distinctive headland and lighthouse of L'Ost-Pic form the southern arm of the Anse de Paimpol. Two small rocky banks lie to the east of L'Ost-Pic, both marked by E-cardinal buoys. Les Calemarguiers lie between half and one mile east of L'Ost-Pic lighthouse, with depths of less than 0.5m on the inshore side and a rocky patch drying 1.8m further out.

Basse St Brieuc bank lies 1¾ miles ESE of L'Ost-Pic, with a depth of 0.5m over its shallowest part. Yachts can safely pass over these banks above half tide, and even near low water you can cut inside Les Calemarguiers ¼ mile off L'Ost-Pic.

## Paimpol approaches

Boats making for Paimpol from St Malo would normally carry a full ebb tide westwards and thus arrive off Paimpol near low water. A rock with less than 1m over it at chart datum lies just over six cables southeast of Les Charpentiers E-cardinal beacon tower and just over one mile northeast of L'Ost-Pic lighthouse. This rock is in the white sector of Porz-Don light and very close north of the direct line between waypoints 47–1 and 47–5, so yachts should take care to avoid it near low water springs.

## Dangers between Paimpol and Ile de Bréhat

A broad area of islets and drying rocks extends up to three miles seawards to form the sheltering north arm of the Anse de Paimpol. Les Charpentiers E-cardinal beacon tower stands near the south-east edge of these dangers, but Les Barbottes Rocks, almost awash at chart datum, lie 3½ cables east of Les Charpentiers tower. Banc de la Cormorandière extends just over 1¼ miles north of La Cormorandière white pyramid, its north tip with only 0.8m over it lying very

close south of the white sector of Men Joliguet light. Yachts approaching Chenal du Ferlas from the east or south-east should make for a position near the Ferlas SE outer waypoint (No 46–17) before closing further with the shore.

## East approaches to Bréhat

There are numerous wide rocky banks to the east and northeast of Ile de Bréhat. They are all well covered above half-tide, but cause uneasy turbulence and steep overfalls during the strongest hours of both the flood and ebb.

Plateau de la Horaine, with the highest area of drying rocks, lies from 3–4 miles northeast of Ile de Bréhat, guarded by La Horaine tower. Plateau des Échaudés is closer to Ile de Bréhat, its shallowest patch drying 2.6m. A narrow passage, Chenal de Bréhat, leads NNW–SSE between Les Échaudés and the Guarine E-cardinal buoy off the east side of Bréhat.

Plateau de Men-Marc'h is a wide shoal area southeast of La Horaine and Les Échaudés. Most of Men-Marc'h is relatively deep, with only a few patches with around 0.5m depth at chart datum; Men-Marc'h Rock itself, on the southeast edge of the plateau, dries 0.6m. There is a passage of deep water just to the south of Plateau de Men-Marc'h and north of Plateau du Ringue-Bras; this route leads in towards the Chenal du Ferlas from the ENE and can be a useful approach to Ile de Bréhat for boats arriving direct from Jersey, provided you allow carefully for any cross-tide.

| ⊕ | | Waypoint name and position | Latitude | Longitude |
|---|---|---|---|---|
| 47 | 1 | Paimpol outer approach, 6.6M 090½°T from Porz-Don lighthouse | 48°47.428′N | 002°51.557′W |
| 47 | 2 | Basse St Brieuc, 2ca 060°T from E-card buoy | 48°46.373′N | 002°53.379′W |
| 47 | 3 | Les Calemarguiers, 2ca 060°T from E-card buoy | 48°47.083′N | 002°54.581′W |
| 47 | 4 | L'Ost Pic inner, 3½ca due E of lighthouse | 48°46.772′N | 002°55.895′W |
| 47 | 5 | Paimpol middle approach, 800m S of Charpentiers beacon tower | 48°47.458′N | 002°56.009′W |
| 47 | 6 | Roche Gueule, 1ca N of red buoy on leading line | 48°47.510′N | 002°57.300′W |
| 47 | 7 | Paimpol outer anchorage, 6ca 216°T from Dénou W pyramid | 48°47.361′N | 002°58.570′W |
| 47 | 8 | Paimpol inner approach, ½M 034°T from Pointe Guilben spot height | 48°47.277′N | 003°00.227′W |
| 47 | 9 | Paimpol entrance, outer pierhead light actual position | 48°47.090′N | 003°02.440′W |
| 47 | 10 | Ferlas SE outer, 3.9M 100°T from Men Joliguet tower | 48°49.420′N | 002°54.394′W |
| 47 | 11 | Ferlas SE inner, ½ca S of Lel ar Serive S-card buoy | 48°49.930′N | 002°58.760′W |
| 47 | 12 | Chenal de Bréhat middle, just E of Guarine E-card buoy | 48°51.613′N | 002°57.525′W |
| 47 | 13 | Cain ar Monse, ¼M 307°T from N-card buoy | 48°50.324′N | 002°57.005′W |
| 47 | 14 | La Chambre, 1ca 230°T from La Chambre S-card beacon | 48°50.095′N | 002°59.708′W |
| 47 | 15 | Rade de Bréhat, 500m 127°T from Men Joliguet tower | 48°49.958′N | 002°59.867′W |
| 47 | 16 | Ferlas middle, 120m S of Receveur S-card beacon | 48°49.630′N | 003°01.960′W |
| 47 | 17 | Trieux River entrance, 6½ca E of Kermouster light | 48°49.550′N | 003°04.210′W |
| 47 | 18 | La Croix inner, 3ca 026°T from La Croix lighthouse | 48°50.499′N | 003°03.051′W |
| 47 | 19 | La Croix outer, 9ca 045°T from La Croix lighthouse | 48°50.870′N | 003°02.290′W |
| 47 | 20 | Grand Chenal inner, 3ca NNW of Rosédo white pyramid | 48°51.770′N | 003°00.930′W |

**Refer to Charts**
Admiralty charts 2027, 3673
Imray C34

in towards a suitable anchorage. Care must be taken to avoid the numerous patches of withies which mark the extensive oyster beds in the Anse de Paimpol.

## Dangers between Paimpol and Ile de Bréhat
A broad area of islets and drying rocks extends up to three miles seawards to form the sheltering north arm of the Anse de Paimpol. Les Charpentiers E-cardinal beacon tower stands near the south-east edge of these dangers, but Les Barbottes Rocks, almost awash at chart datum, lie 3½ cables east of Les Charpentiers tower.

Banc de la Cormorandière extends just over 1¼ miles north of La Cormorandière white pyramid, its north tip with only 0.8m over it lying very close south of the white sector of Men Joliguet light. Boats approaching Chenal du Ferlas from the east or southeast should make for a position near the Ferlas SE outer waypoint (No 46–17) before closing further with the shore.

A narrow but well marked passage, Chenal de la Trinité, cuts inside all these dangers, providing a useful short-cut above half-tide between the Anse de Paimpol and the Chenal du Ferlas just south of Ile de Bréhat.

## COASTAL DANGERS

### L'Ost-Pic
The distinctive headland and lighthouse of L'Ost-Pic form the southern arm of the Anse de Paimpol. Two small rocky banks lie to the east of L'Ost-Pic, both marked by E-cardinal buoys. Les Calemarguiers lie between half and one mile east of L'Ost-Pic lighthouse, with depths of less than 0.5m on the inshore side and a rocky patch drying 1.8m further out.

Basse St Brieuc bank lies 1¾ miles ESE of L'Ost-Pic, with a depth of 0.5m over its shallowest part. Boats can safely pass over these banks above half-tide, and even near

low water you can cut inside Les Calemarguiers ¼ mile off L'Ost-Pic.

### Paimpol approaches
Boats making for Paimpol from St Malo would normally carry a full ebb tide westwards and thus arrive off Paimpol near low water. A rock with less than 1m over it at chart datum lies just over six cables southeast of Les Charpentiers E-cardinal beacon tower and just over one mile northeast of L'Ost-Pic lighthouse. This rock is in the white sector of Porz-Don light and very close north of the direct line between waypoints 47–1 and 47–5, so boats should take care to avoid it near low water springs.

### Anse de Paimpol
Most of the Anse de Paimpol dries at chart datum. Boats arriving in the bay near low water will need to anchor in one of the outer anchorages south or southwest of Ile St Rion until two hours before high water when the Paimpol lock gates open.

When arriving from seaward, most boats come north of Les Calemarguiers E-cardinal buoy to line up on a more or less westerly approach which leaves Les Charpentiers E-cardinal beacon tower about four cables to the north and Gouayan red beacon tower not quite ¼ mile to the south. You then pass north of Roche Gueule red buoy and La Jument red beacon tower before sounding

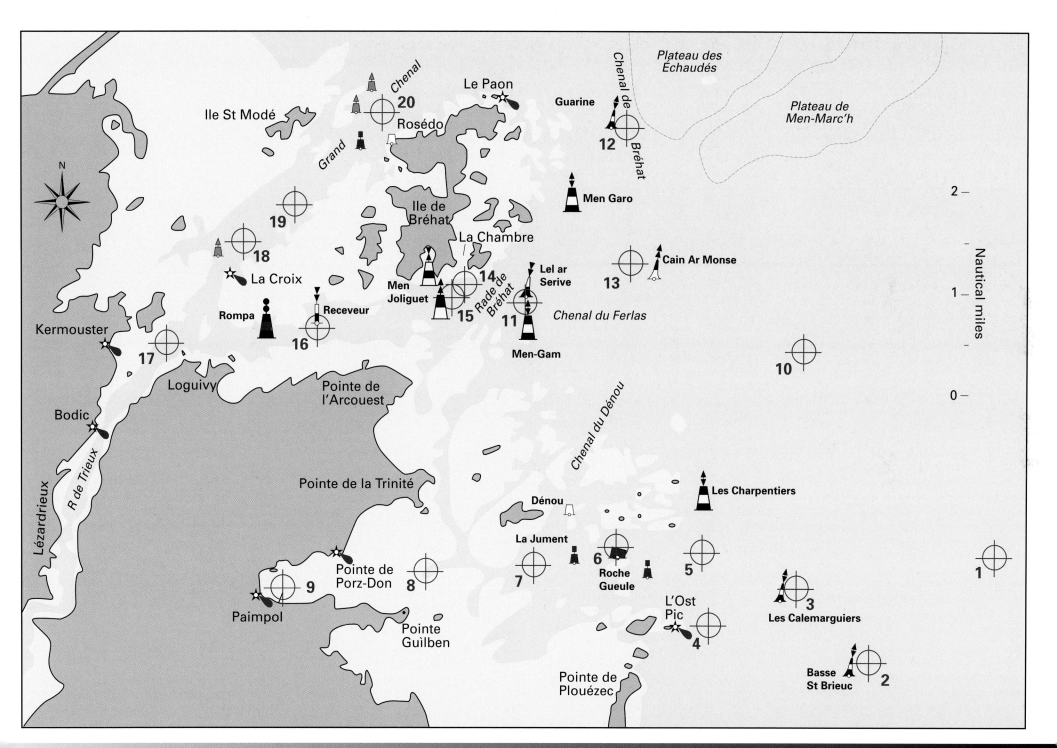

## Chenal de la Trinité

The quickest route between Paimpol and anywhere in the Trieux estuary, this passage may look intricate and impenetrable on the chart, but is well marked and easy to follow above half-tide using Admiralty 3673. Coming from Paimpol, Chenal de la Trinité is simple if you lock out of Paimpol basin an hour or so before high water and motor out through the buoyed approach channel to An Erv Uhel green spar beacon. Then turn northeast towards an isolated danger BRB spar beacon marking Glividy rock, which stands in the southern gap of La Trinité. Slim though it is, Glividy beacon usually stands out well near high water, with most of the background reefs covered. You'll leave several green spars to port on your way up to it.

You can pass either side of Glividy, though near the top of the tide I usually leave it nicely to port and head more or less due north to leave two red spar beacons to starboard and then two more green spars to port. After the second green, carry on north towards Les Fillettes S-cardinal spar (don't confuse it with another S-cardinal, Men Kreiz, further east). When you are about midway between the second green and Les Fillettes, turn northwest and steer for Pointe de l'Arcouest and its prominent white stone mark, but then turn north again past some small boat moorings to steer midway between Arcouest and La Madeleine W-cardinal beacon not quite three cables off it.

After La Madeleine, turn NNE to leave some above water rocks and a small island to starboard, steering to pass a little over a cable east of the stubby Les Piliers N-cardinal beacon tower. Once beyond Les Piliers you are out in Le Ferlas channel south of Ile de Bréhat, and you can either turn west towards Lézardrieux or carry on NNE

towards La Chambre anchorage, off the southeast corner of Bréhat.

On your way through Chenal de la Trinité, you'll have passed over several drying rocky patches and some muddy shoals, all far below your keel near high water. Coming the other way, from the Trieux estuary towards Paimpol, aim to arrive east of Les Piliers tower about two hours before HW. There'll then be plenty of depth through La Trinité and across Anse de Paimpol, and you'll be well placed for locking into Paimpol.

## East approaches to Bréhat

There are numerous wide rocky banks to the east and northeast of Ile de Bréhat. They are all well covered above half-tide, but cause uneasy turbulence and steep overfalls during the strongest hours of both the flood and ebb.

Plateau des Échaudés extends between Ile de Bréhat and the drying reefs of Plateau de la Horaine. The shallowest part of Les Échaudés dries 2.6m. A narrow passage, Chenal de Bréhat, leads NNW–SSE between Les Échaudés and the Guarine E-cardinal buoy off the east side of Bréhat. Plateau de Men-Marc'h is a wide shoal area southeast of La Horaine and Les Échaudés. Most of Men-Marc'h is relatively deep, with only a few patches having around 0.5m depth at chart datum; Men-Marc'h rock itself, on the southeast edge of the plateau, dries 0.6m. There is a passage of deep water just south of Plateau de Men-Marc'h and north of Plateau du Ringue-Bras; this route leads in towards the Chenal du Ferlas from the ENE and can be a useful approach to Ile de Bréhat for boats arriving direct from Jersey, provided you allow carefully for any cross-tide.

## Chenal du Ferlas

The Ferlas channel leads between the south side of Ile de Bréhat and the Brittany mainland just east of the Trieux River. It is well marked and straightforward above half-tide, but care must be taken through parts of the channel near low water. At the east end, Cain Ar Monse Rock, almost awash at chart datum, is marked on its north side by a N-cardinal buoy, although the leading line and the white sector of Men Joliguet normally bring you in four cables or so south of the rock. Opposite Cain Ar Monse, on the south side of the normal leading line, the north tip of Banc de la Cormorandiére has only 0.8m over it at chart datum.

Towards the middle of Chenal du Ferlas, between Ile de Bréhat and Rompa isolated danger beacon tower, there are various patches which are shallow near low water. The south side of the channel is shallow as you approach Roc'h Rouray and there is a patch on the north side with only 0.8m at chart datum, just under one cable south and a shade east of Trebeyou S-cardinal beacon tower. Rompa beacon tower has a small drying rock close off its south side.

## Grand Chenal de Trieux

Once you are abreast Ile de Bréhat, the Grand Chenal de Trieux is straightforward and well marked, sheltered by land and rocks on both sides. However, until you draw south of the north tip of Bréhat, allow for a strong cross-tide across the outer Trieux estuary, especially during the middle hours of the flood.

| ⊕ | Waypoint name and position | Latitude | Longitude |
|---|---|---|---|
| 48 1 | Grand Chenal approach, 8ca NW of Nord Horaine N-card buoy | 48°55.002'N | 002°56.020'W |
| 48 2 | Chenal de Bréhat N, 1¾M 021°T from Le Paon light | 48°53.554'N | 002°58.207'W |
| 48 3 | Chenal de Bréhat middle, just E of Guarine E-card buoy | 48°51.613'N | 002°57.525'W |
| 48 4 | Grand Chenal inner, 3ca NNW of Rosédo white pyramid | 48°51.770'N | 003°00.930'W |
| 48 5 | La Moisie outer, 8ca 343°T from La Moisie beacon | 48°54.598'N | 003°02.587'W |
| 48 6 | La Gaine NE, 1M E of Les Héaux lighthouse on leading line | 48°54.500'N | 003°03.655'W |
| 48 7 | Les Héaux N clearing inner, 1¼M N of lighthouse | 48°55.750'N | 003°05.170'W |
| 48 8 | Les Héaux N clearing outer, 2½M N of lighthouse | 48°57.000'N | 003°05.170'W |
| 48 9 | Roch ar Bel clearing, 4.3M 067°T from Les Héaux lighthouse | 48°56.209'N | 002°59.182'W |

**Refer to Charts**
Admiralty charts 2027, 3673
Imray C34

## COASTAL DANGERS

### Strong cross-tides
The Grand Chenal into the Trieux River is not difficult, but there are dangers several miles from the low-lying coast and you need to allow for the powerful cross-tides that sweep round this corner of Brittany between Les Héaux and La Horaine, especially during the middle hours of the flood. The cross-tide cuts off as you draw abreast the north end of Ile de Bréhat.

### Plateau de la Horaine
Plateau de la Horaine, the most seaward area of shoals and rocks on the east side of the Grand Chenal, lies from 3–4 miles northeast of Ile de Bréhat. The drying dangers on the southwest side of the plateau are guarded by La Horaine tower, but the whole area around these shoals is uneasy with turbulence and overfalls as the tide rushes across it. The north tip of La Horaine is marked by Nord Horaine N-cardinal buoy, the outer buoy for the Grand Chenal.

### Dangers east of Bréhat
There are several other wide rocky banks south of La Horaine and to the east of Ile de Bréhat. These are mostly well covered above half-tide, but again cause uneasy turbulence and steep overfalls during the strongest hours of both the flood and ebb.

Plateau des Échaudés lies between Ile de Bréhat and La Horaine, its shallowest patch drying 2.6m. A narrow passage, Chenal de Bréhat, leads NNW–SSE between Les Échaudés and the Guarine E-cardinal buoy off the east side of Bréhat.

Plateau de Men-Marc'h is a wide shoal area south-east of La Horaine and Les Échaudés. Most of Men-Marc'h is relatively deep, with only a few patches having around 0.5m depth at chart datum; Men-Marc'h rock itself, on the southeast edge of the plateau, dries 0.6m. There is a passage of deep water just to the south of Plateau de Men-Marc'h and north of Plateau du Ringue-Bras; this route leads in towards the Chenal du Ferlas from the ENE and can be a useful approach to Ile de Bréhat for boats arriving direct from Jersey, provided you allow carefully for any cross-tide.

### Outer overfalls
Not quite 3½ miles north and a shade west of the north tip of Bréhat, well to the west of the Grand Chenal approaches, two rocky shoals – Roch ar Bel and Carrec Mingui – have a safe depth over them for boats, but cause turbulent overfalls during the strongest hours of the tide. They should be avoided in fresh winds if you are arriving off the Grand Chenal from the west or leaving the Grand Chenal to round Les Héaux.

### Les Sirlots and Basse Plate
Basse Plate shoals lie about one mile south of Roch ar Bel and Carrec Mingui on the west side of the estuary. Although well covered above half-tide, Basse Plate should be avoided on account of its overfalls and turbulent water, especially during the strongest part of the flood.

The Plateau des Sirlots lies further into the estuary, about ¾ mile south of Basse Plate, and is left clear to starboard as you come in through the Grand Chenal. Les Sirlots green whistle buoy guards the east edge of these shoals and is a strategic mark for the inner part of the estuary.

### West side of Trieux estuary
The west side of the Trieux estuary is a maze of drying rocks and shoals which, providing a natural continuation of the mainland, straggles northeastwards for a good three miles. The long sandspit known as Sillon de Talbert forms the backbone of these dangers and their northeast edge is guarded by several beacons, of which the most seaward is La Moisie E-cardinal beacon tower.

### La Moisie passage
This rather narrow channel leads into the Trieux from the NNW, skirting the edge of the reefs that extend north-east from Sillon de Talber and keeping west of Basse Plate, Plateau des Sirlots and several smaller drying rocks – Ar Mesclek, Pierre Rouge, La Traverse and Roc ar Gazec. The Moisie Passage is useful if you are approaching Lézardrieux from round Les Héaux, or if you are leaving the river bound west along the coast. It needs reasonable visibility and is best taken above half-tide, otherwise the safe corridor becomes very narrow in the northern part, especially between Noguejou Bihan and La Traverse. In fresh onshore winds, it is preferable to use the Grand Chenal.

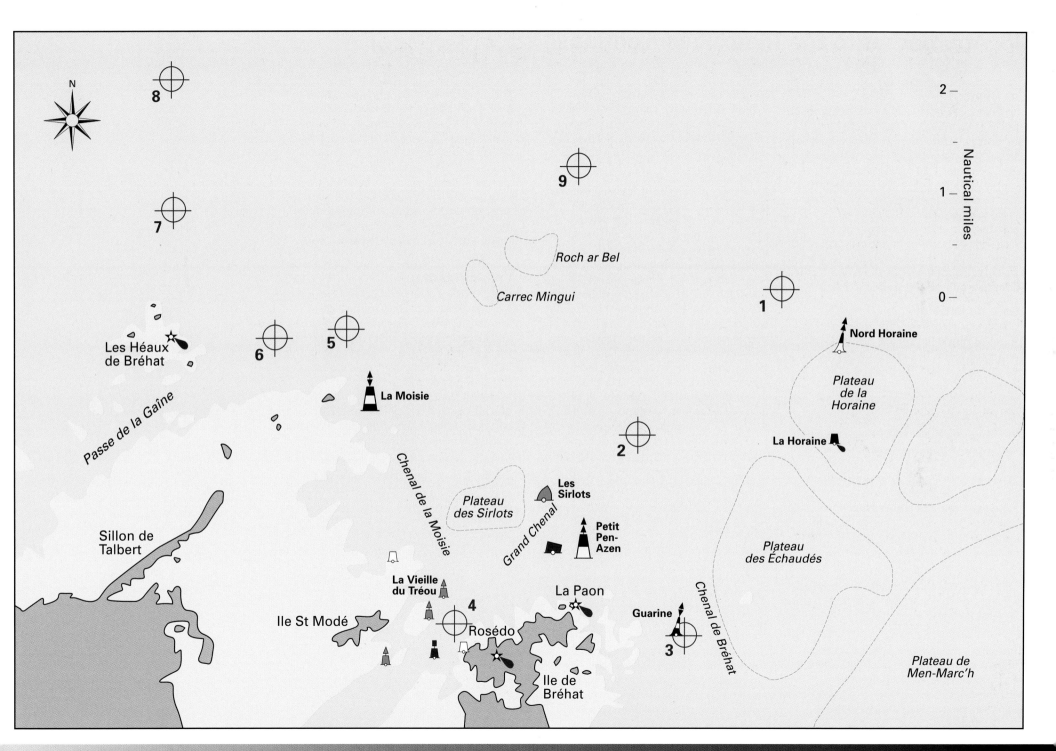

N

Nautical miles

2 —

1 —

0 —

**8**

**7**

**9**

Roch ar Bel

Carrec Mingui

**1**

Nord Horaine

Plateau
de la
Horaine

La Horaine

Les Héaux
de Bréhat

**6**

**5**

Passe de la Gaîne

La Moisie

**2**

Plateau
des Sirlots

Les Sirlots

Grand Chenal

Petit
Pen-
Azen

Plateau
des Échaudés

Chenal de la Moisie

Sillon de
Talbert

La Vieille
du Tréou

La Paon

Guarine

Chenal de Bréhat

**4**

Rosédo

Ile St Modé

Ile de
Bréhat

**3**

Plateau de
Men-Marc'h

### Les Héaux

The cluster of above-water and drying rocks known as Les Héaux de Bréhat are almost the most northerly rocks on the west side of the Trieux estuary. Les Héaux lighthouse is nearly 50m high and provides an unmistakable landfall mark as you approach the Trieux from seaward. When rounding Les Héaux, perhaps bound between Lézardrieux and Tréguier, you must be sure of clearing the various drying dangers which extend WNW of the lighthouse for almost two miles. La Jument N-cardinal buoy is the corner mark for these dangers.

### Passe de la Gaîne

This narrow, rather delicate passage leads inside Les Héaux lighthouse towards the Tréguier estuary. In good visibility though, and above half-tide, Passe de la Gaîne presents no great difficulty for those familiar with the rocks and strong tides along this coast.

Boats entering Passe de la Gaîne at the east end have usually just left the Trieux estuary via Chenal de la Moisie. As you emerge seawards, once Moisie E-cardinal beacon tower is half a mile astern and before Les Héaux lighthouse bears due west true, come to port to make good due west true and so bring the lighthouse fine on the starboard bow.

About a quarter of a mile southeast of Les Héaux lighthouse is a 2m above-water rock, Roc'h ar Hanap. You enter Passe de la Gaîne by steering to make good 241°T and leaving Roc'h ar Harap 1½–2 cables to starboard.

Thereafter, leave the first green beacon a cable to starboard and steer to leave the second green beacon only 150m to starboard. The leading marks for Passe de la Gaîne will be 4–6 miles distant in the Tréguier estuary, a little to the right of Plougrescant church spire. These marks are often hidden in haze until you get much closer, so it's best to steer by the beacons until the transit comes into view.

### Poor visibility

Before we all had GPS it was distinctly dangerous to close this part of North Brittany in poor visibility, but now an instrument approach is perfectly feasible, especially from the north-east by the Grand Chenal. Many yachts coming down from St Peter Port each summer arrive off the Trieux estuary in summer haze or mist, but before drawing inshore it's important to double-check that all your landfall and approach waypoints are entered correctly and you know clearly which is which. For a poor visibility arrival on instruments, enter waypoints carefully, well in advance, all the way into the river at least as far as waypoint 47-17 – Trieux River entrance – given in section 47. The estuary is quite wide as far as La Croix lighthouse and if conditions stay murky all the way in, you don't want to be keying in the river waypoints in a hurry, with rocks looming either side.

Because of the powerful cross-tides around this corner of the coast, it's particularly important in poor visibility to stay closely on track between all the outer waypoints, especially offshore between Roches Douvres and Nord Horaine N-cardinal buoy, and then between Nord Horaine and the waypoint opposite Rosédo white pyramid on the west side of Île de Bréhat. Once you get pushed well off track by strong tides, it can become disorientating on instruments to make the considerable course changes then needed to get back on your safe line. Better to stick carefully to this line all the way in. The cross-tides will cut off as you draw south of Bréhat and then the normal river tides take over. Even in thick murk, by the time you reach the Rosédo waypoint you'll usually glimpse the island coast to port, but don't relax the accuracy of your instrument navigation. The visibility may thicken again further in, and if you've drifted off-track with a sense of premature arrival euphoria it can be disconcerting and confusing to regain control of where you are between waypoints. Keep navigating assiduously until you really arrive.

### Crab-pot buoys

Watch out for crab-pot floats all around the Trieux estuary, especially in the outer approaches where a strong spring tide can pull even the largest buoys under and make them almost invisible. Catching one of these lines round a rudder or skeg can be a serious matter if a boat is then held stern-to the powerful streams, which can touch six knots off this corner of North Brittany. This is perhaps the most cogent argument against a night approach or departure.

In the estuary channels around Ile de Bréhat, the pot buoys tend to be smaller with trailing pick-up lines that can catch you unawares even on calm sunny days when the pilotage all seems straightforward and the whole mood very genial.

| ⊕ | Waypoint name and position | Latitude | Longitude |
|---|---|---|---|
| 49 1 | Roches Douvres west clearing, 3M WNW of lighthouse | 49°07.431′N | 002°53.071′W |
| 49 2 | Roches Douvres east, 3½M due E of lighthouse | 49°06.303′N | 002°43.561′W |
| 49 3 | Barnouic SW, 1.1M W of Roche Gautier W-card buoy | 49°02.013′N | 002°56.039′W |
| 49 4 | Barnouic SE inner, 1½M SE of Barnouic E-card tower | 49°00.572′N | 002°46.828′W |
| 49 5 | Barnouic E clearing, 2½M SE of Barnouic E-card tower | 48°59.764′N | 002°45.789′W |
| 49 6 | Grand Chenal approach, 8ca NW of Nord Horaine N-card buoy | 48°55.002′N | 002°56.020′W |
| 49 7 | Chenal de Bréhat N, 1¾M 021°T from Le Paon light | 48°53.554′N | 002°58.207′W |
| 49 8 | Chenal de Bréhat middle, just E of Guarine E-card buoy | 48°51.613′N | 002°57.525′W |
| 49 9 | Men-Marc'h E approach, 2M 121°T from Men Marc'h buoy | 48°52.174′N | 002°49.202′W |
| 49 10 | Grand Léjon NW, 5M NW of Grand Léjon lighthouse | 48°48.424′N | 002°45.271′W |
| 49 11 | Ferlas SE outer, 3.9M 100°T from Men Joliguet tower | 48°49.420′N | 002°54.394′W |
| 49 12 | Ferlas SE inner, ½ca S of Lel ar Serive S-card buoy | 48°49.930′N | 002°58.760′W |
| 49 13 | Cain ar Monse, ¼M 307°T from N-card buoy | 48°50.324′N | 002°57.005′W |
| 49 14 | Roch ar Bel clearing, 4.3M 067°T from Les Héaux lighthouse | 48°56.209′N | 002°59.182′W |
| 49 15 | La Moisie outer, 8ca 343°T from La Moisie beacon | 48°54.598′N | 003°02.587′W |
| 49 16 | La Gaine NE, 1M E of Les Héaux lighthouse on leading line | 48°54.500′N | 003°03.655′W |
| 49 17 | Les Héaux N clearing inner, 1¼M N of lighthouse | 48°55.750′N | 003°05.170′W |
| 49 18 | Les Héaux N clearing outer, 2½M N of lighthouse | 48°57.000′N | 003°05.170′W |

**Refer to Charts**
Admiralty charts 2027, 2028, 2648
Imray C34

## COASTAL DANGERS

### Passage from Guernsey to Lézardrieux

This popular cruising route to Brittany from Guernsey is easy enough in quiet weather, but can be rough going in fresh winds at spring tides. You can pass either side of Roches Douvres and Plateau de Barnouic, but it's safest to keep down-tide of these dangers, in case of any trouble with engines or something round a prop. Study the tidal stream charts carefully before leaving Guernsey.

The long Grand Chenal into the Trieux estuary is wide and deep, fringed with plenty of rocks. At springs powerful streams pour across the approaches, so a landfall on this corner is always less tense near neaps.

Once you draw south of Ile de Bréhat the estuary is sheltered and easy to follow up to the snug marinas at Lézardrieux. The distance from St Peter Port to the north end of Bréhat is about 42 miles whether you go east or west of Roches Douvres.

Coming east-about you arrive off the estuary at waypoint 49-6, eight cables NW of Nord Horaine N-cardinal buoy on the Grand Chenal leading line. The approach track to waypoint 48-4 follows the charted leading line as far as the NW corner of Ile de Bréhat, opposite Rosédo white pyramid. Thereafter it's easy to follow the marks and beacon towers into the river. Coming west-about Roches Douvres it's convenient to arrive in the estuary at waypoint 48-2 and then turn southwest for waypoint 48-4.

### Roches Douvres

The Roches Douvres plateau is about two miles from west to east and 1½ miles from north to south. The tides set strongly in this area, especially between Roches Douvres and Plateau de Barnouic. It's important to pass a safe distance off, preferably keeping 'down-tide' of the dangers ie passing west-about when the tide is west-going and east-about when the tide is east-going. Note that local magnetic anomalies can be experienced to the east and southeast of Roches Douvres, which may affect an autopilot as well as a steering compass.

### Plateau de Barnouic

This patchy area of rocky shoals about three miles south of Roches Douvres is more spread out than the latter and only has one reef, Roche Gautier, that dries. In some

ways, however, its relative invisibility makes Barnouic potentially more sinister than Roches Douvres in this area of powerful tides. Barnouic E-cardinal beacon tower guards the east edge of the main shoals and the Roche Gautier W-cardinal buoy lies to the southwest of the plateau. The northwest shoals of the plateau have only a metre over them at datum and produce nasty overfalls during the strongest part of the tide.

### Poor visibility

Many yachts come down from St Peter Port each year in summer haze or patchy mist, but before drawing inshore it's important to double-check that all your landfall and approach waypoints are entered correctly and you know clearly which is which. For a poor visibility arrival on instruments, enter waypoints carefully, well in advance, all the way into the river at least as far as waypoint 47-17 – Trieux River entrance – given in section 47. The estuary is quite wide as far as La Croix lighthouse and if conditions stay murky all the way in, you don't want to be keying in the river waypoints in a hurry, with rocks looming either side.

Because of the powerful cross-tides around this corner, it's particularly important in poor visibility to stay closely on track between all the outer waypoints, especially offshore between Roches Douvres and Nord Horaine N-cardinal buoy, and then between Nord Horaine and the waypoint opposite Rosédo white pyramid on the west side of Ile de Bréhat. Once you get pushed well off track by strong tides, it can become

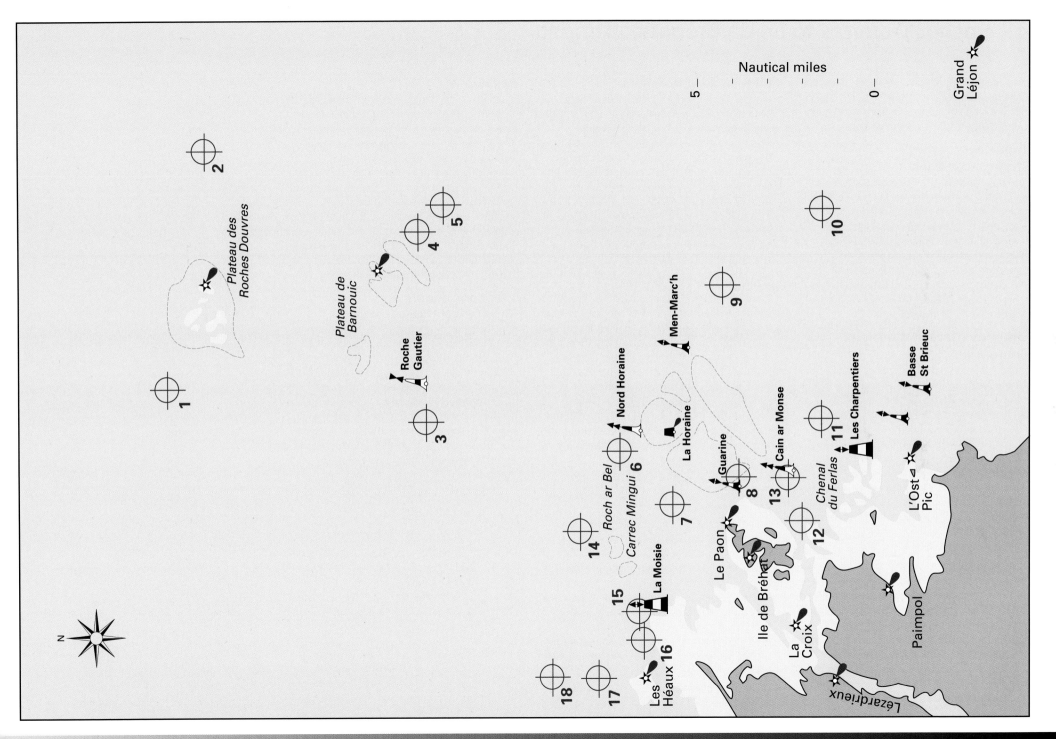

Nautical miles

5

0

Grand Léjon

Plateau des
Roches Douvres

2

Plateau de
Barnouic

4

5

1

Roche
Gautier

3

10

9

Men-Marc'h

Nord Horaine

Roch ar Bel

Carrec Mingui

La Horaine

6

Guarine

7

Cain ar Monse

8

13

Les Charpentiers

11

Basse
St Brieuc

14

Le Paon

12

Chenal
du Ferlas

L'Ost⊲
Pic

15

La Moisie

Ile de Bréhat

La
Croix

Paimpol

16

Les Héaux

17

18

Lézardrieux

N

disorientating on instruments to make the considerable course changes then needed to get back on your safe line. Better to stick carefully to this line all the way in.

## Trieux approaches – strong cross-tides

The approach to the Trieux estuary is not difficult, but there are dangers several miles from the low-lying coast and you need to allow for the powerful cross-tides that sweep round this corner of Brittany between Les Héaux and La Horaine, especially during the middle hours of the flood. Entering the Grand Chenal de Trieux, the cross-tide cuts off as you draw abreast of the north end of Ile de Bréhat.

## Outer overfalls in the Trieux approaches

Basse Maurice, a deepish rocky shoal with 13m over it, lies three miles southwest of the Barnouic Roche Gautier W-cardinal buoy; more or less on the line most yachts take if bound from St Peter Port to Lézardrieux west-about Roches Douvres. There are often overfalls over Basse Maurice, especially with wind over tide, and it's a patch worth avoiding in boisterous weather. In calm conditions, you often see turbulent 'slicks' of oily smooth water near Basse Maurice, caused by the strong tidal stream surging over the shoal.

Not quite 3½ miles north and a shade west of the north tip of Bréhat, well to the west of the Grand Chenal approaches, are two rocky shoals: Roch ar Bel and Carrec Mingui. These have a safe depth over them for yachts, but cause turbulent overfalls during the strongest hours of tide. They should be avoided in fresh winds if you are arriving off the Grand Chenal from the west or leaving the Grand Chenal to round Les Héaux.

## Plateau de la Horaine

Plateau de la Horaine, the most seaward area of shoals and rocks on the east side of the Trieux estuary, lies from 3–4 miles northeast of the Ile de Bréhat. The drying dangers on the southwest side of the plateau are guarded by La Horaine tower, but the whole area around these shoals is uneasy with turbulence and overfalls as the tide rushes across it. The north tip of La Horaine is marked by the Nord Horaine N-cardinal buoy which is the outer buoy for the Grand Chenal de Trieux.

## Dangers east of Bréhat

There are several other wide rocky banks south of La Horaine and to the east of Ile de Bréhat. These are mostly well covered above half-tide, but again cause uneasy turbulence and steep overfalls during the strongest hours of both the flood and ebb. Plateau des Échaudés lies between Ile de Bréhat and La Horaine, its shallowest patch drying 2.6m. A narrow passage, Chenal de Bréhat, leads NNW–SSE between Les Échaudés and the Guarine E-cardinal buoy off the east side of Bréhat.

Plateau de Men-Marc'h is a wide shoal area south-east of La Horaine and Les Échaudés. Most of Men-Marc'h is relatively deep, with only a few patches having around 0.5m depth at datum; Men-Marc'h rock itself, on the southeast edge of the plateau, dries 0.6m. There is a passage of deep water just to the south of Plateau de Men-Marc'h and north of Plateau du Ringue-Bras; this route leads in towards the Chenal du Ferlas from the ENE and can be a useful approach to Ile de Bréhat for yachts arriving direct from Jersey, provided you make careful allowance for any cross-tide.

## Les Héaux

The cluster of above-water and drying rocks known as Les Héaux de Bréhat are almost the most northerly rocks on the west side of the Trieux estuary. Les Héaux lighthouse is nearly 50m high and provides an unmistakable landfall mark as you approach the Trieux from seaward. When rounding Les Héaux, perhaps bound between Lézardrieux and Tréguier, you must be sure of clearing the various drying dangers which extend WNW of the lighthouse for almost two miles. La Jument N-cardinal buoy is the corner mark for these dangers.

## Magnetic anomalies

You can experience local magnetic interference in the sea area immediately south-east of Roches Douvres, an eerie sensation for any navigator. This effect is said to be due to the high ferrous content of the Roches Douvres granite, although I have found that you have to be reasonably close to the plateau before noticing anything odd. These anomalies will affect electronic compasses and autopilot fluxgates as well as ordinary steering and hand-bearing compasses.

| ⊕ | | Waypoint name and position | Latitude | Longitude |
|---|---|---|---|---|
| 50 | 1 | Les Héaux N clearing inner, 1¼M N of lighthouse | 48°55.750'N | 003°05.170'W |
| 50 | 2 | Les Héaux N clearing outer, 2½M N of lighthouse | 48°57.000'N | 003°05.170'W |
| 50 | 3 | La Jument clearing, ¼M N of N-card buoy | 48°55.610'N | 003°08.040'W |
| 50 | 4 | Tréguier outer, 3ca 287°T of Basse Crublent red buoy | 48°54.380'N | 003°11.600'W |
| 50 | 5 | Tréguier inner, 1ca E of Petit Pen ar Guézec green buoy | 48°52.521'N | 003°09.283'W |
| 50 | 6 | La Corne, 1ca due N of La Corne lighthouse | 48°51.451'N | 003°10.623'W |
| 50 | 7 | Perros E outer, ¾M 038°T of Basse Guazer buoy on leading line | 48°52.180'N | 003°20.250'W |
| 50 | 8 | Port Blanc inner, 6ca E of Le Four rock on leading line | 48°51.073'N | 003°19.276'W |
| 50 | 9 | Perros inner, ¼M 207°T of Pierre du Chenal beacon tower | 48°49.068'N | 003°24.847'W |
| 50 | 10 | Perros W outer, ¾M W of Les Couillons de Tomé buoy | 48°50.880'N | 003°26.820'W |
| 50 | 11 | Les Sept Iles E, 2.9M E of Ile Rouzic E tip in Port Blanc W sector | 48°53.940'N | 003°21.700'W |
| 50 | 12 | Les Sept Iles SE, midway between Dervinis and Couillons buoys | 48°51.611'N | 003°26.511'W |
| 50 | 13 | Les Sept Iles S, 1.2M S of Ile aux Moines lighthouse | 48°51.520'N | 003°29.420'W |
| 50 | 14 | Les Sept Iles W, 2¼M W of Ile aux Moines lighthouse | 48°52.723'N | 003°32.816'W |
| 50 | 15 | Les Sept Iles N clearing, 4¼M due N of Ile aux Moines lighthouse | 48°56.970'N | 003°29.400'W |
| 50 | 16 | Ploumanac'h entrance, 2ca NW of Pointe de Mean Ruz lighthouse | 48°50.445'N | 003°29.230'W |

**Refer to Charts**
Admiralty charts 2026, 2027, 2648, 3672
Imray C34

between Pointe du Château and Pointe de Mean Ruz, guarded on their north edge by Bernard green tower, La Fronde green buoy and La Horaine north-cardinal tower.

The Anse de Perros is shallow, most of it drying at chart datum. Depending on the tides, you can anchor or use the waiting buoys between Pointe du Château and Roc'h Hu de Perros red tower. At neaps you can edge further into the bay under Pointe du Château for greater shelter.

## Les Sept Iles
This string of small islands and reefs lies a few miles north of Ploumanac'h and Ile Tomé. The two largest islands, Ile aux Moines and Ile Bono, are close together on the southwest edge of the plateau. Fairly clean on their south sides, they form a natural anchorage which is reasonably sheltered in moderate winds from between north and west.

The powerful Ile aux Moines light is a key mark for a night approach to this coast anywhere between Lézardrieux and Roscoff. Unlit dangers extend 1¾ miles north, nearly 3½ miles ENE and just over a mile west of the lighthouse. Not quite a mile southeast of Ile Bono, Les Dervinis rock (dries 3.2m) is marked on its south side by an unlit south-cardinal buoy.

The tides are strong between Sept Iles and the mainland, especially between Ile aux Moines and Pointe de Mean Ruz. Here the bottom is uneven and relatively shallow in several patches, causing steep overfalls locally, especially near springs with wind-over-tide.

## COASTAL DANGERS

### Approaches to the Tréguier River
There are many drying and above-water rocks between Les Héaux and Tréguier entrance, to which you normally give a wide berth when passing outside Les Héaux, round La Jument N-cardinal buoy and then in through the Grande Passe via Basse Crublent red buoy. Passe de la Gaîne leads inside Les Héaux, a useful short cut between Lézardrieux and Tréguier in quiet conditions, reasonable visibility and above half-tide.

An intermediate channel, Passe de Nord-Est, leads from La Jument N-cardinal buoy inside Le Corbeau rock and Basses du Corbeau. The marks aren't always easy to see and, for the minimal distance saved, most skippers prefer the Grande Passe when approaching Tréguier outside Les Héaux.

### Dangers between Tréguier and Perros
Between Basse Crublent red buoy and Basse Guazer red buoy, various rocky dangers lurk up to 1¾ miles off the low, rather featureless coast. A direct track between Basse Crublent and Basse Guazer buoys leads just outside these dangers, clearing Basse Laéres (dries 0.6m) by barely a cable. Yachts must therefore be careful to stay safely outside this line, especially with onshore winds and during the east-going flood tide, which tends to set inshore.

### Approaches to Perros-Guirec
The northeast approach to Perros-Guirec leads inshore from Basse Guazer red buoy inside Ile Tomé. Basse Guazer shoal lies 1½ miles offshore, but between Guazer red buoy and the red beacon towers in the Anse de Perros, a wide area of reefs on the port hand extends well over a mile offshore between Port Blanc and Kerjean. Yachts using the Passe de l'Est should follow the leading line carefully, holding a direct track between Basse Guazer buoy and the green conical buoy off the south tip of Ile Tomé.

The northwest approach to Anse de Perros is less rocky but better marked and generally more straightforward. Various drying reefs extend up to ¾ mile west of Ile Tomé, marked at the extremity by Bilzic red beacon tower. Les Couillons de Tomé reef, half a mile off the northwest tip of Ile Tomé, is guarded by a W-cardinal buoy.

On the south side of Passe de l'Ouest there are several drying reefs well out in the bay

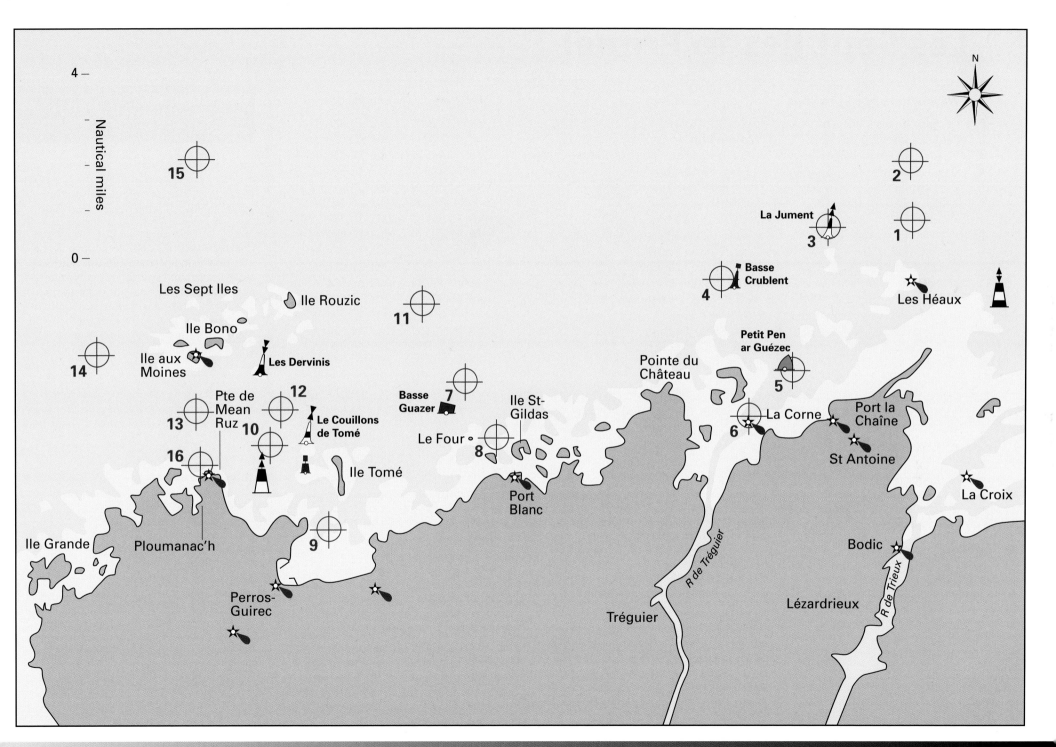

4 —

Nautical miles

0 —

15

2

1

La Jument

3

Basse Crublent

4

Les Héaux

Les Sept Iles

Ile Rouzic

11

Petit Pen
ar Guézec

Pointe du
Château

5

Ile Bono

Les Dervinis

Basse
Guazer

7

Ile St-
Gildas

La Corne

Port la
Chaîne

Ile aux
Moines

14

6

St Antoine

12

Pte de
Mean
Ruz

Le Couillons
de Tomé

Le Four

8

La Croix

13

10

Port
Blanc

16

Ile Tomé

Bodic

9

Ile Grande

Ploumanac'h

Perros-
Guirec

Lézardrieux

R de Tréguier

R de Trieux

Tréguier

# 51 Les Sept Iles to Primel

| ⊕ | Waypoint name and position | Latitude | Longitude |
|---|---|---|---|
| 51 1 | Les Sept Iles S, 1.2M S of Ile aux Moines lighthouse | 48°51.520'N | 003°29.420'W |
| 51 2 | Les Sept Iles W, 2¼M W of Ile aux Moines lighthouse | 48°52.723'N | 003°32.816'W |
| 51 3 | Ploumanac'h entrance, 2ca NW of Pointe de Mean Ruz lighthouse | 48°50.445'N | 003°29.230'W |
| 51 4 | Trégastel entrance, 1½ca NW of Ile Dhu red beacon | 48°50.478'N | 003°31.398'W |
| 51 5 | Les Sept Iles SW, 3½M 250°T from Ile aux Moines lighthouse | 48°51.553'N | 003°34.412'W |
| 51 6 | Bar all Gall, ¼M NW of Bar all Gall W-card buoy | 48°49.967'N | 003°36.491'W |
| 51 7 | Triagoz South, 1¾M due S of Triagoz lighthouse | 48°50.530'N | 003°38.787'W |
| 51 8 | Les Triagoz west clearing, 5M due W of Triagoz lighthouse | 48°52.281'N | 003°46.392'W |
| 51 9 | Méloine NE, 2½M 019°T of La Méloine Grande Roche | 48°48.919'N | 003°45.604'W |
| 51 10 | Trébeurden NW outer, 1.3M 247°T from Bar all Gall buoy | 48°49.290'N | 003°37.038'W |
| 51 11 | Trébeurden W inner, 6ca 236°T from Ar Veskleg rock | 48°46.165'N | 003°37.624'W |
| 51 12 | Trébeurden approach, 150m S of Ar Gourédec S-card buoy | 48°46.333'N | 003°36.593'W |
| 51 13 | Le Crapaud W, ¼M W of Le Crapaud W-card buoy | 48°46.673'N | 003°40.964'W |
| 51 14 | Le Crapaud SW, ½M SW of Le Crapaud W-card buoy | 48°46.321'N | 003°41.121'W |
| 51 15 | Le Crapaud S, 1.3M S of Le Crapaud W-card buoy | 48°45.370'N | 003°40.590'W |
| 51 16 | Lannion outer, 4M W of Beg Léguer lighthouse | 48°44.310'N | 003°39.964'W |
| 51 17 | Lannion inner, 1M W of Beg Léguer lighthouse | 48°44.310'N | 003°34.422'W |
| 51 18 | Lannion entrance, 100m N of inner green beacon tower | 48°43.838'N | 003°33.248'W |
| 51 19 | Roc'h Parou clearing, ¾M 066°T from Gouliat N-card buoy | 48°42.880'N | 003°37.940'W |
| 51 20 | Locquirec approach. ½M E of Le Château rock E edge | 48°41.967'N | 003°37.565'W |
| 51 21 | Méloine South, 1.6M S of La Méloine Grande Roche | 48°44.849'N | 003°46.895'W |
| 51 22 | Primel approach, on leading line 8ca from pierhead | 48°43.506'N | 003°49.929'W |
| 51 23 | Méloine West, 3ca W of Méloine W-card buoy | 48°45.559'N | 003°51.131'W |

**Refer to Charts**
Admiralty charts 2026, 2745
Imray C34

distance offshore, and also because the only buoy off this section of coast, the Bar all Gall W-cardinal, is not moored right on the corner of the off-lying dangers but well round to the south of some of them.

## Plateau des Triagoz

This low group of drying and above-water rocks lies four miles west of Les Sept Iles, marked on its south side by a lighthouse. Triagoz lighthouse is useful for gauging your position as you come round the rocky corner of mainland between Ploumanac'h and Trébeurden. Cruising west with the west-going tide, be careful not to be set too close to Triagoz as you hold offshore to avoid the coastal dangers. You would normally need to be turning south of west just as the Bar all Gall W-cardinal buoy bears south.

## Le Crapaud shoals

This wide area of rocky shoals extends from about a mile to over two miles west of Ile Molène. The shallowest danger, Le Crapaud rock, dries 3.9m on the north side of this plateau. Boats coming round from the east towards Trébeurden can cut between Le Crapaud shoals and Ile Molène with care, using waypoints 51-9 and 51-10 and making good due south between them to keep ½ mile west of Ar Veskleg rock. If in doubt though, take the outside passage west of Le Crapaud, dropping safely south of the shoal area before heading ENE towards the northwest tip of Ile Milliau and the entrance to Trébeurden.

## COASTAL DANGERS

### Les Sept Iles

This string of small islands and reefs lies just offshore a few miles north of Ploumanac'h and Ile Tomé. The two largest islands, Ile aux Moines and Ile Bono, are close together on the SW edge of the plateau. They form a natural anchorage which is open to the south and east but reasonably sheltered in moderate winds from between north and west.

The powerful lighthouse on Ile aux Moines is a key mark if you are approaching this stretch of coast at night anywhere between Lézardrieux and Roscoff. Unlit dangers extend 1¾ miles ENE and just over a mile west of the lighthouse. Les Dervinis, an isolated rock drying 3.2m not quite a mile southeast of Ile Bono, is marked on its south side by an unlit S-cardinal buoy.

The tides are very strong locally between Les Sept Iles and the mainland, especially in the narrows between Ile aux Moines and Pointe de Mean Ruz. The bottom is uneven and relatively shallow in several patches through this strait, and this can cause steep overfalls locally, especially near springs with wind-over-tide.

## Dangers between Ploumanac'h and Trébeurden

The rather austere corner of North Brittany mainland between Ploumanac'h and Trébeurden is well littered with off-lying rocks, which need to be given a wide berth as you come round the coast inside Les Sept Iles and Plateau des Triagoz.

This can be a tricky corner for gauging safe distances off, partly because there is no prominent landmark on the mainland, partly because of the strong tidal streams whose direction can vary depending on your

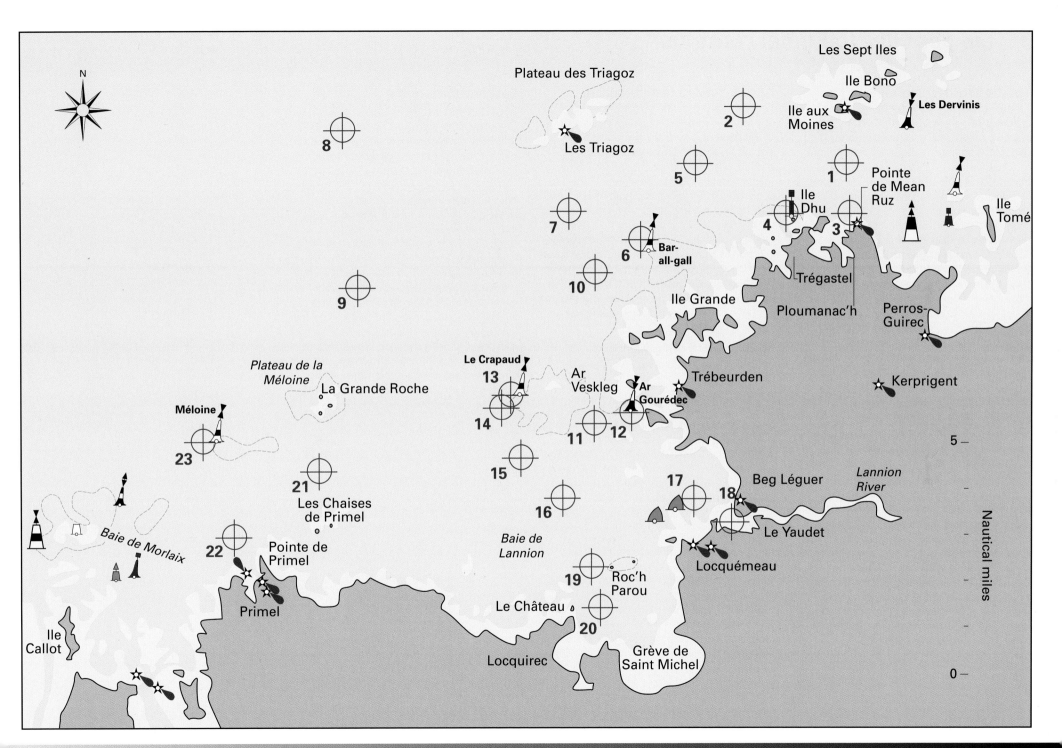

Les Sept Iles

Plateau des Triagoz

Ile Bono

**Les Dervinis**

Ile aux
Moines

2

8

5

Les Triagoz

1

Pointe
de Mean
Ruz

Ile Tomé

Ile
Dhu

7

4

3

Bar-
all-gall

6

Trégastel

10

Ile Grande

Ploumanac'h

Perros-
Guirec

9

Le Crapaud

Ar
Veskleg

Trébeurden

13

Ar
Gourédec

Kerprigent

Plateau de la
Méloine

La Grande Roche

14

Méloine

11    12

15

5 —

23

17

Beg Léguer

*Lannion
River*

21

Les Chaises
de Primel

16

18

*Baie de
Lannion*

Le Yaudet

Nautical miles

22

Pointe
de Primel

19

Roc'h
Parou

Locquémeau

Baie de Morlaix

Le Château

20

Primel

Locquirec

Grève de
Saint Michel

Ile
Callot

0 —

## The Trébeurden channels

As well as detailing the rocky hazards around this corner of North Brittany, it's worth emphasising that the shallow channels between Trébeurden, Ile Molène and Ile Grande have some fabulous sandy beaches and several fascinating neap tide anchorages. In quiet summer weather this area is a holiday paradise for all kinds of boats, sheltered all around by islands and reefs. With Trébeurden marina as a base, you can have great fun exploring these secret places, even in the dinghy if conditions are calm. The French SHOM chart 7124 is worth having. A mile opposite Trébeurden you can anchor off a glorious beach at the southeast corner of Ile Molène. Approach from the SSE from about a cable west of An Ervennou west-cardinal beacon, ideally a couple of hours before low water when the various reefs east of Molène are clearly exposed.

Further north, most boats can anchor and just stay afloat at dead neaps about four cables southwest of Ile Grande, slightly northwest of a line between Karreg Jentil S-cardinal beacon and Karreg ar Meg E-cardinal tower. This spot is reasonably sheltered in westerlies and northwesterlies, especially below half-tide. About a quarter of a mile northeast of Karreg ar Meg is the long stone landing jetty at the southwest tip of Ile Grande, a wild but fascinating spot well off the beaten track. Boats that can take the ground safely can approach the jetty near high water, anchor near the local boats and dry out on the wide area of firm sand off the end of the jetty.

## Approaches to Lannion River

There are various off-lying rocks in the approaches to the Lannion River, especially if you come round from Trébeurden. Les Roches lie almost a mile southwest of Ile Milliau, with the isolated heads of Le Four (drying 1m and 3.5m) another six cables or so further south-west. Bonnieg (dries 4.9m) and Le Taureau are about a mile seaward of Pointe de Bihit, but the south tip of Le Taureau, which is almost 2m above water, is the southern-most danger on the port hand as you approach the Lannion estuary from the west. On the south side of the Lannion approaches, the drying reefs north of Pointe de Séhar are guarded by Locquémeau and Kinierbel green buoys.

## Plateau de la Méloine

This long tail of rocks and rocky shoals runs NE–SW a few miles offshore in the east approaches to the Bay of Morlaix. The northeast outlier is Pongaro Rock, just awash at datum, which lurks about 1¼ miles northeast of the main cluster of above-water rocks. The southwestern dangers are Les Trépieds, a couple of miles WSW of the main rocks, guarded on their west side by Méloine W-cardinal buoy.

## Les Chaises de Primel

This distinctive line of rocks extends northeast from Pointe de Primel for a couple of miles. The most prominent of the outer rocks, Le Pigeonnier is 10m high, but drying dangers extend for ½ mile beyond Le Pigeonnier and must be given a wide berth if you are approaching the Bay of Morlaix from the east inside Plateau de la Méloine, especially if coming across from Trébeurden or Lannion.

## East entrance to the Morlaix estuary

The Chenal de Tréguier is relatively shallow and should only be taken above half-flood, but is the shortest way into the Morlaix estuary if you arrive from the east inside Plateau de la Méloine. Leave Les Chaises de Primel and Pointe de Primel each about three quarters of a mile to the south before making for waypoint 52-3, two cables ENE of La Pierre Noire green beacon. Leave La Pierre Noire beacon 300m to starboard and head towards a pair of beacon towers two miles into the estuary – Grand Aremen green and Petit Aremen red. This track leaves Jaune du Large rock (with a red-and-white painted mark) a quarter mile to port and Tourghi green beacon two cables to starboard. Pass midway between Grand and Petit Aremen, leave La Chambre green beacon tower 100m to starboard, and then come to starboard to enter the river

| ⊕ | | Waypoint name and position | Latitude | Longitude |
|---|---|---|---|---|
| 52 | 1 | Primel approach, on leading line 8ca from pierhead | 48°43.506'N | 003°49.929'W |
| 52 | 2 | Méloine West, 3ca W of Méloine W-card buoy | 48°45.559'N | 003°51.131'W |
| 52 | 3 | Chenal de Tréguier outer, 2ca ENE of La Pierre Noire beacon | 48°42.639'N | 003°51.929'W |
| 52 | 4 | Chenal de Tréguier inner, 3½ca 010°T from Ile Noire lighthouse | 48°40.700'N | 003°52.440'W |
| 52 | 5 | Grand Chenal outer, 2ca NE of Pot de Fer E-card buoy | 48°44.370'N | 003°53.800'W |
| 52 | 6 | Stolvezen, 2ca NW of Stolvezen red buoy | 48°42.789'N | 003°53.623'W |
| 52 | 7 | Grand Chenal inner, ½M 356°T from Ile Louet lighthouse | 48°40.920'N | 003°53.380'W |
| 52 | 8 | Les Duons south, ½M S of Les Duons white pyramid | 48°43.160'N | 003°55.318'W |
| 52 | 9 | Bloscon inner approach, 5½ca 030°T from Bloscon pierhead | 48°43.708'N | 003°57.279'W |
| 52 | 10 | Bloscon outer approach, 1.1M E of Astan E-card buoy | 48°44.914'N | 003°55.998'W |
| 52 | 11 | Batz inner north clearing, 2½M N of Ile de Batz lighthouse | 48°47.213'N | 004°01.594'W |
| 52 | 12 | Chenal de Batz west inner, 130m N of Basse Plate beacon tower | 48°44.320'N | 004°02.530'W |

**Refer to Charts**
Admiralty charts 2026, 2745
Imray C34, C35

## COASTAL DANGERS

### General

The Bay of Morlaix, some three miles wide between Primel and the Plateau des Duons, is littered with rocks and islets but well marked with buoys and beacon towers. The two main entrance channels, the Grand Chenal and Chenal de Tréguier, lead south through the cordon of dangers into the sheltered but mostly shallow lower reaches of the Morlaix River. In reasonable visibility, you can enter the estuary by the Grand Chenal at any state of tide, by day or night, to anchor or pick up a mooring close east of Pen Lann point.

### Plateau des Duons

This outer group of rocks lies about 1½ miles east of the east end of the Chenal de Batz and effectively separates the approaches to the Morlaix estuary and the approaches to Roscoff and the Penzé River. The northeast corner of Plateau des Duons is guarded by Pot de Fer E-cardinal buoy, while the main body of reefs is surmounted by a white pyramid. It is easy enough to cut south of Les Duons when passing between, say, Port de Bloscon and the Grand Chenal de Morlaix.

### Chenal de Tréguier

The eastern-most channel into the Morlaix estuary is relatively shallow and should only be taken above half-flood, but provides the shortest way in if you are coming round from Primel, or if you are approaching Morlaix from the east inside Plateau de la Méloine. The Chenal de Tréguier can be taken at night with care, using the leading lights on Ile Noire and up on La Lande.

### Grand Chenal de Morlaix

The Grand Chenal, although rather narrow between Ile Ricard and the extensive reefs around Ile aux Dames, is deep for most of its length and can be taken by most boats at any state of tide, by day or night. In poor visibility, however, the Chenal de Tréguier is usually a safer bet, especially if you arrive from the east.

### Chenal Ouest de Ricard

This western-most channel into the Morlaix estuary, just west of the Grand Chenal, carries the deepest water of all three entrance channels but is only feasible in daylight.

### Approaches to the Penzé River

The various rocky shoals at the entrance to the Penzé River form a kind of outer bar. It is best for strangers to treat these as drying at least a metre The best time to approach Penzé is about half-flood, when it is straightforward to come in between Guerhéon green and Le Cordonnier red beacon towers and follow the marked channel south into the river.

### Ile de Batz

The north-facing coast near Roscoff and the Ile de Batz just opposite are well littered with rocky dangers. The Chenal de Batz between Roscoff and the island is shallow at its east end, but is well marked and straightforward enough with at least a couple of hours' rise of tide. Seaward of Ile de Batz, the dangers extend up to a mile offshore.

Most boats on passage between Morlaix and L'Aberwrac'h will find the Chenal de Batz easier and quicker than keeping outside Ile de Batz, especially as one will be leaving Morlaix, perforce, near high water. Similarly, yachts carrying a fair stream eastwards from L'Aberwrac'h will normally arrive off Batz with plenty of depth in the Chenal de Batz.

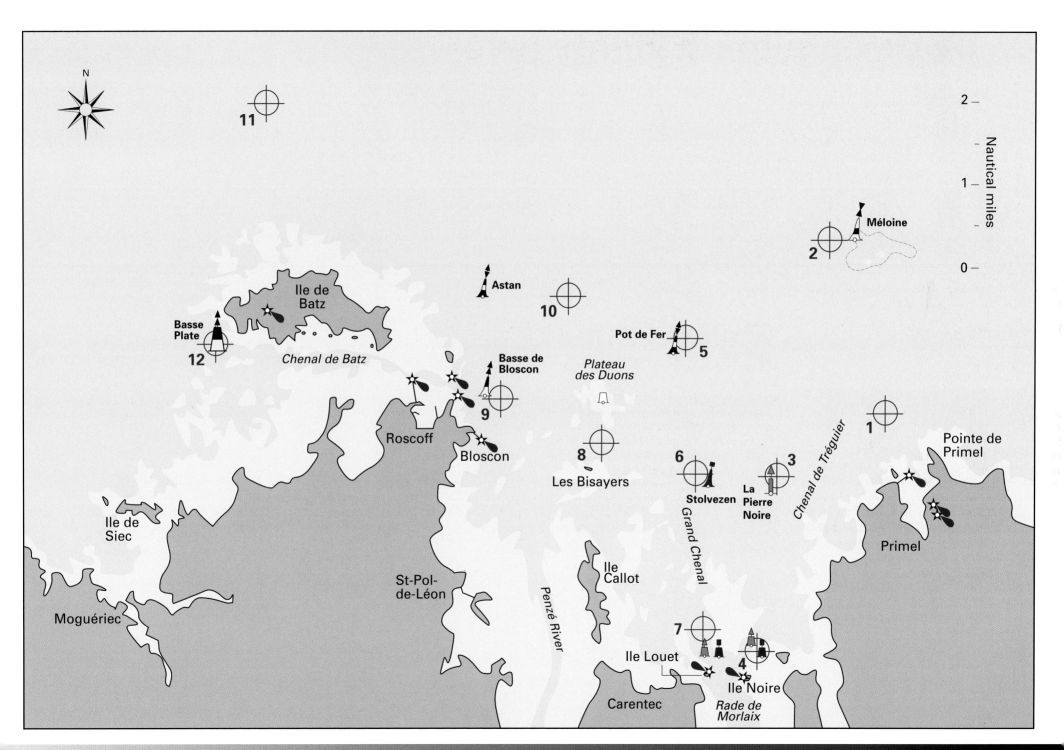

N

2 —

1 —

Nautical miles

0 —

11

Méloine

2

Astan

10

Ile de
Batz

Basse
Plate

12

Chenal de Batz

Pot de Fer

5

Basse de
Bloscon

Plateau
des Duons

9

Roscoff

Bloscon

8

Les Bisayers

6

Stolvezen

La
Pierre
Noire

3

Chenal de Tréguier

1

Pointe de
Primel

Ile de
Siec

Primel

Ile
Callot

Grand Chenal

St-Pol-
de-Léon

Penzé River

Moguériec

7

Ile Louet

4

Carentec

Ile Noire

Rade de
Morlaix

| ⊕ | Waypoint name and position | Latitude | Longitude |
|---|---|---|---|
| 53 **1** | Batz inner north clearing, 2½M N of Ile de Batz lighthouse | 48°47.213′N | 004°01.594′W |
| 53 **2** | Batz outer north clearing, 4M N of Ile de Batz lighthouse | 48°48.713′N | 004°01.594′W |
| 53 **3** | Chenal de Batz west inner, 130m N of Basse Plate beacon tower | 48°44.320′N | 004°02.530′W |
| 53 **4** | Chenal de Batz west outer, 3M W of Ile de Batz lighthouse | 48°44.713′N | 004°06.146′W |
| 53 **5** | Anse de Kernic offing, 4M N of Benven rock | 48°44.050′N | 004°13.860′W |
| 53 **6** | Pontusval outer, 1.7M N of Pontusval E-card buoy | 48°43.120′N | 004°19.320′W |
| 53 **7** | Pontusval E-card buoy, actual position | 48°41.420′N | 004°19.320′W |
| 53 **8** | Pontusval entrance, 50m W of An Neudenn beacon tower | 48°40.671′N | 004°19.145′W |
| 53 **9** | Aman ar Ross N-card buoy, actual position | 48°41.880′N | 004°27.030′W |
| 53 **10** | Lizen Ven Ouest W-card buoy, actual position | 48°40.530′N | 004°33.630′W |

### Refer to Charts
Admiralty charts 2025, 2026
Imray C35

### Poor visibility
Poor visibility is not uncommon towards the west end of this stretch of coast. Boats on passage between Ile de Batz and L'Aberwrac'h can sometimes find conditions much hazier off Ile Vierge than they were further east. However, it is not difficult to pick your way between Aman ar Ross and Lizen Ouest buoys, and then make for ⊕54–3 before turning south for ⊕54–4 and Le Libenter W-cardinal buoy at the entrance to L'Aberwrac'h.

## COASTAL DANGERS

### Ile de Batz
The north-facing coast near Roscoff and the Ile de Batz just opposite are well littered with rocky dangers. The Chenal de Batz between Roscoff and the island is shallow at its east end, but is well marked and straightforward enough with at least a couple of hours' rise of tide. Seaward of Ile de Batz, the dangers extend up to a mile offshore.

Most boats on passage between Morlaix and L'Aberwrac'h will find the Chenal de Batz easier and quicker than keeping outside Ile de Batz, especially as one will be leaving Morlaix, perforce, near high water. Similarly, yachts carrying a fair stream eastwards from L'Aberwrac'h will normally arrive off Batz with plenty of depth in the Chenal de Batz.

### Dangers between Ile de Batz and Ile Vierge
The North Brittany coast between Roscoff and Ile Vierge is rather featureless and austere, with off-lying dangers extending over two miles offshore in parts, particularly down towards Ile Vierge. It is prudent to stay on or outside a direct line between Ile de Batz lighthouse and Aman ar Ross N-cardinal buoy, or say between ⊕53–4 and 53–9 in the table above.

Shallow draught boats venturing into Pontusval should make for ⊕53–6 before turning inshore for ⊕53–7, which is the Pontusval E-cardinal buoy.

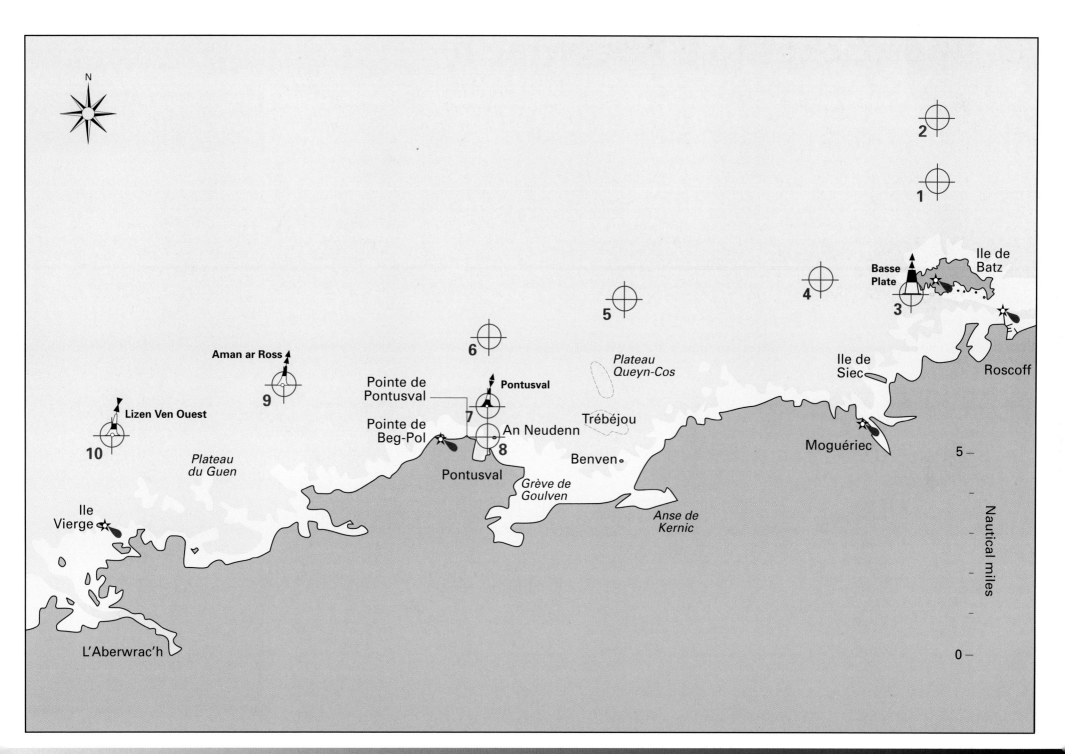

N

**2**

**1**

**4**

Basse
Plate

Ile de
Batz

**3**

**5**

Roscoff

Ile de
Siec

**6**

Plateau
Queyn-Cos

Aman ar Ross

Trébéjou

Pointe de
Pontusval

**Pontusval**

Moguériec

**9**

**7**

5 —

Lizen Ven Ouest

Pointe de
Beg-Pol

An Neudenn

**10**

**8**

Benven

Nautical miles

Plateau
du Guen

Pontusval

Grève de
Goulven

Anse de
Kernic

Ile
Vierge

0 —

L'Aberwrac'h

| ⊕ | Waypoint name and position | Latitude | Longitude |
|---|---|---|---|
| 54 1 | Aman ar Ross N-card buoy, actual position | 48°41.880'N | 004°27.030'W |
| 54 2 | Lizen Ven Ouest W-card buoy, actual position | 48°40.530'N | 004°33.630'W |
| 54 3 | L'Aberwrac'h north approach, 1.2M 348°T of Le Libenter buoy | 48°38.628'N | 004°38.830'W |
| 54 4 | L'Aberwrac'h entrance, 1½ca SW of Le Libenter buoy on leading line | 48°37.357'N | 004°38.605'W |
| 54 5 | L'Aberwrac'h middle, 1M 280°T from Ile Vrac'h lighthouse | 48°37.061'N | 004°36.046'W |
| 54 6 | L'Aberwrac'h inner, ¼M 308°T from La Palue directional light | 48°36.051'N | 004°34.111'W |
| 54 7 | Corn Carhai clearing, 1¼M 340°T from Corn Carhai lighthouse | 48°36.366'N | 004°44.588'W |
| 54 8 | Grande Basse de Portsall W clearing, 1¼M W of W-card buoy | 48°36.701'N | 004°48.010'W |
| 54 9 | Basse Paupian W-card buoy, actual position | 48°35.310'N | 004°46.270'W |

**Refer to Charts**
Admiralty charts 1432, 2025, 2026
Imray C35

## COASTAL DANGERS

### Poor visibility

Poor visibility is not uncommon towards the west end of this stretch of coast. Boats on passage between Ile de Batz and L'Aberwrac'h can sometimes find conditions much hazier off Ile Vierge than they were further east. However, it is not difficult to pick your way between Aman ar Ross and Lizen Ven Ouest buoys, and then make for ⊕54–3 before turning south for ⊕54–4 and Le Libenter W-cardinal buoy at the entrance to L'Aberwrac'h.

### Le Libenter

Yachts arriving off L'Aberwrac'h from the east must make the final approach to Le Libenter W-cardinal buoy from due north or just west of north ie making for ⊕54–3 before turning south for ⊕54–4. This is to stay well clear of Le Libenter reef, a dangerous plateau over which the sea breaks heavily at the least provocation.

### Approaches to L'Aberbenoît

L'Aberbenoît is easy enough to enter in moderate weather with sufficient rise of tide, but should be avoided in a heavy northwesterly swell, when the relatively small buoys and beacons of the approach channel will be difficult to identify in good time. The outer mark for L'Aberbenoît is La Petite Fourche W-cardinal buoy, which lies about six cables SSW of Le Libenter buoy.

### Roches de Portsall

This dangerous area of rocks, right on the northwest corner of Brittany, is where the tanker Amoco Cadiz came to grief notoriously in the late 1970s. These reefs are marked by Corn Carhai lighthouse, but drying rocks extend not quite ½ mile north of the lighthouse.

Yachts and motorboats rounding this corner will normally pass a good mile north of Corn Carhai, making towards the Grande Basse de Portsall W-cardinal buoy although not necessarily keeping outside it. ⊕54–7 and ⊕54–9 make useful turning points for this corner, although the Grande Basse de Portsall buoy is a useful landfall mark if you are arriving off the north end of the Chenal du Four direct from across the Channel.

### Swell

This far northwest corner of Brittany is often subject to a heavy swell from between west and northwest, even in quite moderate winds. This can make the area feel more menacing than it really is, and the deep troughs of the swell can sometimes make it difficult to pick out landmarks from some distance offshore.

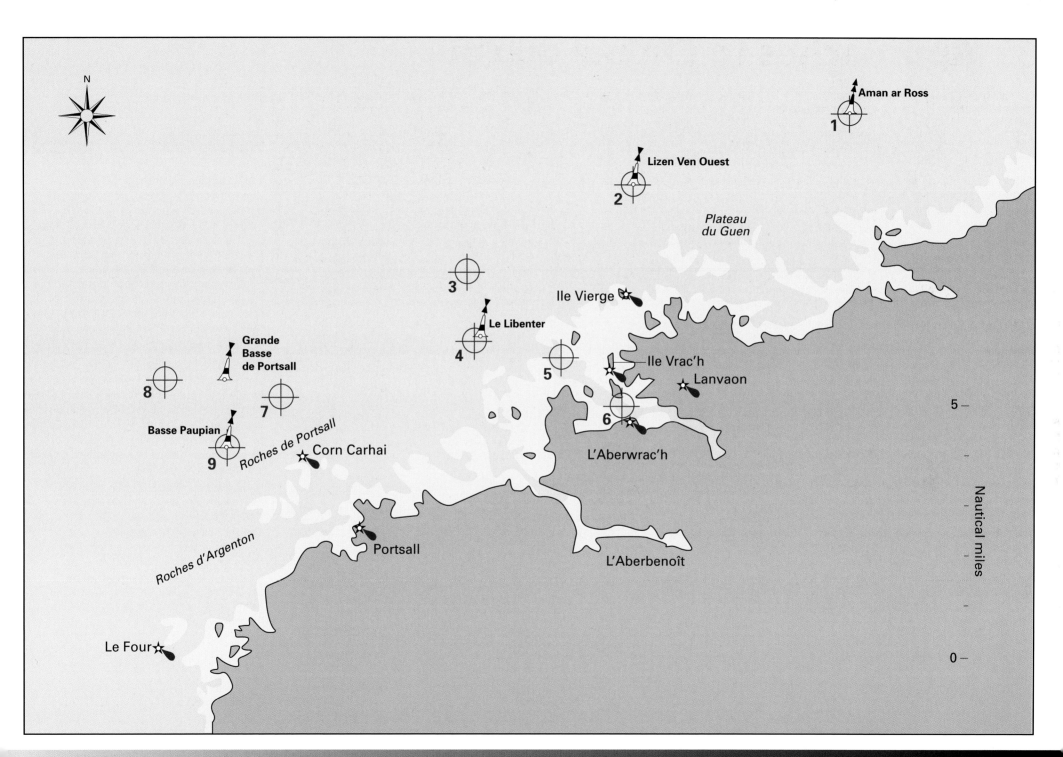

N

Aman ar Ross
1

Lizen Ven Ouest
2

Plateau du Guen

3

Ile Vierge

Le Libenter
4

5

Grande Basse de Portsall

Ile Vrac'h

Lanvaon
6

8

7

Basse Paupian
9

Roches de Portsall

Corn Carhai

L'Aberwrac'h

Roches d'Argenton

Portsall

L'Aberbenoît

Le Four

Nautical miles

5

0

| ⊕ | Waypoint name and position | Latitude | Longitude |
|---|---|---|---|
| 55 1 | Corn Carhai clearing, 1¼M 340°T from Corn Carhai lighthouse | 48°36.366'N | 004°44.588'W |
| 55 2 | Grande Basse de Portsall W clearing, 1¼M W of W-card buoy | 48°36.701'N | 004°48.010'W |
| 55 3 | Basse Paupian W-card buoy, actual position | 48°35.310'N | 004°46.270'W |
| 55 4 | Portsall outer, 3¼M 266°T from Portsall directional lighthouse | 48°33.610'N | 004°47.150'W |
| 55 5 | Portsall inner, ½M 266°T from Portsall directional lighthouse | 48°33.807'N | 004°43.016'W |
| 55 6 | Le Four inner, 6ca W of Le Four lighthouse | 48°31.380'N | 004°49.222'W |
| 55 7 | Le Four west clearing, 1M W of Le Four lighthouse | 48°31.380'N | 004°49.835'W |
| 55 8 | L'Aberildut outer, 2½M 263°T from L'Aberildut directional light | 48°27.940'N | 004°49.290'W |
| 55 9 | L'Aberildut inner, 130m S of Le Lieu red beacon tower | 48°28.170'N | 004°46.640'W |
| 55 10 | La Valbelle, 200m W of La Valbelle buoy on leading line | 48°26.420'N | 004°50.190'W |

## Refer to Charts

Admiralty charts 1432, 3345
Imray C35

## COASTAL DANGERS

### General

The Chenal du Four is a well-marked passage between the far northwest corner of Brittany and the off-lying islands of Ushant, Moléne, Quéménès and Béniguet. It provides the most common route for yachts cruising between the English Channel and the Bay of Biscay. The Chenal du Four is wider than it appears from a small-scale chart and is quite straightforward in reasonable visibility, by day or night, so long as you carry the tide in your favour.

You often meet a somewhat forbidding Atlantic swell in the north approaches between L'Aberwrac'h and Le Four lighthouse, especially off the Roches de Portsall, but further south the islands provide some shelter and the swell usually dies away.

### Roches de Portsall

This dangerous area of rocks, right on the northwest corner of Brittany, is where the tanker Amoco Cadiz came to grief notoriously in the late 1970s. These reefs are marked by Corn Carhai lighthouse, but drying rocks extend not quite ½ mile north of the lighthouse.

Yachts rounding this corner will normally pass a good mile north of Corn Carhai, making towards the Grande Basse de Portsall W-cardinal buoy although not necessarily keeping outside it. ⊕55–1 and ⊕55–3 make useful turning points for this corner, although the Grande Basse de Portsall buoy is a good landfall mark if you are arriving off the north end of the Chenal du Four direct from across the Channel.

### Roches d'Argenton

This long tail of drying and above-water rocks lies up to a mile offshore and stretches northeast from Le Four lighthouse for more than two miles. Yachts coming down from Basse Paupian W-cardinal buoy should not make for Le Four lighthouse directly but for a clearing position safely off to the west, in order to be sure of keeping well off Roches d'Argenton.

### Les Liniou

This distinctive group of mainly above-water rocks are the next features you see as you draw south of Le Four lighthouse. In moderate weather Les Liniou provide useful steering marks because it is safe to pass ½ mile west of the outer above-water rocks. From here you can make good just west of south towards La Valbelle red buoy which marks the entrance to the southern, usually more sheltered part of the Chenal du Four.

### Plateau des Fourches

This rather nasty plateau of reefs lies about a mile south of the normal leading line approach to L'Aberildut. You need to take particular care to clear Plateau des Fourches if cutting close inshore to cheat the tide in the Chenal du Four; perhaps while northbound towards L'Aberildut when the stream in the Four is already running south. With any swell in the offing, the sea breaks heavily over Plateau des Fourches below half-tide.

### Poor visibility

It is not uncommon to meet poor visibility in the Chenal du Four, particularly towards the north end even having passed Le Conquet in quite sunny conditions. With GPS, this is not such a trial as it once was, so long as you keep your head and work systemically from waypoint to waypoint.

Having come up through the Chenal du Four in murky visibility, it is not usually difficult to find Le Libenter buoy with GPS and thus to enter L'Aberwrac'h safely. However, when approaching L'Aberwrac'h entrance from the west in mist or fog, it is vital to find Le Libenter buoy before proceeding any further east. The buoy's mournful whistle can be a surprising help in the final approach.

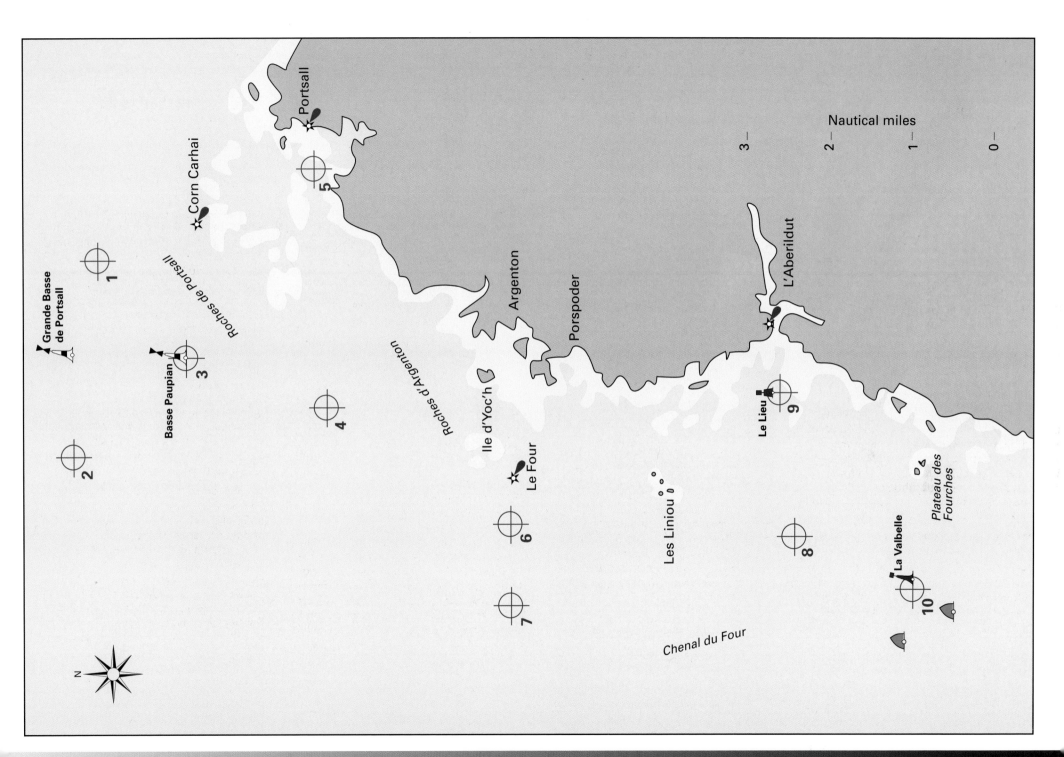

Nautical miles

3 — 2 — 1 — 0

Portsall

Corn Carhai

Grande Basse
de Portsall

**1**

Roches de Portsall

Basse Paupian

**3**

**5**

**2**

**4**

Rochés d'Argenton

Argenton

Porspoder

Ile d'Yoc'h

Le Four

L'Aberildut

Le Lieu

**9**

**6**

Les Liniou

**8**

Plateau des
Fourches

La Valbelle

**7**

**10**

Chenal du Four

N

# Chart List

## Admiralty charts

| | |
|---|---|
| 26 | Harbours on the South Coast of Devon |
| 28 | Salcombe Harbour |
| 30 | Plymouth Sound and Approaches |
| 31 | Harbours on the South Coast of Cornwall |
| 32 | Falmouth Harbour |
| 34 | Isles of Scilly |
| 60 | Alderney and the Casquets |
| 147 | Plans on the South Coast of Cornwall |
| 148 | Dodman Point to Looe Bay |
| 154 | Approaches to Falmouth |
| 323 | Dover Strait Eastern Part |
| 438 | Boulogne-sur-Mer |
| 536 | Beachy Head to Dungeness |
| 777 | Land's End to Falmouth |
| 807 | Guernsey and Herm |
| 808 | East Guernsey - Herm and Sark |
| 883 | Saint Mary's and the Principal Off-Islands |
| 1112 | Cherbourg |
| 1114 | Approaches to Cherbourg, Cap de la Hague to Pointe de Barfleur |
| 1136 | Jersey - North Coast |
| 1137 | Approaches to St Helier |
| 1138 | Jersey - East Coast |
| 1148 | Isles of Scilly to Land's End |
| 1267 | Falmouth to Plymouth |
| 1349 | Ports in the Baie de Seine |
| 1351 | Approaches to Calais |
| 1354 | Ports of Fécamp and Le Tréport |
| 1355 | Dieppe |
| 1432 | Le Four to Ile Vierge |
| 1613 | Eddystone Rocks to Berry Head |
| 1634 | Start Point to Brixham |
| 1652 | England - West Coast, Selsey Bill to Beachy Head |
| 1828 | Dover to North Foreland |
| 1892 | Dover Strait Western Part |
| 1900 | Whitsand Bay to Yealm Head including Plymouth Sound |
| 1967 | Plymouth Sound |
| 2021 | Harbours and Anchorages in the West Solent Area |
| 2022 | Harbours and Anchorages in the East Solent Area |
| 2025 | Portsall to Anse de Kernic |
| 2026 | Anse de Kernic to Ile Grande |
| 2027 | Ile Grande to Ile de Bréhat |
| 2028 | Ile de Bréhat to Plateau des Roches-Douvres |
| 2029 | Ile de Bréhat to Cap Fréhel |
| 2035 | Western Approaches to The Solent |
| 2036 | The Solent and Southampton Water |
| 2037 | Eastern Approaches to the Solent |
| 2038 | Southampton Water and Approaches |
| 2041 | Port of Southampton |
| 2044 | Shoreham Harbour and Approaches |
| 2045 | Outer Approaches to The Solent |
| 2135 | Pointe de Barfleur to Pointe de la Percée |
| 2136 | Pointe de la Percée to Ouistreham |
| 2146 | Approaches to Le Havre and Antifer |
| 2148 | Approaches to Fécamp and Dieppe |
| 2154 | Newhaven Harbour |
| 2172 | Harbours and Anchorages on the South Coast of England |
| 2253 | Dartmouth Harbour |
| 2255 | Approaches to Portland and Weymouth |
| 2290 | River Exe and Approaches including Exeter Canal |
| 2345 | Plans in South West Cornwall |
| 2450 | Anvil Point to Beachy Head |
| 2451 | Newhaven to Dover and Cap d'Antifer to Cap Gris-Nez |
| 2454 | Start Point to The Needles including Off Casquets TSS |
| 2565 | Saint Agnes Head to Dodman Point including the Isles of Scilly |
| 2610 | Bill of Portland to Anvil Point |
| 2611 | Poole Harbour and Approaches |
| 2613 | Cap de la Hague to Fécamp |
| 2615 | Bill of Portland to The Needles |
| 2647 | Ile d'Ouessant to Ile de Batz |
| 2648 | Roches de Portsall to Plateau des Roches Douvres |
| 2669 | Channel Islands and Adjacent Coast of France |
| 2700 | Approaches to Saint-Malo |
| 2745 | Baie de Morlaix Ile de Batz to Pointe de Primel |
| 3315 | Berry Head to Bill of Portland |
| 3345 | Chenal du Four |
| 3418 | Langstone and Chichester Harbours |
| 3653 | Guernsey to Alderney and adjacent coast of France |
| 3654 | Guernsey Herm and Sark |
| 3655 | Jersey and Adjacent Coast of France |
| 3656 | Plateau des Minquiers and adjacent coast of France |
| 3659 | Cap Fréhel to Iles Chausey |
| 3672 | Harbours on the North West Coast of France |
| 3673 | Ile de Bréhat and Anse de Paimpol Entrance to Le Trieux |

## Imray charts

| | |
|---|---|
| C3 | Isle of Wight |
| C4 | Needles Channel to Bill of Portland |
| C5 | Bill of Portland to Salcombe Harbour |
| C6 | Salcombe to Lizard Point |
| C7 | Falmouth to Isles of Scilly and Trevose Head |
| C8 | Dover Strait |
| C9 | Beachy Head to Isle of Wight |
| C10 | Western English Channel Passage Chart |
| C12 | Eastern English Channel Passage Chart |
| C14 | Plymouth Harbour and Rivers |
| C15 | The Solent |
| C31 | Dover Strait to Le Havre |
| C32 | Baie de Seine |
| C33A | Channel Islands (North) |
| C33B | Channel Islands and North Coast of France |
| C34 | Cap d'Erquy to Ile de Batz |
| C35 | Baie de Morlaix to L'Aber-Ildut |
| Y58 | River Fal |

## Small format chart packs

| | |
|---|---|
| **2200** | **The Solent** |
| 2200.1 | Isle of Wight |
| 2200.2 | Christchurch to the Solent |
| 2200.3 | Eastern Approaches to the Solent |
| 2200.4 | Chichester and Langstone Harbours |
| 2200.5 | Portsmouth Harbour and Approaches |
| 2200.6 | Central Solent |
| 2200.7 | Southampton Water |
| 2200.8 | West Solent |
| 2200.9 | Isle of Wight and Solent Plans |
| 2200.10 | Rivers and Marinas in Southampton Water |
| **2300** | **Dorset and Devon Coasts** |
| 2300.1 | Isle of Wight to Start Point |
| 2300.2 | Western Approaches to the Solent |
| 2300.3 | Poole Harbour to Bill of Portland |
| 2300.4 | Lyme Bay |
| 2300.5 | Poole Harbour |
| 2300.6 | River Exe |
| 2300.7 | Exmouth to Salcombe |
| 2300.8 | Teignmouth and Tor Bay |
| 2300.9 | River Dart |
| **2400** | **West Country** |
| 2400.1 | Land's End to Trevose Head |
| 2400.2 | Approaches to the Isles of Scilly |
| 2400.3 | Isles of Scilly |
| 2400.4 | River Camel |
| 2400.5 | Salcombe |
| 2400.6 | River Yealm |
| 2400.7 | River Fowey to Lostwithiel |
| 2400.8 | Start Point to Fowey |
| 2400.9 | Fowey to Lizard Point |
| 2400.10 | Lizard Point to Land's End |
| 2400.11 | Helford River |
| 2400.12 | Falmouth Harbour |
| 2400.13 | Plymouth Harbour |
| 2400.14 | Saint Mary's, Tresco and Surrounding Islands |
| **2500** | **Channel Islands** |
| 2500.1 | Alderney to Iles Chausey |
| 2500.2 | Alderney to Guernsey |
| 2500.3 | Guernsey, Herm and Jethou |
| 2500.4 | Guernsey to Jersey |
| 2500.5 | Jersey (St Helier) to Carteret |
| 2500.6 | Alderney to Jersey |
| 2500.7 | Jersey to Granville |
| 2500.8 | St Malo approaches |
| 2500.9 | East Guernsey, Herm and Sark |
| 2500.10 | Approaches to Channel Islands |

# Index

# Captions for photos

p8: Jetée des Fontaines de Bas beacon, Les Minquiers.
p9: Entering the Trieux River by the Grand Chenal.
p12: Violet Channel fairway buoy off Jersey's south-east corner.
p28: St Michael's Mount and its tiny drying harbour.
p30: St Anthony Head and Falmouth entrance.
p32 top: St Mawes Castle on the east side of Falmouth entrance.
p32 bottom: Mylor Yacht Harbour on the River Fal.
p34 top: Coastguard lookout on the east side of Fowey entrance.
p34 bottom: Gribbin Head beacon and the approaches to Fowey.
p36: Eddystone lighthouse and the stump of the old tower.
p38: Plymouth Sound and Drake's Island.
p42: Dartmouth harbour looking towards Kingswear.
p44: Tanker at anchor in Tor Bay.
p46 top: Portland Bill lighthouse from the inner passage.
p46 bottom: Entering the River Exe.
p48: Portland Marina and the National Sailing Academy.
p50: Entering Lulworth Cove.
p52 left: Anvil Point lighthouse.
p52 right: Old Harry off Handfast Point.
p54 top: The Needles lighthouse.
p54 bottom: Looking across Keyhaven towards Hurst Point and the IOW.
p56 left: Hamstead Ledge green buoy near Newtown River entrance.
p56 right: Approaches to Lymington looking towards the IOW.
p60 clockwise from top left: Beaulieu River entrance beacon; Bosham near high water; Upper Emsworth Channel; Hythe marina village; Upper reaches of the Hamble; Shipping in the Solent; The Royal Oak at Langstone; Sparks Marina on Hayling Island.
p60 centre: The Itchenor ferry in Chichester Harbour.
p61 clockwise from top left: Chichester Harbour channels; Eling Harbour up the River Test; Entrance to Portsmouth Harbour; HMS Warrior at Portsmouth; Eric and Susan Hiscock's lifeboat at Yarmouth; IOW ferry approaching Wootton Creek; J-class elegance in the Solent; Pile moorings off Lymington town.
p61 centre: No Man's Land fort in the East Solent.
p62: Horse Sand Fort in the East Solent.
p64: The dramatic south coast of the Isle of Wight.
p68: Beachy Head and its famous lighthouse.
p72: The amazing Goodwin Sands.
p74: Cross-Channel ferry entering Calais.
p76: Boulogne harbour entrance channel.
p78: Dieppe harbour and marina.
p80: Entrance to Deauville-Trouville.
p84: Ouistreham harbour and the tidal lock into the Caen Canal.
p86: The river channel leading inland to Carentan lock and marina.

p90: Pointe de Barfleur and its dramatic lighthouse.
p94: Alderney lighthouse on Quénard Point.
p100 clockwise from top left: Longis Bay anchorage, Alderney; Carteret port de plaisance; Hanging Rock on Alderney's south coast; A tight squeeze at Guernsey's Beaucette Marina; St Peter Port harbour; Visitors' berths at Diélette; Herm's glorious harbour beach; Snug inside Beaucette Marina.
p100 centre: Alderney lighthouse on Quénard Point.
p101 clockwise from top left: Colourful waterfront at St Peter Port; La Grande Grève anchorage on Sark's west coast; Victoria Marina, St Peter Port; Rosaire anchorage off Herm's south-west corner.
p107 clockwise from top left: Noirmont Point on Jersey's south coast; Low tide lagoons in Les Écrehou; St Helier harbour's prominent chimney; St Helier's sheltered visitors' marina; St Helier harbour entrance; St Helier breakwater and the Platte Rock beacon; La Corbière lighthouse, Jersey; Moored off Marmotière islet in Les Écrehou.
p107 centre: Beau Port bay on Jersey's south-west coast.
p110: Pierre d'Herpin lighthouse.
p114: The comfortable, well-placed marina at St Cast.
p119: St Quay marina in Baie de St Brieuc.
p122: Snug visitors' berth in Binic's friendly locked marina.
p123: Looking south across Port Clos, Ile de Bréhat.
p127 clockwise from top left: Rosédo white pyramid on Ile de Bréhat; L'Ost-Pic lighthouse near Paimpol; Approach to Port de la Corderie, Ile de Bréhat; The author's gaff cutter Stormalong anchored in La Chambre; Paimpol lock; Le Croix lighthouse in the Trieux River; Ghosting towards Lézardrieux; Paimpol's very Breton waterfront.
p127 centre: Rocky channels west of Ile de Bréhat.
p131 clockwise from top left: La Moisie E-cardinal beacon in the Trieux estuary; Approaching La Vieille du Tréou green beacon at the south end of the Moisie Passage; Les Héaux lighthouse from Passe de la Gaîne; Pointe du Paon, the NE tip of Bréhat.
p135: Roche Douvres' pink granite lighthouse
p141 clockwise from top left: Les Sept Iles from westward; The sill at Ploumanac'h inner harbour; Local boats in Trégastel; The sleepy Lannion River; Approach channel to Ploumanac'h; Rocky entrance to Ploumanac'h; Local boats in Ploumanac'h; Trébeurden marina sill near low water.
p141 centre: Trébeurden marina.
p144: The channel south of Ile de Batz.
p146: Ile Vierge lighthouse.